Claude McKay

Claude McKay

A Black Poet's Struggle for Identity

Tyrone Tillery

AMHERST

The University of Massachusetts Press

Copyright © 1992 by The University of Massachusetts Press

All rights reserved

Printed in the United States of America

LC 91-25135

ISBN 0-87023-762-4

Designed by David Ford

Set in Mergenthaler Caledonia

Printed and bound by Thomson-Shore, Inc.

Library of Congress Cataloging-in-Publication Data
Tillery, Tyrone, 1946–
    Claude McKay : a black poet's struggle for identity /
Tyrone Tillery.
        p.   cm.
    Includes bibliographical references and index.
    ISBN 0-87023-762-4 (alk. paper)
    1. McKay, Claude, 1890–1948.   2. Authors,
American—20th century—Biography.   3. Authors,
Jamaican—20th century—Biography.   4. Identity
(Psychology) in literature.   5. Afro-Americans in
literature.   I. Title.
PS3525.A24785Z89   1991
811'.54—dc 20   91–25135
    [B]   CIP

British Library Cataloguing in Publication data are
available.

For the Tillerys—
but especially for Wesley, my father
and Tyrone, my son

Contents

Preface

*T*HE 1920s witnessed an extraordinary flowering of literary and artistic creativity among African Americans. Critics hailed the emergence of a "New Negro," who took pride in the black race and its African heritage, and whose writings exposed and attacked discrimination, explored black folk culture, and strove to create a unique African-American literature. Yet for all its vitality, the cultural movement best known as the Harlem Renaissance was fraught with tensions: between the ideal of Africa and the reality of America; between the lure of a romanticized rural past and the demands of an alien urban present; between the need to affirm the uniqueness of black culture and the desire to achieve acceptance by the majority white culture.

Perhaps more than any other Harlem Renaissance figure, Claude McKay embodied these contradictory impulses. A Jamaican immensely proud of his peasant heritage, he abandoned his homeland, immigrated to the United States, and embarked on a career as a writer. A political radical contemptuous of all things middle class, he embraced and later rejected communism, and eventually converted to Roman Catholicism. A poet whose verse breathed militance, anger, and alienation, he dreamed of transcending racial categories and developed his closest relationships with white intellectuals.

Not surprisingly, contemporary judgments of McKay reflected these paradoxes. He was derided as a "racial opportunist," a "black fascist," a propagandist, and a charlatan. Yet he was also widely regarded as a literary genius and became the first black writer to make the best-seller list.

This book is an interpretation of the life and work of Claude McKay. My aim is twofold: to offer a psychological portrait of a complex, deeply conflicted literary figure, and to use McKay's life as a vehicle for analyzing the larger problems of identity, vocation, and politics that confronted black intellectuals and artists during the interwar years. Drawing upon a wide range of archival sources, including recently declassified government documents, I explore the roots of McKay's political radicalism. I also provide an analysis of the contrasting meanings of race in the Caribbean and the United States, the literary politics of Harlem in the 1920s, and the ambivalence that characterized relations between black and white intellectuals in McKay's time.

The paradox of Claude McKay cannot be reduced to any simple formula. He was at once an enfant terrible who took pride in the Negro's cultural heritage and an intellectual who strove for acceptance in predominantly white circles. He was a radical intent on transforming his adopted country who nevertheless left the United States temporarily for the Soviet Union. Yet these tensions, as I will show, cannot simply be ascribed to personal or psychological problems; ultimately, they were rooted in the ambiguous social and cultural position of the black artist and political radical of the early twentieth century.

Acknowledgments

*I*T IS A pleasure to be able to thank some of the many individuals and institutions who have generously helped me in the development and preparation of this book. I am indebted to my mentors August Meier and the late Elliott Rudwick for sharing with me, as a graduate student at Kent State University, their extraordinary knowledge of African-American history. Professor Ernest Allen, Jr., of the University of Massachusetts provided me with invaluable help in understanding the "New Negro." Steven Mintz of the University of Houston not only read through the various drafts of the manuscript and offered excellent advice, but, more important, he gave me the encouragement scholars hope to receive from a fellow colleague.

I would also like to thank a number of other individuals who have contributed in their own ways toward the completion of this book. Copyeditor Philip G. Holthaus's thoroughness improved the overall quality of the work. Jenny Corbin, the manuscript typist in the Department of History at Wayne State University, deserves my gratitude for her willingness to retype the pages through their many drafts. Colleague Alan Raucher read the manuscript early in its preparation and offered valuable advice. Special thanks also go to Clark Dougan, senior editor at the University of Massachusetts Press, whose kindness and support I have greatly appreciated through the long process of preparing this book for publication.

In addition, I also would like to thank the many people at the various research institutions for their cooperation. Among them: Andy Simons at the Amistad Research Center, Tulane University, New Orleans; Esme Bhan at the Moorland-Spingarn Research Center, Howard University, Washington, D.C.; Saundra Taylor at the Lilly Library, Indiana University, Bloomington, Indiana; Patricia C. Willis at the Yale Collection of American Literature, Beinecke Rare Book and Manuscript Library, Yale Library, New

ACKNOWLEDGMENTS

Haven, Connecticut; and the staff at the Houghton Library, Harvard University, Cambridge, Massachusetts.

Finally, I would like to express a special thanks to my son, Tyrone Dwight Tillery, whose love for his "Popi" made the completion of the McKay manuscript all the more important. At the age of ten he has a wisdom far beyond his years.

Claude McKay

1

In Search of Larger Worlds

*L*ATE IN 1912 Claude Festus McKay prepared to leave Jamaica for the United States. At twenty-three he already had become something of a Jamaican "Robert Burns."[1] A pioneer in writing Jamaican dialect poetry, and author of two volumes of verse, *Songs of Jamaica* and *Constabulary Ballads,* he had reached the point at which the development of his intellectual and creative ambitions required a world larger than Jamaica. Yet, as he departed, McKay carried with him the intellectual and psychological baggage of a culture that left an indelible mark on his intellectual and social development.[2] Both his eventual successes and his future failures can be traced to the strong influences exerted on him as a child and young man in Jamaica.

Claude was born on September 15, 1890, in the tiny village of Sunny Ville, nestled in the remote hills of Clarendon parish. Sunny Ville sat in a triangle of land formed by two streams—one so large the peasants called it a river.[3] The hills and streams of Jamaica formed an important part of the peasants' lives. Life, it was believed, was inseparably "linked with streams," which nourished the Jamaican peasant's soul, and provided a point of reference for the native son who happened to wander from his native soil. Written in the Jamaican dialect, McKay's poem "To Clarendon Hills and H.A.H." captures much of this feeling:

> Love Clarendon Hills, Dear Clarendon Hills,
> Dear Clarendon Hills,
> Oh I feel de chills,
> Yes, I feel de chills
> Coursin' t'rough me frame
> When I call your name,
> Dear Clarendon hills,
> Loved Clarendon hills.[4]

For McKay, the rivers also represented the innocence and purity of youth, unspoiled by the intrusion of age and the encroachment of civilization. After leaving Clarendon, McKay nostalgically declared in the poem "Sukee" that he would forever love the river and vowed to return one day, never to leave its bosom again. The Sukee was a place of "blissful swims," of jumping off the old plank and swimming naked, unburdened by the pains of life that so marked his later experience.[5]

The youngest of eight children, McKay was born to Thomas Francis and Ann Elizabeth McKay, pillars of the local Baptist church and respected leaders of the black peasant community.[6] Claude's father was the undisputed head of his family. Thomas was a descendant of the West African nation of Ashanti, and often held the family transfixed telling wonderful stories of African traditions and customs, but more important to him he was also the product of the intense Christian fundamentalist indoctrination he had received as a youth. Thomas never strayed from the straight and narrow moral road: he tried to live a completely honest life, avoided the use of curse words, and totally abstained from drinking and dancing. He coaxed a good living from the difficult soil, growing cacao, coffee, bananas, sugar cane, and other tropical fruits and plants.[7]

Many Jamaican peasants believed that such things as hurricanes, floods, diseases, and other natural catastrophes were caused by the Obi or Obeah, a West African god, but Thomas McKay scorned such ideas. He prided himself in believing that people could be hurt only by the machinations of others, not by magic. He placed his faith in religion, his reason, and his reverence for Anglo-Saxon justice. His contact with people tended to be formal and distant, but his appreciation of Anglo-Saxon justice won him the respect of the villagers, and he was often called upon to adjudicate quarrels among the other peasants. A more serious consequence of his puritanical personality was his inability to develop a close relationship with his children, especially with Claude.[8]

Claude's mother presented a contrasting personality. He remembered his mother as being physically quite brown, with two wonderful strands of hair reaching down to her shoulders when plaited. Like her husband a descendant of slaves, but from Madagascar, McKay's mother was less demanding in her relationships and freely gave love and warmth to her children and to all who knew her. McKay's love of his mother and of the natural habitat of

Jamaica constituted his strongest and fondest memories of his boyhood.[9] In McKay's poem "My Mountain Home," written in the Jamaican dialect, he invites us on a tour to show us where he was born. There among the banana field and corn, on a lonesome mountain road one Sunday morning before service, his mother gave birth to him. As McKay put it,

De mango tree in yellow bloom,
  De pretty akee seed
De mammee where de John-to-whits come
  To have their daily feed,

Show you de place where I was born,
  Of which I am so proud,
'Mongst de banana-field an' corn
  On a lone mountain-road.

One Sunday marnin' 'fo' de hour
  Fe service-time come on,
Ma say dat I be'n born to her
  Her little las'y son.[10]

McKay's tour of his mountain home concludes, as many of his poems do, with a vow to return to where the wild ferns grow and to his most beloved and hallowed spot, "where my dear mother rest."[11]

The contrast of growing up with a warm and loving mother and a cold and distant father had a profound effect on Claude McKay. Like his mother, he was more concerned with the emotional and aesthetic things life had to offer. However, much like his father, he had trouble with interpersonal relationships. From the beginning it was difficult for Claude McKay to reconcile these extremes of personality. His need for the visualization of the beautiful things of life made it increasingly impossible for him to live under the roof of a man with such opposite inclinations. Consequently, when Claude was eight, McKay's mother decided to send him to live with his oldest brother, Uriah Theophilious, a schoolteacher in the northwestern part of the island.[12]

McKay's brother, besides being the local schoolteacher, was an amateur journalist, a country correspondent who wrote for the city newspapers. Uriah possessed an impressive library, a rarity for the average Jamaican, containing all the great English masters and several translations of ancient works. With Uriah's encourage-

5

ment, McKay spent much of his time reading novels, histories, biblical literature, and most of the works of William Shakespeare. As Claude was later to recall, "that was a great formative period in my life—a time of perfect freedom to play, read and think as I liked."[13]

Although Uriah provided McKay with an unfettered environment to expand his intellectual horizons, he could also display the strict disciplinarian traits of his father. While Claude was a student in his brother's school, he was attracted to Agnes, a pretty, light mulatto, and through a friend began sending her love letters. Eventually, Uriah intercepted some of the letters; finding them to be too passionate for someone of McKay's age, he soundly whipped him.[14]

In 1901 Claude and Uriah returned to their native village, where Uriah accepted a position as teacher in the primary school. Under the guidance of his brother, McKay prepared for the examinations to become an elementary school teacher himself. But after passing an examination for the Government Trade Scholarship in 1906, he received a three-year state stipend to enter the trade school at Kingston.[15]

On January 7, 1907, not long after McKay had started school, Kingston was hit by a terrible earthquake. The sixteen-year-old McKay, lying on the bed in his underwear when the earthquake struck, was impressed by the destruction left in the earthquake's aftermath: "I went out that afternoon to go to the center of the city, where my cousin lived. . . . the bricks had piled up in the streets. There were dead bodies all around, groans of those who were trapped, and the stench of burning bodies, turned me back." Afterward, Claude moved to the provincial village of Browns Town, where he prepared for his certification as a wheelwright. But after two uninspired years, Claude was convinced that he would never be any good at a trade and returned home again to Sunny Ville, where, as he put it, he "farmed rather half-heartedly."[16]

He had been home for less than six months when his mother died. Her death was a bitter blow to McKay. She had given Claude the love and affection his father was incapable of bestowing. She made Claude feel a sense of self-worth and may have sent him away to his brother's to protect him from the harsh judgments of the elder McKay. In his poem "My Mountain Home" McKay remembered the time his mother sent him to the spring. "I was so happy feelin' then," he wrote, "Dat I could do something."[17]

His mother's death and his lack of interest in farming prompted McKay to once again set off for Kingston, where, after a short stint working in a match factory, he impulsively joined Jamaica's constabulary.[18] Initially, McKay's experience on the force was not unpleasant. Reflecting on the time spent in the force, McKay wrote, "As constituted by the authorities the Force is admirable, and it only remains for the men themselves and especially the sub-officers to make it what it should be, a harmonious band of brothers."[19] The force not only provided McKay with close friends and, perhaps, even a lover, it exposed him to one of the first in a series of strong male figures who would play an important role in his life. In a poem dedicated to an inspector who was leaving the force, McKay's attraction to and respect for strong male father figures is evident. Titled "To Inspector W. E. Clark," the poem begins:

> Farewell, dear Sir, a sad farewell!
> An, as across the deep you sail,
>   Bon voyage we wish you:
> We love you deepest as we can,
> As officer an' gentlemen,
>   With love sincere an' true.[20]

The thought of never meeting the inspector again brought an aching pain to the impressionable McKay.

At first, McKay greeted the constabulary with a "heart that was light and gay."[21] He developed an intense relationship with a comrade he identified in a poem only as Bennie; this relationship made his first five months on the force tolerable, if not pleasant. In the poem "Bennie's Departure" Claude describes this close bond and the emotional devastation he felt when Bennie suddenly left the constabulary. The loss of Bennie continued to affect McKay long after he left the constabulary:

> Where'er I roam, what'er the clime,
> I'll never know a happier time;
> I seemed as happy as could be,
> When—everything was torn from me.
> De fateful day I 'member still
> De final breakin' o' my will,

Again de sayin' o' good-bye,
My poor heart's silent wilin' cry;
My life, my soul, my all be'n gone,
And ever since I am alone.[22]

It may well be that Bennie's friendship with McKay filled the emotional void left by the recent death of his mother. Once Bennie departed, the harsher aspects of the constabulary—the brutality and corruption, the discipline of a semimilitary life, and the policeman's preoccupation with making cases—increasingly revolted McKay. He was left alone to face "de Depot's black strife."[23]

Basically, Claude did not have the "heart of a Constab."[24] As an officer on the police force, McKay was distrusted by his fellow blacks, who considered all policemen tools of the upper classes. As Claude put it,

Tis grievous to think dat, while toiling on here,
My people won't love me again,
My people, my people, me owna black skin—
De wretched t' ought gives me such pain.[25]

His temperament was such that he was pained by the daily injustices he witnessed as a constable. Unable to rebel openly against the constabulary hierarchy, McKay poured his feelings out in poems that became the basis for the volume of *Constabulary Ballads.*[26] Upon McKay's release from "misery,"[27] he looked forward to returning to the hills of Clarendon to forget his "too too rash act" of joining the constabulary force.[28]

He returned to Clarendon parish in 1911. By now he was a handsome man of medium height and build, "whose eyebrows arched high up and never came down."[29] But McKay's third return home would also be short-lived. Several things had taken place in his life that made it impossible for him to remain in Clarendon parish or even on the island of Jamaica. One was his growing awareness, whether admitted or not, that his identification with the Jamaican peasantry was always more wishful than real. Possessing qualities uncharacteristic of the Jamaican peasant, he gradually came to realize that he needed a larger world in which to operate. His artistic creativity and intellectual independence set him apart from most of his fellow Jamaicans.

Claude had become interested in writing poetry during his elementary school years. His early poems were composed in traditional English style. One day, while working as an apprentice wheelwright, he instinctively dropped the English form and thereafter wrote a number of poems about peasant life in the Jamaican dialect.[30]

The poems that were later gathered as *Songs of Jamaica* were colorful and offered vivid descriptions of the life of the peasant. Life for the average Jamaican peasant was difficult, characterized by the "hard times" of trying to keep the sheriff away from the door for nonpayment of taxes; working like a mule for the buccra (white man); struggling to make a crop grow and wondering whether God had cursed the "black naygur"; or sending one's children to school without food or clothes to wear.[31] In a moment of weakness the Jamaican peasant might ask:

> De many pleasures? Wh's de gain?
> I'll tell you of a grindin' pain
> Deat companies de birt,'
> An' runs wid vengeance mirt'
> De life, till it is slain.[32]

In spite of a life whose daily food was often pain, the Jamaican peasant, McKay observed, approached it with a resignation that bordered on stoicism: "We needn' fold we han' an' cry,/Nor vex we hart wid groan and sigh/De best we can do is fe try."[33] The Jamaican peasant could be happy when it rained, when he lacked food to put on the table, or even when he was in the hospital. Indeed, when the angel of death visited the peasant, he could accept it with resignation, for it was his fate to do the best he could, regardless of life's overwhelming obstacles.

However, there was compensation for those who suffered, whether from life's natural misfortunes or from the oppression of man. "For every smallest wrong dere is a right," McKay wrote in the poem "Compensation." Oppression might endure for a time but in the end there was a cure for every ill.[34]

McKay's poetic ability had brought him the attention and encouragement of several prominent whites. Tom Redcam, a native-born Jamaican poet of Irish descent who found his inspiration in the life and history of Jamaica, was one early source of support. Born in 1870, he became editor of the *Jamaican Times*. While

9

editor, Redcam offered encouragement to younger writers and found space for their work, including the poems of the young black man from Clarendon. Redcam published some of McKay's dialect verse and later helped to secure publication of his first two collections of poems.[35]

Even more helpful was Walter Jekyll, an English planter. Born into an upper-class family in Surrey, England, Jekyll had been educated at Harrow and Trinity College, Cambridge University. After receiving his master's degree, he entered the ministry, when he soon found himself embroiled in a debate over religion and science. Ultimately, he rejected religion and renounced his holy orders. When McKay met him, Jekyll was in his late fifties and had resided in Jamaica for several years, most recently in the Blue Mountains.[36]

His interest in McKay was partly a reflection of a growing recognition among some white Jamaicans that native Jamaica constituted a storehouse of material for artistic expression. Jekyll convinced Claude to focus his artistic talents on creating dialect poetry and prose. He himself had been traveling the island seeking from Jamaican peasants the African stories called annancy tales. Like Redcam, Jekyll viewed the Negro as a born actor to whom gesture, which gave emphasis to work, came naturally.[37] In his collection *Jamaican Song and Story*, published in 1907, Jekyll commented that the book was a tribute to his love of Jamaica and its dusky inhabitants with their winning way and their many good qualities, including their supreme virtue of "cheerfulness."[38]

Jekyll had heard about a "Negro peasant who wrote poetry" and wanted to meet him. He was intrigued by the idea of a black who wrote poetry, and one who was writing in the Jamaican vernacular about Negro folktales and tall tales, typically despised as old-fashioned and shunned by better educated members of the black community.

Jekyll's recognition of McKay's natural attributes proved crucial to Claude's development as a writer and intellectual. His praise and support stimulated McKay's creativity and through his contacts McKay was able to get some poems published in the leading newspaper, the *Daily Gleaner*. According to McKay, his dialect poetry created an immediate sensation. With Jekyll's help, McKay eventually published his dialect poems under the title

Songs of Jamaica (1912). The volume sold over two thousand copies and won the Mulgrave Silver Medal, a prize established by a British family for the best representation of Jamaican literature.[39]

At the time of these visits with Jekyll in the Blue Mountains, McKay was serving as a member of the constabulary and was a very emotionally troubled man. The recent loss of the two people he loved most, his mother and Bennie, rendered Claude very vulnerable and confused. His life thus far had been one of disappointment and pain. The early happy days, he wrote of in the poem "My Mountain Home," had slipped quickly away, and he now found himself a "man among strange folks in a strange land." He continues:

> My little joys, my wholesome min' [mind],
> Dey bullied out o' me,
> And made me daily mourn an' pine
> An' wish dat I was free.
>
> Dey taught me to distrust my life,
> Dey taught me what was grief;
> For months I travailed in de strife,
> 'Fo' I could find relief.[40]

The strange land McKay referred to was certainly the city of Kingston, and the difficulties were those he was now experiencing on the force. At this point, what McKay wanted most was to find a place "far in de country" where he could hide from life's pain and restore his spirits. From the safety and sanctuary of a home in nature he could "view de wul" and learn of all "its doin's to de full" without fear.[41] He found this plan of retreat at Jekyll's home in the Blue Mountains.

McKay spent much of his spare time studying at Jekyll's cottage. During these visits he began to understand the aesthetics of the Jamaican dialect and often marveled that his white mentor had been one of the first to discover its beauty. Under Jekyll's tutelage, McKay's curiosity about the world beyond the small island grew. He was introduced to the great German philosophers—Kant, Hegel, and Nietzsche—and acquired a fondness for German poetry, which Jekyll would first read to him in the original language before translating it into English.

Jekyll increasingly became a source of inspiration and fascination to McKay. The older Jekyll sensed McKay's confusion and insecurity and offered him the opportunity to nourish his talent as a poet at a very crucial time in his life. Jekyll's life-style too, particularly his apparent willingness to break with class and race distinctions, intrigued McKay. On one occasion, for example, the governor paid Jekyll an unexpected visit. Perceiving the rather intimate relationship between McKay and Jekyll, the governor attempted to embarrass Claude by making some crass remarks about race and class. Jekyll refused to participate and the governor left hurriedly. As a native, McKay was quite astounded by Jekyll's willingness to stand by him, for he was "just a peasant." But Jekyll explained that English gentlemen always liked peasants; it was the ambitious middle class that they could not tolerate.[42]

McKay's relationship with Walter Jekyll constituted one of the more complex chapters in his life. Some have chosen to suggest that it may have been a homosexual relationship and that the younger man was seduced by the older, more experienced Jekyll.[43] Nothing in McKay's correspondence or his writings provides evidence for this idea, but it must be admitted that McKay himself was bisexual. Writing to Harold Cruse of her relationship with McKay in 1924, Josephine Herbst commented, "McKay was bisexual, although he had none of the mannerisms of most homosexuals." She could personally attest to his bisexuality, for she had contracted syphilis from him.[44] It is entirely possible that McKay's feelings for Jekyll were simply those of a student for an admired mentor. Throughout his life McKay would be attracted to strong men, such as Max Eastman of the *Liberator*, Frank Harris, editor of *Pearson's Magazine*, and Bishop Henry Sheil of the Catholic church. But it would not be far fetched to suggest that in Jekyll's case, at least, a physical relationship supplemented the mentor-student relationship.

Though Jekyll exhibited a form of class snobbishness, he was always a warm and generous father figure to McKay. As if to punctuate the nature of this relationship, McKay listed Jekyll as his father on his school records while he was a student at Kansas State College in 1914.[45]

Whatever the reasons, the influence Jekyll exerted on McKay's intellectual development and personality was immense, the result being a peculiar combination of social inclinations. Despite his own peasant origins, McKay adopted certain English aristocratic characteristics. Throughout his life he behaved much like Jekyll in his relationships with other people. As McKay would later recall, "All through my life, wherever I have travelled, I have always managed to preserve some form of personal aloofness even if I were living in the poorest neighborhood."[46] Like Jekyll, McKay always tolerated members of the lower class better than he did members of the aspiring middle class. Further, throughout his life, McKay's best friends would resemble Jekyll: they would be white, somewhat radical, economically well off, but usually living bohemian or quasi-bohemian lives.

McKay also appears to have internalized much of Jekyll's philosophical outlook about the world. On numerous occasions Jekyll expressed his dislike for modernism and industrialism. He was particularly critical of the United States, whose rapid industrialization threatened the equilibrium of the world. From his mentor in Jamaica's Blue Mountains, McKay acquired attitudes that later nourished his own criticism of capitalistic societies.[47]

Of equal importance in McKay's intellectual and social development was contact with British influence in Jamaica. British culture intruded upon and often overwhelmed much of the indigenous black culture. From a very early age, black Jamaicans were subtly shaped to become "black Britons"—in theory if not in actuality. Such conditioning involved learning to believe that freedom had come from the hands of Queen Victoria. McKay remembered participating each year along with thousands of other Jamaicans in the celebration of the queen's benevolent deed. As they danced and sang in the queen's honor, the descendants of Africans enslaved by Europeans recited the verse "Rule, Britannia, Britannia rules the waves,/For Britons never shall be slaves."[48]

McKay once wrote that the educational system "was so directed that we really and honestly believed that we were little black Britons." At the elementary level, education had been extended to all classes and races. But the high schools followed English models: they were intended only for children of wealthy parents, mostly from white families. Fortunately for McKay, his grammar school years had been spent with his brother Theophilious.[49]

The Jamaican peasant's education was heavily laced with British propaganda. Strong emphasis was placed on loyalty to the king and queen. Such identification with, and emulation of, the British system created serious problems of identity for Jamaicans. Sisyphus-like, they were doomed, striving to be a part of the system and yet in actuality finding themselves powerless and removed from their own society. This manifested itself in the difficulty of native Jamaicans to develop and preserve a distinctly Jamaican culture.[50]

English culture in general cast a long shadow over the psyche of all Jamaicans. They spoke the king's language, accepted British values, vicariously admired British power, imitated the British system of government, and learned to accept the British stratification of social classes. As McKay wrote, "Jamaicans have striven so hard to be like the English that the little island is known as 'little England.'"[51]

McKay had ambivalent feelings about the British influence on black Jamaicans. In *Songs of Jamaica* in 1912, McKay declared of Jamaica:

> Dere is no land dat can compare
> Wid you where'er I roam;
> In all de wul' none like you fair,
> My native land, my home.[52]

Jamaica, McKay exclaimed, was the "nigger's place," and although critics often derided it as a "no land race," it was his native land, his home.[53] Yet, in the same volume, in a poem entitled "Old England," he expressed equally strong emotions about longing to travel to view the "homeland England," where "rests de body of our Missis Queen Victoria de Good."[54]

Throughout his life he respected and admired the British empire and its culture. In an unpublished manuscript written near the end of his life, "My Green Hills of Jamaica," McKay still expressed admiration for the British. He believed that Jamaicans had acquired from the British their democratic spirit and respect for law and order. This could be seen clearly in the conduct of the constabulary and its administrative officials: "They would not," he remarked, "take bribes and indulge in grafting. . . . In fact, as I remember it, there was no graft in the entire governmental system of Jamaica."[55]

McKay concluded that, unlike black Americans, who were poorly treated by whites, black and colored Jamaicans were treated with respect by the British. They could, for instance, serve in the legislative council. In truth, the majority of legislators where whites and mulattoes, but blacks did sometimes win election. Negroes were conspicuous and exercised a great deal of influence in all Jamaica's affairs, according to McKay.

McKay was particularly impressed by the "sense of dignity" bequeathed to blacks by British culture. It did not matter, he asserted, that the overwhelming majority of the black population was poor, for "people might stand a little loss of property with good grace if they are not entirely stripped of all their human dignity." Furthermore, McKay wrote, "An Englishman actually believes that his house, however poor, is his castle and so also has conveyed to the Jamaican peasant that feeling of security, in which he believes that his hut is his castle."[56]

For most of his life McKay believed that the extreme poverty of black Jamaicans could be explained by laws of economics or the variations in natural conditions that determined the ebb and flow of agricultural prosperity. He firmly believed that the great mass of peasants did not feel oppressed as a result of their color because anyone with talent could rise out of the masses and his or her economic condition. Writing to James Weldon Johnson in the late 1920s, McKay remarked, "In my village, I grew up on equal terms with white, mulatto and black children of every race because my father was a big peasant and belonged. The difference on the island is economic, not social." Moreover, despite widespread poverty, McKay claimed, Jamaica had spiritual values that were lacking in the United States. No race problem existed and, if one did, it arose from the friction between blacks and near-whites.[57]

Since he believed that racism played little or no part in relations among the various racial groups in Jamaica, McKay also believed that the black Jamaican peasant, unlike African-Americans, never suffered from an inferiority complex. "No black Jamaican," McKay argued, "even imagines he is not adequately protected under British law. No British West Indian bears that mark of futility, frustration, despair and neurosis among the educated class which is branded on every American Negro from California to New York and from Texas to Washington." According to McKay, the absence of racism in the British West Indies explained why those blacks who fled the poverty of the islands to live in the United States preferred to retain their British citizenship rather than become American citizens—a bias that caused McKay serious difficulty later in America.[58]

All these comments about Jamaica and the British empire must be viewed with great care, for they were written near the end of McKay's life and may be more nostalgic than accurate. The Jamaica described in his "Green Hills" manuscript was never so idyllic, either during his childhood or at the time of the writing of the manuscript.

In the period of McKay's childhood, Jamaica had barely stepped out of the shadow of slavery. Emancipation had meant little for the overwhelming majority of the black population. Following the abolition of slavery in 1833, the tiny white majority continued to rule as it always had, and did what it could to prevent the black peasants from achieving economic independence. The white ruling class simply refused to sell land in small parcels to individuals. What land was acquired by the peasants was purchased by missionary bodies in large tracts and then either leased or resold as small holdings to blacks. Some blacks obtained land as squatters, but in inaccessible places in the hills. Other black Jamaicans, for one reason or another, were unable to escape the old estates and eventually became Jamaica's landless proletariat.[59]

Since the majority of the population was black, whites feared the potential strength of this population. Therefore, they took a number of measures to assure control for the next ten decades. As it happened, a color class hierarchy had already evolved in Jamaica. The children born of miscegenation had become a social problem by the middle of the eighteenth century. White planters often rewarded their black concubines with freedom; even more often, they freed the children born from such unions. Frequently, manumissions were accompanied by the granting of property to the colored children born to these interracial unions. By 1763 such property was valued at £3 million, a situation that caused fear among whites of a growing wealthy colored population. This fear led to the passage of an act declaring that money passing from a white to a Negro or mulatto (colored) person should not exceed £1,000.

The white elite eventually recognized that it could use the

colored class to check the aspirations of the darker classes. By granting preferential treatment and opportunity to mulattoes, the whites created a division between the colored and the black classes. Such practices had originated in the preemancipation era, but they remained in force until well into the twentieth century.[60]

By the time McKay was born, this racial hierarchy had already crystallized. At its apex stood the white minority in whose hands was concentrated all social, economic, and political power. The colored class constituted a sort of "managerial" and buffer zone between the whites and blacks. While both the mulatto and black Jamaicans suffered from white control, there was far more friction between the two nonwhite groups than between nonwhites and whites. Since lesser degrees of color carried special privileges in education and economics, the mulatto class viewed the black masses as a threat to their privileged position.[61]

Little of this intraracial resentment ever surfaced as open conflict, owing partially to the imposition of an English class system that cosmetically covered over the racial motives behind the social and economic structure in Jamaica. For many black Jamaicans it was difficult, if not impossible, to admit to racial cleavages; to do so would be to admit their inferior status as a group. Consequently, most Jamaicans refused even to discuss color or shade prejudice. Only when some incident occurred and acted as a catalytic agent did individuals publicly give vent to their accumulated feelings.[62]

For Jamaicans of dark complexion, like Marcus Garvey or McKay, the subtleties of color, class, and culture were invariably associated with pain and ambivalence. Garvey articulated this hurt in the boldest terms. While in Jamaica, he accused mulattoes of frustrating his plans to establish local schools modeled after Booker T. Washington's Tuskegee Institute. He once remarked, "I was openly hated and persecuted by some of these colored men of the island who did not want to be classified as Negroes but as white."[63] After coming to American Garvey erroneously assumed that nonwhite society in the United States was similar to nonwhite society in Jamaica and therefore projected a similar pattern of racial stratification—concluding that in both countries it was easier for blacks to secure support from whites than from mulattoes in the matter of implementing racial betterment programs.

17

Garvey was adamant in his contempt for mulattoes, but also exhibited considerable ambivalence when it came to whites. At times he uttered high praise for aristocratic whites, noting, for example, how as a child he had played freely with the best white children of his parish. But Garvey also cited his recognition of white domination of Jamaica as the major factor in his decision to leave Jamaica. In light of the deep levels of frustration and hopelessness experienced by black Jamaican peasants, Garvey felt that mounting a worldwide assault on white domination from Jamaica was doomed to failure, so Garvey came to America to accomplish what he could not do in his native land. He brought with him his British culture and his sense of Jamaican class and color stratifications.[64]

Unlike Garvey, McKay seems to have been psychologically incapable of openly confronting the problems that beset the black Jamaican. Instead, he spent much of his life fleeing from them. While Garvey could publicly acknowledge the racial animosities in Jamaica and their implications for black Jamaicans, McKay denied the realities of race relations in Jamaica. Like Garvey, he was quick to point out that when he was a child he had had many white playmates.[65] That fact, he more than once reminded African Americans, was the essential difference between himself and them. "I was brought up to use the same language to a white person as a colored," he instructed a black during the 1920s, "without carrying a chip on my shoulder."[66] It seems extraordinary that in his "Green Hills" manuscript McKay would continue to deny that color played any sort of significant role in determining the socioeconomic status of black Jamaicans or that black Jamaicans suffered no sense of inferiority on account of being black. He could hardly have escaped the opprobrium of color in Jamaica anymore than anyone else.[67]

Occasionally, in private, McKay did reveal the pain he felt over Jamaica's color problem. After he published his novel *Home to Harlem* (1928) and gained temporary financial success, he wrote to his brother expressing concern about the education and job opportunities available to his daughter, Ruth Hope, who, like McKay, had a dark complexion. In his letter McKay indicated to Theophilious that the black population had fewer opportunities than mulattoes, and that he feared that Ruth would not be able to secure a decent job. His brother assured him that while it was true that mulattoes received preferential treatment, ability also counted. He said that he felt that a girl of her "complexion" would be able to get a decent job anytime.[68] Theophilious's optimism about Ruth and her color seemed to have been short-lived. A few years later he wrote to Claude complaining about the barriers in Jamaica against darker-complexioned blacks, declaring that "Jamaica is all white and brown. There is no scope for one."[69]

Ellen Tarry knew firsthand the anguish, and sometimes rage, McKay felt about color. Tarry, an aspiring writer of extremely fair complexion, was befriended by McKay in the late 1930s. "Yellow Negroes," she recounted, headed McKay's list of dislikes, closely followed by "people who spouted religiosity," and "Reds." In spite of her color, according to Tarry, McKay opened closed doors in the literary market for her. Yet, without warning, McKay would sometimes lose control and in her presence launch an unwarranted attack on "light" people. Once, in the company of James Weldon Johnson, also a rather fair-skinned black, McKay inexplicably lashed out at Tarry: "Just look at you. You're sitting there as white as alabaster. Why don't you buy yourself some brown powder?" Later, a mutual friend who had known McKay in Jamaica attempted to justify his behavior by indicating that such outbursts were the result of indignities McKay suffered at the hands of a mulatto superior in the Jamaican constabulary.[70]

That McKay never reconciled Jamaican color ambivalence may account for the different political roads Garvey and he traveled. Garvey became a racial chauvinist in the 1920s, while McKay sought refuge in the working-class radical movements of socialism and communism. However, after suffering the pain of racism in the United States, McKay increasingly stressed the importance of "race" within the communist movement during the twenties and ultimately embraced race chauvinism in the thirties.

Clearly, notwithstanding his protestations to the contrary, McKay was marked by the ambivalences and tensions concerning color that all black Jamaicans felt. However, with the encouragement of white Jamaicans such as Redcam and Jekyll and his own intellectual independence, he was able to partially break free from his British conditioning. By 1912 McKay realized he needed to see the world beyond Jamaica. As he later noted, "Jamaica was too small for high achievement. There, one was isolated, cut off from the great currents of life."[71]

McKay never mentioned a racial motive for leaving Jamaica. But as Kenneth Ramchand notes in his study of the West Indian novel, "the doors which would have been shut to an equally talented Negro were open to the white-skinned." A Negro's future as a writer, Ramchand suggests, would have been severely limited in the colony of his birth.[72] When it was suggested by Henrietta Vinton Davis—an African-American singer on tour in Jamaica, who was a friend of Booker T. Washington—that McKay might attend Tuskegee and study agriculture, he seized the opportunity. He immediately consulted Jekyll, who initially objected for fear that America would exert a corrupting influence on the young author. Eventually he consented, reasoning that Tuskegee would provide McKay with the education that would enable him to return to Jamaica, make a good living, and still pursue his poetry.[73]

McKay, the proverbial "marginal man," left Jamaica not knowing that he never would return. He was among the first in a long line of emigrating West Indian writers.[74] He would have to suffer through the unexpected problems of adjustment in a new and sometimes unsympathetic milieu, and at the same time continue his struggle to reconcile or break free from his British leanings; his Jamaican-rooted hostility toward the "light skinned"; and his appropriated contempt for the black middle class—all while pursuing his true vocation, that of a "creative writer."[75]

2

In Search of Moorings

MC K AY A R R I V E D in Charleston, South Carolina, in the summer of 1912. It was the first stop on his way to Alabama's famous black industrial college, Tuskegee Institute.[1] There McKay joined other blacks, many of Hispanic background, to study agronomy.[2] From the outset, McKay experienced difficulty in adjusting to his new environment. Within six months he became so disenchanted that he left Tuskegee to attend Kansas State College in Manhattan, Kansas. His reasons for leaving Tuskegee remain obscure. Most students of McKay have accepted the explanation he himself offered in an article published five years later in *Pearson's* magazine. McKay remarked that he had departed from Tuskegee because of its "semi-military machine existence."[3] Few acquainted with Tuskegee under the leadership of Booker T. Washington would deny the school's concern for discipline and order, but McKay's departure from the institution may have been prompted by reasons other than the one he suggested.

From all indications, he actually found the discipline of the school distressingly lax. A few months after his arrival McKay sent an article to the *Daily Gleaner,* Jamaica's largest newspaper, in which he observed that the morals of the students were being affected by the close contact of the boys and girls in the dining halls and on the ball field.[4] His criticism troubled Tuskegee's administration, who wished to prevent harm to their school's positive public image. Washington's secretary, Emmett Scott, ordered an inquiry into McKay's accusations. John Whittaker, a trustee at the school, headed the investigation and concluded that, while McKay was considered a serious student with a "keen and observant eye," he had a tendency to be too critical. Nevertheless, Whittaker advised taking steps to ensure that the social life of the students should not detract from their studies.[5]

The following poem, written in memory of Booker T. Washington, makes no mention of the oppressive and restrictive environment McKay cited as reason for his abrupt departure:

CLAUDE McKAY

In Memoriam: Booker T. Washington

I vividly recall the noon-day hour
    You walked into the wide and well-filled hall:
    We rose and sang, at the conductor's call.
Dunbar's Tuskegee hymn. A splendid tower
of strength, as would a gardener on the flower
    Nursed tenderly, you gazed upon us all
    Assembled there, a serried, sable wall
Fast mortared by your subtle fact and power.
O how I loved, adored your furrowed face!
    And fondly hoped, before your days were gone,
    You would look in mine too with paternal grace.
        But vain are hopes and dreams!—gone: you are gone,
        Death's hand has torn you from your trusting race,
        And O! We feel so utterly alone.[6]

McKay's poem projects the image of a student who revered the fatherly strength and assurance Washington provided his students.

If McKay's published explanation of his departure from Tuskegee is suspect, what were his actual motives for leaving the school? A number of causes probably combined to influence his decision to quit Tuskegee. One was McKay's age. Though only twenty-three, he was older than most of the students at Tuskegee. He had already published two volumes of poetry and was, as Whittaker suggested, unusually serious about the school as well as about his own expectations. It is also probable that Tuskegee's practical curriculum did not appeal to McKay, whose real motive for attending the school had been to further his creative writing career. After discovering that Tuskegee would contribute little toward that goal, he became dissatisfied and left.

Moreover, as protective as Tuskegee's administration sought to be, McKay was ill at ease in a country where race played such an overwhelming role in the relations of its people. Tuskegee could not hide or completely isolate him from what he described as the "implacable hate of my race." Familiar with prejudice of the English sort, "subtle and dignified," rooted—at least cosmetically—in class distinction, he was unprepared for the "primitive animal race hatred" so many whites directed toward American blacks.[7]

Since, at least in his own mind, race and color were factors "hardly taken into account," in Jamaica, McKay must have been uncomfortable living amidst the obviously racist, often hostile, whites of the Deep South.[8] He was estranged even from African Americans. "There is always an unfamiliar something between people of different countries and nationalities, however intimate they may become," McKay later wrote of himself and an African-American woman.[9] As a black man of African descent, McKay was disgusted by white animosity regarding his black brothers, but as a Jamaican "black Briton" he also felt culturally and psychologically distanced from his American brothers and sisters.

Like other West Indies immigrants, he brought with him certain ill-conceived notions about his black counterparts in America. The *Daily Gleaner* had on occasion talked about African Americans, in the process revealing considerable ignorance concerning the life-style of American blacks. Typical of such articles was one titled "Dress of Negroes in New York." Reprinted from a New York dispatch, the article discussed what was apparently a mystery to many islanders: how the Negro could afford to dress so resplendently. The newspaper concluded from an incident involving a lawsuit brought by a black woman against her Pullman-porter husband that most Negroes were porters who made enormous tips with which they bought expensive clothing.[10] Unfortunately, many foreigners and even some Americans formed their perception of the African American from just this sort of misinformation. McKay's own boyhood recollection was that, in the popular mind, Negroes were more or less clowns. He remarked, "All those that we saw in Kingston on the street were the happy go lucky clowning types who sang coon songs for White men and they seemed to like it."[11]

At Kansas State College, McKay's frustrations continued. Although he stayed at the college for two years, taking courses ranging from sociology to how best to purchase feed, his grades reflected less-than-enthusiastic interest in the study of agronomy. The courses in which he performed most poorly were subjects directly related to agriculture.[12] McKay's social life at Kansas was little better than it had been at Tuskegee. As a West Indian, he moved rather uneasily among the small midwestern African-American middle class.[13] However, thanks to an undisclosed "English benefactor" (probably Jekyll), he received a gift of $2,000 and extricated himself from his uncomfortable situation. With this gift, McKay set off for the Negro Mecca, Harlem.[14]

Despite his disappointment and frustration, McKay's brief stay at the two American educational institutions marked an important phase in his development. The experience finally laid to rest any further notions he had that his destiny lay as a tiller of the soil or as a teacher of agronomy, an idea he had suggested to Jekyll before leaving Jamaica. Jekyll, who anticipated McKay's eventual return to Jamaica, had cautioned Claude that a poet could not sustain himself in an agricultural society unless he was at least partially connected to the soil. McKay's abandonment of agronomy clearly precluded such a connection.

At both schools, McKay had been forced to come to terms with the realities of his psychological and intellectual makeup. He learned that he was not temperamentally suited to the disciplined and regulated world of academia. Emotionally, McKay needed freedom and flexibility. As he put it some years later, "After a few years of study at the Kansas State College I was gripped by the lust to wander and wonder. The spirit of the vagabond, the daemon of some poets, had got hold of me. I quit college. I had no desire to return home."[15] Moreover, McKay was instinctively a loner who found himself an "outside observer" at Tuskegee and Kansas. His loner personality, which would always remain a major obstacle to McKay's establishing close relationships with African Americans, undoubtedly was complicated by his West Indian origins.

In any case, McKay's decision to travel to New York could not have been a more logical one for a poet in 1914. The intellectual and cultural center of white America was then rapidly becoming the intellectual and cultural center of black America.[16] In a few years Harlem would become a great magnet for black intellectuals, pulling them from every corner of the country.[17] For a West Indian, migration to New York was equally appropriate. During the first two decades of the twentieth century thousands of West Indian immigrants sought new homes in the rapidly emerging black metropolis of New York's Harlem. Leaving the islands of Jamaica, Haiti, Puerto Rico, and Trinidad, black immigrants traveled to Harlem in hopes of finding better social and economic opportunities.

As with previous generations of foreign immigrants, West Indians faced a number of problems that made assimilation into the mainstream of American life difficult. First, the immigrant brought a cultural heritage very different from that of most Americans. Second, and in contradistinction to the typical immigrant of previous generations, the West Indian immigrant was nonwhite and, like other racial minorities in America, was subject to social and economic proscriptions.

Such proscriptions were particularly vexatious to British West Indians, who prided themselves on being British citizens, entitled to the same respect and courtesy received by immigrants from England. Compared to many other immigrant groups, the black British immigrants were well educated: few, if any, were illiterate. They also enjoyed a reputation for skill and success in business.[18] Not surprisingly, they were angered and terrified to discover America's reality of lynchings, Jim Crowism, and discrimination. They openly resented being called "George" or "boy" by whites.[19]

Ironically, the race conflict was sharpest between the black British West Indians and African Americans.[20] By the 1920s, these tensions had reached crisis proportions in the form of heated debates, abusive exchanges in newspapers, proposals from African Americans for the restriction of further West Indian immigration, and even schemes for the redistribution of West Indians to other parts of the country.[21]

Several factors accounted for the conflict between the two nonwhite groups. Most important was the difference in their perception of "race." For African Americans, race was synonymous with color; color was the all-consuming reality of their lives. It was the starting point for the discussion of the African-American experience, past and present. Race/color was the inevitable sociopolitical arbiter, and any approach to the problems of discrimination and oppression must proceed along "race" lines. W. E. B. Du Bois epitomized this feeling for African Americans when he wrote that "the problem of the twentieth century is the problem of the color line."[22]

Most black Americans shared Du Bois's judgment concerning the role of race in American society and expected nonwhite foreigners to be just as race-conscious. They were impatient with, and intolerant of, British West Indians who did not view race as the defining problem for all people of color.

Many West Indians openly refused to be grouped with African Americans, whom they considered less refined than themselves. West Indians often went to extremes to maintain the difference between themselves and their American counterparts. For instance, most British West Indians refused to give up their British citizenship. When immigrants were faced with racial discrimination, it was not to American authorities but to the British embassy that they appealed.[23] The British West Indians tended to view racial discrimination less as a matter of race than of class prejudice. Consequently, West Indian immigrants tended to believe that individual or group "uplift programs" were the best way to combat discrimination. Thus, during the first two decades of the twentieth century, British West Indians combined their resources to purchase real estate, and also worked to achieve professional status within the black community; indeed, one-third of the black professionals in Harlem were West Indian. West Indians as a group were also the most significant depositers in Harlem's postal banks.[24]

West Indians' economic success, their consequent independence, and their reputation for clannishness aroused American blacks' resentment. West Indians were accused of exhibiting a pseudosuperiority complex that hurt the efforts of black Americans to confront racism and achieve first-class citizenship. American blacks charged that British West Indians, while keeping their British citizenship, took jobs from American blacks, the same blacks who actively fought for such employment opportunities through voting and other racially oriented tactics that the West Indians benefited from, but did not support.[25] If there was some basis for the accusations made by American blacks, their ridicule and stereotyping of the British West Indians exacerbated the problem. Derision of the West Indian accent and habits of dress, along with the caricaturing of the immigrants as "Monkey chasers," drove British West Indians closer together.[26]

Despite attempts by some African Americans and West Indians to bridge the gap and to promote intraracial harmony, antagonisms persisted. Neither group seemed capable of understanding or sympathizing with the other's cultural and psychological characteristics: the British West Indians continued to distinguish themselves from African Americans, often perpetuating certain stereotypes of their own, while African Americans persisted in considering the British West Indians as "outsiders."[27] George Schuyler, author and social critic, reflected the American black consensus when he stated that West Indians were "foreigners" and were not as realistic as the American Negro. Their leaders, he suggested, were given to flights of fancy and extremism uncommon among American blacks, whom he considered more firmly grounded.[28] Such black American prejudice led to widespread opposition to British West Indian involvement in economics, politics, or literature.

McKay's initial experience in New York looked more like a textbook example of the West Indian immigrant seeking economic and social mobility than the experience of a writer or poet. Soon after his arrival, McKay, in partnership with another individual, purchased a restaurant in Brooklyn.[29] On July 30, 1914, he married Eulalie Imelda Edwards, a childhood Jamaican sweetheart. A few months later, he had lost both his business and his wife. According to McKay, his wife wearied of life in the city and returned to Jamaica. He attributed the failure of his business to "high living" and "bad business" practices.[30]

Basically, however, he did not possess the qualities necessary to be either a successful proprietor or a devoted husband. The responsibilities that accompany marriage presented limitations to which McKay could not conform. Seven years later, while in the company of some friends, McKay had a chance encounter with his former wife. One of his friends expressed surprise at the revelation that McKay had been married. Embarrassed, McKay remarked that he had married when a domestic partnership seemed necessary to his existence. He went on to explain that he was not suited for marriage because he was a "truant by nature and undomesticated in the blood."[31] This was certainly an honest self-evaluation. He never saw his only child, Eulalie Ruth Hope, and made little effort to provide financially for her.[32]

As it happened, these marital and financial failures proved to be a boon to his career as a creative writer. He was forced by these events to recognize his own psychological underpinnings and needs. McKay now drifted from place to place working as a porter, houseman, janitor, butler, and waiter—anything that provided him with enough money for food and shelter.[33] Freed from the "fetters" of business and marriage, he could focus on what had been his primary objective for coming to America: the fulfillment of his desire to be a successful poet.

Black Harlem had a catalytic effect on McKay. Failure with middle-class pursuits forced McKay to live down among the rough body of the great serving class of African Americans. Living alongside them he experienced an exhilaration unlike anything he had felt in Jamaica. As McKay described it, "their spontaneous ways of acting on and living for the moment, the physical and sensuous delights, the loose freedom in contrast to the definite peasant patterns by which I had been raised—all served to feed the riotous sentiments smoldering in me and cut me finally adrift from the fixed mooring my mind had been led to respect, but to which my heart had never held."[34]

Much like early twentieth-century white bohemians who had impulsively turned their backs on nineteenth-century Victorian morality, McKay imbibed Harlem culture, especially its nightlife. The intimacy, warmth, and native excitement of the cabarets located on 135th Street between Fifth and Seventh avenues enthralled McKay. Though he spent most of his time traveling through New England as a railroad dining-car waiter, he always looked forward to the return trip to black Harlem: "There, coming off the road like homing birds, we trainmen came to rest awhile and fraternize with our friends in the city—elevator runners and porters—and snatch from saloon and cabaret and home a few brief moments of pleasure, of friendship and of love."[35]

McKay's involuntary vagabondage inspired him to begin writing poetry again. The return to such creative endeavors was fraught with constraints and pitfalls. This was especially true for the period 1916 to 1919, when the older established schools of literature were being challenged by groups of literary radicals advocating different philosophies concerning style and content. The most conspicuous of these groups was headed by James Oppenheim, editor of *Seven Arts* magazine. Oppenheim's group believed that socialism would lead to a reconstruction of American society and with it a new culture, a new literature, and new art forms. They were uncertain about the exact nature of this new culture, but Oppenheim's group knew that it would be "modern." Their idea of modern was best expressed in their attitude toward poetry: the modernist flew in the face of tradition and wrote without regard for existing forms or style. The modern poet would use simpler language, even slang.[36]

A new literary movement was also beginning to appear in the black community, a movement that was characterized by its emphasis on the African-American racial heritage. This literary movement, while most conspicuous to the black community itself, had not escaped the attention of whites, both liberal and radical. In fact, much of the initial encouragement for the new kind of black literature came from whites such as Joel E. Spingarn, one of the early leaders of the National Association for the Advancement of Colored People. He urged blacks to preserve their cultural heritage, while at the same time seeking full integration in all other arenas of the larger society. To this end, Spingarn and the NAACP in March 1913 established the annual Spingarn Award, to be given to the Negro who "shall have reached the highest achievement in his field of activity."[37]

While whites such as Spingarn sought to encourage blacks to write about themselves and the entire black experience, literary radicals of Oppenheim's persuasion were more interested in publishing material from blacks that dealt exclusively with racial themes. This was the situation McKay faced when he began to write poetry again. McKay's poetry was not solely concerned with racial themes. Thus, he became frustrated and disillusioned when pressures were brought to bear on him to conform to the new trends advocated by some literary radicals.

For example, when McKay sent a number of poems to the editors of *Seven Arts,* Oppenheim replied that he liked the spirit of the poems but not the sonnet form in which they were written. McKay disagreed with Oppenheim's position and wrote privately to Spingarn expressing his frustration and confusion. He complained that, in the context of his training, the form was correct. In truth, his attempts to use free form had failed, but the sonnet he found admirable for a moment's thought. He understood that he had a tendency to be diffuse and repetitive, and he felt that tight rhythmic and metric forms helped him check these faults.[38]

Despite Oppenheim's reservations about McKay's form, *Seven Arts* accepted two of his poems for its December 1917 issue. This success did not lessen McKay's disappointment at Oppenheim's

CLAUDE MCKAY

attitude and his circle's intolerance of the classic literary traditions. [39] Even more disturbing to McKay than his conflict with Oppenheim concerning form were the increasing restrictions placed on his choice of subject matter. Writing to William Stanley Braithwaite, the black assistant literary editor of the *Boston Transcript* in 1916, who had recently won national recognition for his books *Lyrics of Life* (1904) and *The House of Falling Leaves* (1908), McKay explained his concern:

> When I was in New York I sent a sonnet on the race problem to a prominent newspaper editor who answered that he would like to print it and asked for more of my work. I sent him other verses but there was no other on the race question. I would not let myself believe it was on that account they were sent back, but recently I sent some verses to a popular magazine. The editors wrote that they appreciated the poems and would like to publish some part of the work of my race but not just that sort of verse, there was only one poem that contained anything about race. [40]

The popular magazine McKay referred to was probably *Seven Arts*, since it had published "Harlem Dancer" and "Invocation" in 1917, which though traditional sonnets in form were clearly racial in theme. [41]

They were the first published fruits of McKay's Harlem "baptism." "Harlem Dancer" described the young black prostitutes of Harlem, whose "perfect half-clothed bodies swayed like a proudly swaying palm." It continues:

> Upon her swarthy neck black shiny curls
> Luxuriant fell; and tossing coins in praise,
> The wine-flushed, bold-eyed boys, and even the girls,
> Devoured her shape with eager, passionate gaze;
> But looking at her falsely-smiling face,
> I knew her self was not in that strange place. [42]

"Invocation," on the other hand, extolled the virtues of ancient Ethiopia, "before the white God said: Let there be light." McKay invoked ancestral spirits to bring the ancient music to his modern heart:

> Let fall the light upon my sable face
> That once gleamed upon the Ethiopian's art;
> Lift me to thee out of this alien place
> So I may be, thine exiled counterpart,
> The worthy singer of my world and race. [43]

"Harlem Dancer" and "Invocation" immediately identified Mc-Kay—under his nom de plume "Eli Edwards"—as a poet with a "sincere gift."[44] In subject matter and theme, the two poems anticipated the creativity of the Harlem Renaissance. Braithwaite offered "Harlem Dancer" as a successful example of Negro poets' attempts to use folk material and indigenous racial literature.[45] Though Braithwaite spoke for the consensus, dissenters like Allison Davis complained that "Harlem Dancer" had stimulated an unhealthy obsession with cabarets.[46]

McKay agonized over his suspicion that certain publishers desired work dealing only with race. Dejectedly, he wrote Braithwaite that "this has set me wondering whether Fine Art is not beyond nation or race—if one's mind can be limited to one's race and its problems when Art is as sublime as he who gave it to man." As a rule, racial issues did not inspire him. Few of the things he had written, he pointed out to Braithwaite, were on racial themes. Concern about possible typecasting moved McKay to ask Braithwaite whether it was better that poems with racial themes be eliminated from those he submitted to publishers.[47] When Mc-Kay wrote of this exchange with Braithwaite twenty years later, he indicated that it had been Braithwaite who had initiated the suggestion he write and send to magazines only poems that did not reveal his racial identity. He characterized Braithwaite's supposed advice as "grim and terrible."[48] Such "misremembrance"—to be charitable—or conscious reconstruction of his past is characteristic of McKay: his reminiscences and interpretations of his past are always shaped by present concerns.

McKay's reservations concerning racial themes did not stem from any denial of the desirability of poems or literature on racial themes. His seminal work using the Jamaican dialect is testimony to this truth. His concern, evidently, was that white intellectuals would force black writers into a "racial groove." This was unacceptable to a man who refused to view the world only in terms of color. He had already commented on this to Spingarn, remarking that he thought that the attitudes of whites toward writers of other races were wrong, that they (whites) were always searching for a singular racial quality that did not exist. He believed in the fraternity of great writers in which race would have no defining part.[49]

McKay cited Spingarn an example of how unsympathetic and unfair was the attitude of whites toward nonwhite writers. Oppenheim had asked his opinion of Vachel Lindsay's *Congo*, which Oppenheim liked. McKay told him he did not care much for it because it was superficial and expressed no real sympathy, unlike Wordsworth's sonnet on Toussaint L' Ouverture, which could be interpreted as a fitting tribute to any great soul who had been wronged. In McKay's judgment, Lindsay reveled in the picturesque and bizarre. McKay conceded that it was not easy for white writers to empathize deeply with black people, but also indicated that it could be done if there were enough sympathy and strength of will. He concluded, "Mrs. Stowe understood this and Whitman also. . . . many think Negro art should be ragtimy and barbaric, but it is a false conception." He admitted that he revered traditional poetic conventions. What appealed to McKay in literature was independent of race and nationality. It was, he told Spingarn, "The human feeling that transcends racial boundaries."[50]

McKay's correspondence with Spingarn and Braithwaite reveals an extremely confused writer. A published writer of some note in his native land, he was fearful of rejection by American publishers. For these reasons McKay published his *Seven Arts* sonnets under the nom de plume "Eli Edwards" and signed most of his correspondence to Braithwaite between 1916 and 1919 with the pseudonym "Rhonda Hope."[51] In a moment of painful introspection McKay confided to Spingarn, "I often have to stop working and take stock of myself and ask, am I on the right track? Am I moving forward or have I fallen behind. But I find myself in a quandary for no answer is forthcoming."[52]

McKay's introduction to Frank Harris, editor of *Pearson's Magazine* in 1918, did little to relieve him of his "Gordian Knot." Harris was anxious to meet a "Negro who wrote poetry while waiting upon tables working for the railroad." McKay was impressed with Harris and later described him as the "embodiment of a romantic illuminary of the writing world," who aroused his intellect like Byron and Heine, Victor Hugo and Rimbaud. On a more pragmatic level, McKay was happy to meet the editor who had announced that the purpose of *Pearson's* was to "reach and discover the obscure talents of America who were perhaps discouraged, engaged in uncongenial work"—certainly McKay felt he was among those talents.[53]

After reading some of McKay's poems, Harris pronounced Mc-

Kay a poet of rare talent, but one who had not yet given his best. Citing McKay's "The Lynching," a sonnet later published in *Harlem Shadows*, Harris indicated that McKay had not risen to the heights and stormed heaven like Milton in his "On the Late Massacre in Piedmont." Harris urged that McKay, as an African, had to accomplish things for both himself and his race—to write literature that came from his guts to express the "sublime human cry of anguish and hate against man's inhumanity to man."[54]

The following year McKay provided Harris with evidence that he was a poet of rare talent and deserved to be included among the ranks of the "poetic elect." "If We Must Die" exploded out of McKay during the turbulent days of the "Red Summer," in which scores of African Americans were beaten and killed. In "Harlem Dancer," McKay had spoken with a soft voice, full of poetic beauty. The clashes between blacks and whites in 1919, however, brought forth a different voice, one of defiant despair, bitterness, and invective.[55] McKay infused the sonnet with the fear and terror he felt in the midst of the "Gehenna." Traveling on the railroad had become so perilous for a black man that McKay began carrying a revolver. Never again would McKay be as close to African Americans as he was during this period. "We did not separate from one another gaily to spend ourselves in speakeasies, and gambling joints," he recalled. "We stuck together, some of us armed, going from railroad station to our quarters. We stayed in our quarters all through the dreary ominous nights, for we never knew what was going to happen."[56]

The Red Summer was a traumatizing ordeal for McKay and countless other blacks. At times merely remaining sane seemed to be a "tour de force." For some, like Howard University professor Carter G. Woodson, who helplessly witnessed the brutal execution of an African-American male in Washington, D.C., the memory of that long hot summer lasted a lifetime.[57] And though McKay never experienced any violence firsthand, newspaper accounts of murderous shootings and hangings inspired him to write "If We Must Die."

Yet, the poem represented only an emotional and temporary abandonment of the philosophical outlook McKay had held since his childhood in Jamaica—that of viewing man's experience from the universal, rather than the racial. It did not signify, as some have suggested, that at this juncture he had freed himself to concentrate on the black man's isolation and despair in the midst of Western society.[58] Since 1913, McKay had been aware of the intense race hatred that existed in America. Occurrences of discrimination and physical abuse against blacks had at first horrified him and then pushed him to the edge of returning such hatred in kind. But he saw hatred as such a miserable feeling that he refused to allow his perspective on humankind to be distorted by it. Moreover, he did not view race hatred and oppression as peculiar only to whites against blacks in America. As McKay put it the year before writing the famous sonnet:

> Looking about me with bigger and clearer eyes I saw that this cruelty in different ways was going on all over the world. Whites were exploiting and oppressing whites even as they exploited and oppressed the yellows and blacks. And the oppressed, groaning under the lash, evinced the same despicable hate and harshness toward their weaker fellows. I ceased to think of people and things in the mass—why should I fight with mad dogs only to be bitten and probably transformed into a mad dog myself? I turned to the individual soul, the spiritual leaders, for comfort and consolation. I felt and still feel that one must seek for the noblest and best in the individual life only: each soul must save itself.[59]

McKay's class orientation made it difficult—if not impossible—to interpret events taking place in the post–World War I period only in terms of race. By the time McKay wrote "If We Must Die," he was already deeply involved with radical labor philosophy. At the beginning of 1919 McKay quit his job on the railroad, entered a factory in New York as a semiskilled worker, and joined the revolutionary Industrial Workers of the World.[60] "The World War had ended," he wrote, "but its end was a signal for the outbreak of little wars between labor and capital."[61] It was also the beginning of the federal government's efforts to hunt down and destroy systematically radicals like those in the IWW, who were committed to the overthrow of capitalism.[62]

Years later McKay would go to great lengths to point out that the poem was written for all men who were being abused, brutalized, and murdered, whether they were black, brown, yellow, or white.[63] Ironically, no poem better illustrates McKay's universal outlook than his sonnet "If We Must Die":

If we must die, let it not be like hogs
Hunted and penned in an inglorious spot,
While round us bark the mad and hungry dogs,
Making their mock at our accursed lot.
If we must die, O let us nobly die,
So that our precious blood may not be shed
In vain; then even the monsters we defy
Shall be constrained to honor us though dead!
O kinsmen! we must meet the common foe!
Though far outnumbered let us show us brave,
And for their thousand blows deal one deathblow!
What though before us lies the open grave?
Like men we'll face the murderous, cowardly pack,
Pressed to the wall, dying, but fighting back![64]

It is remarkable that this poem that was hailed as the personifica-tion of a new spirit of race militancy contained no specific mention of race. Nowhere does *black, colored, Negro,* or any other word appear that would indicate an exclusive appeal to an audience of African Americans. The poem was universal enough for Winston Churchill to have quoted from it at the conclusion of his oration before the American Congress when he was seeking American involvement in World War II (ironically, just twenty years earlier, the poem had been censored by the Justice Department and denounced as inflammatory and seditious by the Congress).[65] That the poem was first submitted to and published in the *Libera-tor,* a white radical publication, further indicates that the poem had been intended for a wider audience than just the black com-munity, few of whom read the *Liberator.*

Some have chosen to disregard McKay's statement concerning his intent with "If We Must Die" because it was made years later. Yet, interestingly, during the period of its composition Braith-waite described McKay as a "genius" meshed in a dilemma. Braithwaite thought that McKay seemed to "waver between the racial and the universal notes" in his poetry. Unfortunately, Braithwaite chose to interpret McKay's poetry, especially "If We Must Die," only as "strident propaganda."[66] It is entirely conceiv-able that while writing this poem, McKay was still committed to writing literature that spoke to the human condition in general. Joining Braithwaite in appraising the universal thrust of McKay's poetry was James Weldon Johnson. Writing in *Black Manhattan,*

Johnson exclaimed, "But there was among them a voice too powerful to be confined to the circle of race, a voice that carried further and made America in general aware; it was of Claude McKay." Here, Johnson continued, was a true poet of great skill and wide range, who turned from creating the mood of poetic beauty in the absolute and began pouring out cynicism, bitterness, and invective.[67]

The black community's embrace of "If We Must Die" as its own is wholly understandable. America's entry into World War I had summoned black Americans to a supreme challenge: to "close ranks" with white Americans to save the world for democracy, while temporarily putting aside their own historic grievances. How could America launch a crusade to destroy tyranny and spread democracy throughout the world without providing justice for the black millions in America during the postwar period?[68] But before the war had even ended, in East St. Louis, Houston, and countless other places, the black hope of full citizenship was dashed to bits. W. E. B. Du Bois, whose *Crisis* editorial "Close Ranks" had been most responsible for rallying the African-American community to the national cause, now on May 7, 1919, urged blacks "to fight a sterner, longer, more unbending battle against the forces of hell in our own land." But even the *Crisis* editor's exhortatory words,

> We return
> We return from fighting.
> We return fighting[69]

could not express the emotions African Americans felt: anger, disillusionment, protest, and challenge. McKay's sonnet, though seemingly an incongruous medium for pouring out cynicism and bitterness, was not compromised as Du Bois had been in his "Returning Soldiers."[70] Moreover, Max Eastman may have been correct in his critical estimation that McKay was a great lyric genius of his race.[71] In "If We Must Die" that genius satisfied what sociologist Horace Cayton has described as "a deep hunger in the hearts of more than a million American Negroes," in the postwar period.[72] The poem was reprinted in black magazines and newspapers and established McKay as "a poet of his people."[73] It was committed to memory; recited at school exercises and public meetings; and discussed at private gatherings. Its impact as a harbinger and symbol of a transition in black letters continued to affect black writers even a generation after it first appeared. Writer M. Carl Holman remembers that during his high school years he yearned to write a poem as defiantly bitter as McKay's "If We Must Die."[74]

Cedric Dover, McKay's close friend, struck a note of profound truth when he remarked, "Ironies are the ways of history." While McKay appreciated the honor bestowed upon him by the black community, he was nonetheless uncomfortable at being cast in the role of a race poet representing the African American. As he put it, "And for it ["If We Must Die"] the Negro people unanimously hailed me as a poet. Indeed, that one grand outburst is their sole standard of my poetry."[75] Such praise, he feared, bordered on racial patronage and not on appreciation of his ability as a poet and intellectual. What he desired most in 1919 was to be the "individual soul" who sought what was noblest and best in the life of the individual. He put his faith in the maxim "each soul must save itself," which had expressed his approach to life and literature since his boyhood days in Jamaica.

Despite his sudden rise to prominence, he continued to be perplexed and concerned over the restraints placed on the black artist. But for better or worse, McKay had become an important symbol of the new cultural movement and was recognized as the first voice in a new chorus of black writers and artists. Unfortunately for McKay, his future career as a creative writer would too often be judged less by the quality of his work than by the sociopolitical aspects of "race" contained in them.

3

The Problems of a Black Radical: 1919–1923

*M*CKAY'S RESISTANCE to becoming "racially grooved" in his choice of literary subject matter was part of a personal struggle to earn recognition, without consideration of race, for his gifts as a writer. In his writing he tried to appeal to a wider audience, seeking to place art and intellect above color. Likewise, in the post–World War I period he applied this same philosophy to politics, economics, and personal relationships. This was best reflected in McKay's efforts to initiate a fruitful relationship with white bohemian radicals in the years after the war. McKay tended to be intellectually more iconoclastic and rebellious than most African Americans, and white bohemia seemed to offer him a milieu more compatible with his own temperament.

McKay immediately confronted two powerful dilemmas. Involvement in the world of radical journalism, both in America and Great Britain, forced him to examine his relationship with the white bohemian radicals he so emulated. At the same time, his experience on the staff of the radical American magazine the *Liberator* raised questions about the relationship between race and class in analyzing the depressed status of blacks. Bitter personal humiliations increasingly pushed McKay in the direction of stressing the importance of race within the context of the working-class radical movement. Ultimately, his insistence on a sharply defined racial perspective alienated him from his radical colleagues.

McKay began to read many of the radical and bohemian literary magazines soon after he moved to New York. "Because of my eclectic approach to literature and my unorthodox ideas of life," he recalled, "I developed a preference for the less conservative literary organs. The *Masses* was one of the magazines which attracted me when I came from out West to New York in 1914." According to McKay, "there was a freshness in its sympathetic and iconoclastic items about the Negro."[1]

The *Masses*, established in 1911, had become the journalistic center of the white bohemian rebellion against middle-class America. It described itself as "frank, arrogant, and impertinent, searching for true causes; it was the loud rough voice of the younger generation." The *Masses* was a free-for-all proponent of revolution; under the editorship of Max Eastman, it was noted for its mélange of wit, learning, bold new art and literature, and crusade for socialism.[2] The magazine fascinated McKay. He recalled one issue that carried a powerful cover drawing showing blacks being tortured on crosses in Georgia.[3] This drawing, featured in the August 1915 issue, was one indication of white socialists' overt attempt to raise consciousness about America's racial problems. The *Masses* itself had recently been criticized by a party member for its habit of publishing jokes and cartoons that depicted blacks in a derogatory manner. The entire editorial board of the *Masses* met to consider this criticism. Though some believed that the artists criticized were not guilty of racism, the board agreed to take care not to publish anything that might be misinterpreted by racist whites or race-sensitive blacks. The cover drawing of a black crucifixion was thus indicative of a more serious commitment by the *Masses* to the problems of blacks. A few issues later, it published Mary White Ovington's emotional story "The White Brute," which described the ordeal of a black bride taken from her black husband and raped by a white man.[4]

The *Masses*'s general approach to the question of oppressed blacks so impressed McKay that he submitted a number of poems for publication. None was accepted. McKay never offered any reason for their rejection; it is possible, as McKay later suspected, that his poems were not radical enough for the *Masses*. Undaunted, he tried other white bohemian magazines. Finally, in 1917, as mentioned earlier, he successfully placed some poems with *Seven Arts*, despite the editor's reservations about his conservative style. Soon after, he appeared in *Pearson's*, where he continued to build his friendship with Harris.[5] However, it would be with Max Eastman that he found a kinship of mind and developed a relationship as important as the earlier one with Walter Jekyll.

Eastman first came to McKay's attention as editor of the *Masses*, where he had acquired quite a reputation as an intellectual. As a leader of the more political wing of the Greenwich Village rebellion, Eastman believed that Marxism provided the proper underpinning for reconstructing society along scientific lines. Although many of his associates considered him to be a romantic, Eastman frequently lectured on the duty of being scientific and the value of social engineering.[6] McKay did not have an opportunity to meet Eastman during his editorship at the *Masses* for, with America's entrance into World War I, the *Masses* became a key target of government persecution. Eastman and other members of the staff were tried for conspiracy. Although they were eventually acquitted, the magazine folded. It was subsequently resurrected in 1918 by Eastman and his sister, Crystal, as the *Liberator.*[7]

Crystal Eastman had read some of McKay's poems, and she invited him down to the *Liberator* for an interview with Max. Eastman impressed McKay as a pure intellectual in conversation and critical opinion. He was delighted that during the interview Eastman at his home at Croton-on-Hudson in upstate New York. This visit brought back memories of his first trip to visit Jekyll in the Blue Mountains of Jamaica. Even Eastman's life-style reminded McKay of the eccentric Jekyll, who lived as easily in the Eastman at his home at Croton-on-the-Hudson in upstate New York. This visit brought back memories of his first trip to visit Jekyll in the Blue Mountains of Jamaica. Even Eastman's life-style reminded McKay of the eccentric Jekyll, who lived as easily in the world of radicals as in that of aristocrats. Following his return to New York City, he wrote Eastman to express some of this admiration, "I love your life—more than your poetry, more than your personality. It would have done your heart good to hear that chauffeur speak of your splendid and beautiful life." It was refreshing to see Eastman live so unaffectedly free, not striving to be like the masses, as some radicals did.[8] When not in Croton-on-Hudson, Eastman resided in a rented house in Greenwich Village near Washington Place. There he and his sister collected a kind of family of white intellectuals.[9] From their first encounter and despite periodic disagreements, Eastman and McKay always maintained mutual respect for one another.

As editor of the *Liberator,* Eastman opened the door to the rest of bohemian society for McKay. In spite of its radical orientation, the magazine achieved a degree of popular success, doubling its circulation during the first month of publication to over 60,000 copies. The magazine's declaration— "We issue the *Liberator* into a world whose possibilities of freedom and life for all are now certainly immeasurable"—appealed to a broad cross section of people. Even the widow of William Lloyd Garrison, publisher and editor of the original, abolitionist *Liberator*, praised the magazine and commented that she was glad to see the old name revived for such a good cause.[10]

McKay shared her enthusiasm. Though he had some reservations about the reaction of blacks to "If We Must Die," the thought of being published in the *Liberator* and having his name associated with the magazine pleased him enormously. "I was keen," he wrote, "about the poem appearing in the *Liberator*, because of the magazine's high literary and social standard." "The *Liberator*," he continued, "was a group magazine. The list of contributing editors was almost as exciting to read as the contributions themselves. There was a freshness and a bright new beauty in those contributions, pictorial and literary, that thrilled. And altogether, in their entirety, they were implicit of a penetrating social criticism which did not in the least overshadow their novel and sheer artistry. I rejoiced in the thought of the honor of appearing among that group."[11]

His work's appearance in the *Liberator* seemed to McKay the culmination of a five-year struggle to find a milieu compatible with his intellectual temperament. However, publication also brought less-welcome attention from the Justice Department's committee investigating African-American radicalism and sedition. The department regarded "If We Must Die" and his emotional reaction to postwar events as inflammatory and seditious. The government was convinced that McKay was attempting to induce blacks to see "red" and pointed as evidence to an exchange of letters in the *Negro World* between McKay and W. H. Ferris, literary editor for the Garvey paper. During this exchange McKay had suggested that "Every negro who lays claim to leadership should make a study of Bolshevism and explain its meaning to the colored masses. It is the greatest and most scientific idea afloat in the world today that can easily be put into practice by the proletariat to better its material and spiritual life."[12]

Justice Department pressure may have accounted for McKay's sudden decision to leave the United States and travel to England. Though McKay later wrote that his departure had been the result of an unexpected opportunity to take advantage of an all-expense-paid trip and of his childhood desire to visit his "true cultural homeland," he had a lifelong tendency to rewrite his own history—as we have already seen—and tended to supply idealistic reasons for practical decisions in his retrospective explanations. Certainly, the increasingly hostile environment must have made the trip seem like a good idea.[13]

He arrived in England late in 1919, eager to see the famous streets, places, and chimneys pouring smoke. All these things were in evidence, but so too were the bigotry and coldness that permeated English society. McKay's spiritual homecoming coincided with an outburst of Negrophobia. During the war England had experienced a sharp increase in the number of black immigrants from the West Indies and Africa. These immigrants were confronted with blatant discrimination. White workers feared black competition for jobs, did not want to work alongside blacks, and accused blacks of sexual aggression against white women. White-black confrontations eventually erupted in a series of race riots. In the summer of 1919 racial violence broke out against local black minorities in Liverpool, Cardiff, Manchester, Newton, and Hull. Again, McKay was confronted with the ugly specter of race.[14] Disappointed, he remarked, "Had I been a Black Diogenes exploring the white world with my African lamp, I could have proclaimed: I saw Bernard Shaw! Otherwise I did not get a grand thrill out of London."[15]

McKay found refuge in two clubs of intellectuals representing a wide spectrum of ideologies. He was particularly attracted to the International Club, where men and women conversed, debated, and argued over contemporary political issues. Of all the diverse subjects debated, the often uncompromising and serious discussions of Marxist ideology most attracted McKay.

He had become familiar with Marxist ideology by reading the *Masses* and *Liberator,* but this was the first time he found himself in the midst of people who discussed the subject so intensely. The more he listened, the more convinced he became of the necessity of making an earnest effort to fully understand Marxism. He found the task tedious, but Marx's prediction of a revolution and the events taking place in Russia and the world fascinated McKay. "The world," he mused, "was in the beginning of passing through a great social change, and I was excited by the possibilities." He wondered if those who believed that Marx was the true prophet of the new social order were right. History had taught him that the face of the world had been changed before by an obscure prophet. "After all," he remarked, "I had no reason to think that the world I lived in was permanent, solid, and unshakable: the World War had just come to a truce."[16]

But the club also provided McKay with more immediate and practical rewards. As the only "African" (a description he took the liberty of applying to himself), he became a kind of celebrity, assuming the role of liaison between whites and other blacks. At the club McKay met an impressive array of Europe's international radicals, among them Sylvia Pankhurst, editor of London's radical *Workers' Dreadnought*, an organ of the working-class movement.[17] He needed no introduction, for the *Workers' Dreadnought* had already reprinted some of McKay's poems from the *Liberator*. The newspaper took great pains to describe him as a black proletarian who wrote poetry while working as a waiter in an American dining car.

During the *Workers' Dreadnought*'s brief existence, Pankhurst had shown an interest in the problems of black workers. On occasion she used the *Workers' Dreadnought* to criticize white workers who exhibited racial prejudices. The article "Stabbing of Negroes in the Dock Area," for example, demonstrates the Pankhurst approach. In it she denounced unemployed whites who could not afford white prostitutes for attacking blacks who could. She suggested that it would be far better for whites to join with blacks, who were also victims of a capitalist society and who shared the same problems of unemployment.[18]

McKay appreciated Pankhurst's sympathetic attitude toward blacks. Since his arrival in England, he had become progressively more disturbed about English prejudice toward blacks, which at times seemed to equal the intensity of white American racism—particularly when it involved the subject of the black man's sexuality. He remarked bitterly, "I think the Anglo-Saxon mind becomes morbid when it turns on the sex life of the colored people."[19]

It had been this concern that brought McKay to the personal attention of Pankhurst. McKay had become outraged over a *Daily Herald* attempt to create a national sensation by initiating a campaign against the French employment of black troops in the occupation of Germany in the postwar period. Headlines such as "Black Scourge in Europe," "Black Peril on the Rhine," "Brutes in French Uniforms," and "Sexual Horrors Let Loose by France" reminded McKay of America's South. Outraged that black men had been used to arouse the moral righteousness of the English in favor of the Germans against the French, he wrote to the editor, George Lansbury, to protest this vicious propaganda. For political reasons, Lansbury refused to print McKay's letter, but at the suggestion of a friend he did send it on to the *Workers' Dreadnought*.

Pankhurst not only printed the letter but offered McKay a job as field reporter for the *Workers' Dreadnought*. She hoped that as a black radical he would be able to provide a fresh point of view. For his first assignment, he was sent to the English docks to dig up information among colored seamen. He later recalled that his first attempts at writing what was essentially propaganda lacked radical intensity. The magazine then assigned a young Finn named Erkki Veltheim, referred to as "Comrade Vie," to give McKay instructions about writing in the proper radical manner.[20]

McKay never became proficient as a field reporter, but he did provide the *Workers' Dreadnought* with its first in-depth analysis of African Americans and radicalism. In "Socialism and the Negro" he stated his belief that socialism and the working-class revolution were of immense importance and benefit to African Americans. He suggested that the majority of blacks were being misled by such organizations as the National Association for the Advancement of Colored People. Composed of the "old conservative Quaker aristocracy of New England and Pennsylvania, liberal capitalists and commercial Jews," the association was myopic when it approached the race problem in America. According to McKay, the group had failed to recognize that the Negro question was fundamentally an economic, not a racial, problem. Foolishly, the association felt the solution to the race problem could be solved by admitting into white society the few blacks who had attained education and wealth, or by pleading with the capitalists for the improvement of the political and social status of "colored folks."[21]

McKay contended that the problems faced by black Americans were rooted in the oppressive character of the capitalist system and, conversely, that its solution rested on the African American's willingness to accept a Socialist system such as the one being created in Russia. He believed some progress had already been made. Beginning with World War I, the Socialists and the Industrial Workers of the World had, with the aid of the *Messenger* and *Liberator* magazines, done some constructive work among blacks that was now bearing fruit. The rank and file, he insisted, had been very responsive to the "new truths." Black workers were always willing to meet white workers halfway in the fight against capitalism; owing to the seeds of hatred sown by the master class, however, the two groups were still reluctant to take the step that would result in a Socialist triumph.[22]

Organizations like the NAACP and the professional class of African Americans shared responsibility with the capitalists for impeding Socialist progress in recruiting black workers. They either disapproved of socialism altogether or trifled with socialism from an opportunistic-racial standpoint. Pointing to W. E. B. Du Bois as a case in point, McKay remarked, "Dr. Du Bois has flirted with the socialist idea from a narrow opportunistic racial standpoint; but he is in spirit opposed to it." "If our negro professionals are not blindly ignorant," McKay continued, "they should realize that there will never be any hope—no sound material place in the economic life of the world—for them until the negro masses are industrially independent."[23]

McKay did not confine his critique to blacks and whites in America. Whether in the United States, Europe, or Africa, the problem was always the same: the working classes were manipulated by the capitalist class. Not only had capitalism pitted whites against blacks, but it also encouraged some groups of blacks to fight against other blacks. Referring to an article written by Lettow-Vorbeck, a German commander, who recounted the courage of his black troops in East Africa during World War I, McKay exploded,

> England also used her black troops, and the whole nasty business shows to what depths Capitalism will descend to maintain its supremacy. Ignorant black men were pitted against their brothers to fight for a cause that was alien to them. While the Capitalist may forgive each other their mistakes (Germany and

England) it was the workers who keep on hating each other on account of race differences, nation and color. The exploiting classes world wide would set black against black, white against black and turn about face if necessary to keep their power. If for nothing more than sheer self-preservation.[24]

Capitalistic imperialism, he concluded, had to be challenged by a united front of black and white workers. To achieve this united front, it would be necessary for the Socialists to step in and bridge the gulf between the two groups exploited by the capitalists. Serving notice to the capitalists, he remarked that "There is plenty of work to be done, and no time should be lost, for who knows when the storm will break?—when rivers of blood will flow, bearing the souls of white and black workers into eternity?"[25]

Analytically, McKay's discussion offered nothing new about the relationship of blacks and socialism. He was merely echoing the official position of the Socialists that the exploitation of blacks was only an extreme form of the exploitation of all workers under capitalism. Like other Socialists, he dismissed the notion that the "Negro problem" had its roots in racial antipathy or social caste, and accepted the belief that its solution could be realized only through socialism. Nor was he the first black to advocate the cause of socialism. A number of African Americans had reached a similar conclusion. A. Philip Randolph and Owen Chandler, writing in the *Messenger,* agreed that socialism offered the best means of opposing colonialism and imperialism. "Socialism," the *Messenger* proclaimed, "is the only weapon that can be used to clip the claws of the British lion and the talons of the American eagle in Africa, the British West Indies, Haiti, the Southern states and at the same time reach the monster's heart."[26]

What is most significant about McKay's discussion is the responsibility he placed on the NAACP and certain African Americans for the problems Socialists faced in recruiting blacks. Although well-intentioned, his argument mixes misinformation, specious reasoning, and naïveté. For example, his characterization of NAACP members was far too simplistic and misleading. The early leaders of the association came from diverse backgrounds and held varying economic and political philosophies. Joel E. Spingarn, for instance, was Jewish; Oswald Garrison Villard was the grandson of the great abolitionist William Lloyd Garrison; and William English Walling, though a southerner and a descendant of a slave-owning family, was a Socialist. Others, such as Mary White Ovington and Charles Edward Russell, were avowed economic radicals. Neither Ovington nor Russell had been "palpably ignorant" that solving the Negro problem involved economics or even a socialist approach. However, despite the socialist leanings of some of the founders of the NAACP, the association itself emphasized the attainment of full civil and political rights under the existing socioeconomic system, to the virtual exclusion of a program of black economic uplift. And though Ovington and Russell argued that it was necessary to divorce the cause of blacks from that of socialism or participation in any radical movement until they had acquired complete freedom, it is unlikely that under any circumstances the NAACP would have engaged in any radical political movement.[27]

McKay's criticism of African Americans and their role in obstructing socialism lacked sophistication. Blacks attracted to the socialist ideology faced much the same dilemma as many white economic radicals: race was simply too overwhelming to permit a serious revolutionary approach to their problems. For African Americans, this had been further complicated by the longstanding fear that contemporary white radical movements would move along the same path followed by earlier movements. Blacks were painfully aware that Thomas Watson, James K. Vardaman, and Samuel Gompers had combined "radical reform" programs with bitter and reactionary hatred of African Americans, and they wondered whether the Socialist party would follow the same path.

This concern gave Du Bois's ambivalence on socialism the appearance of "racial opportunism."[28] As early as 1907 Du Bois had attempted to place the race question in a larger framework: he recognized that the root cause of oppression, whether expressed as the economic exploitation of white workers or the social exploitation of blacks by whites, was economic. Yet, he never professed a doctrinaire Marxist approach to socialism and described himself as a "socialist of the path." His form of lukewarm socialism was characteristic of an influential minority of blacks and liberal whites.[29]

McKay failed to recognize that, if Socialists wanted to win the support of blacks, they needed to analyze the specific problem confronting blacks in terms of their status as a racial minority and not merely in terms of their status as workers. Furthermore, his experience in Jamaica made it difficult for him to understand that, because of race, the black American's political and economic orientation was more pragmatic than doctrinaire. Any group or movement that proposed to speak in behalf of black workers without appreciating the complexity of race was doomed to fail. The Socialist party's inability to grasp this truth helps to explain why the vast majority of black workers remained so indifferent to or even unaware of socialism. But certainly the NAACP and the professional class of African Americans had not failed to grasp the connection between racial and economic exploitation.[30]

Following the publication of the "Lettow-Vorbeck" article, the British government conducted a series of raids and shut down the *Workers' Dreadnought*. Without money or a job, McKay decided to return to the United States.

England had been an emotional disappointment for McKay. Its turbulent racial milieu had even deprived him of the satisfaction he might have derived from the publication of his first book of poetry since leaving Jamaica. English reviews of his *Spring in New Hampshire* (1920) were generally condescending and often flippant about the notion of a Negro writing poetry. McKay was particularly vexed by the *Spectator's* critic, who expressed "relief" that McKay, described as "a pure-blooded Negro," had written a work that did not overstep the barriers which would have put white racial instincts against him. McKay left "Old England" in the spring of 1921.[31] Back in America, he gladly accepted an invitation to join the staff of the *Liberator*, first as a correspondent and then as a coeditor.

For a while his return to America and his position on the *Liberator* staff provided McKay with the best of both worlds. Intellectually, the *Liberator's* radical and iconoclastic approach appealed to McKay. Writing to H. L. Mencken, he remarked, "Our gang here holds divergent views on politics too—what holds us together is that we are all rebellious and have a vague idea of some revolutionary change, however far away it may be. . . . Although keeping with the revolutionary idea, we are sort of general muck-rakers."[32]

48

At the *Liberator*, he worked with a group of people who seemed oblivious of color. Joseph Freeman, a member of the *Liberator* staff, recalled that in general the office was full of explosive personalities, and while the staff was dominated numerically by Anglo-Saxons, no racial or national distinctions ever appeared between them. Traditional racial barriers were transcended not only in friendship, but even in the intimate relations of love and marriage. Freeman felt that on a small scale the *Liberator* represented that ideal society they all desired, one in which no racial barriers could possibly exist.[33]

When his day at the *Liberator* ended, McKay returned to his old apartment on 131st Street in Harlem. There he could experience the "rare sensation" of being just one black among many, and loiter along Seventh Avenue enjoying the aroma of spareribs, corn pone, sweet potatoes, and fried chicken.[34]

These were heady days for McKay—rosy and filled with romance. He discussed poetry with E. E. cummings, lunched on Park Row with Carl Van Doren, one of the editors of the *Nation*, and enjoyed the company of the celebrated Charlie Chaplin at Eastman's home at Croton-on-Hudson. McKay was immensely flattered when Chaplin included his poem "The Tropics of New York" in his book *My Trip Abroad*. McKay recalled that "friends vied with friends in giving me invitations to their homes for parties and in offering tickets for plays and concerts." He was introduced to Greenwich Village tearooms and gin mills which, as he put it, "were not crazy with colorphobia." McKay often reciprocated by giving some of his *Liberator* friends tours of the cabarets and cozy flats of Harlem.[35]

When not entertaining white notables, McKay used his position as assistant editor, and the *Liberator* offices, to gather many of Harlem's black radicals. One such gathering included Hubert Harrison, Harlem street-corner lecturer and agitator, Grace P. Campbell, a pioneer black member of the Socialist party, Richard Moore and W. A. Domingo, editors of the *Emancipator*, a radical Harlem weekly, and Cyril Briggs, founder of the African Blood Brotherhood and editor of the *Crusader*, its organ.[36]

Except for Robert Minor, white Communist and artist for the *Liberator*, all of the principals at this important mid-1921 meeting were members of the African Blood Brotherhood, whose name derived from the African rite of fraternization by mingling drops of blood. Founded by Briggs in the fall of 1917 as "a revolutionary secret order," the Brotherhood was strongly linked to the struggle for a "free Africa." However, the Brotherhood considered the fight to secure the democratic rights of American blacks a vital prerequisite for developing a strong political force to campaign for the liberation of Africa. Under the general heading of "immediate protection and ultimate liberation," the Brotherhood called for armed resistance to lynching, unqualified voting rights for blacks in the South, a struggle for equal rights and opposition to all forms of discrimination, and the organization of Negroes into established trade unions. It protested against trade-union discrimination and advocated the organization of separate Negro unions in those trades where blacks were denied membership in white unions. Its objectives were quickly expanded to include cooperation with white workers who were fully class-conscious and honestly working for a United Front for all workers. The Brotherhood also called for the self-determination of blacks in states where they constituted a majority.[37]

While the extent of McKay's participation in the African Blood Brotherhood is uncertain, his charter membership is not surprising. Most of the original members of the Brotherhood were both West Indians and Socialists like Briggs, Moore, Otto Hall, and Otto Huiswood.[38] They were part of a small but influential segment of the New Negro movement who linked anticolonialism with militant protest against the treatment of blacks in the United States. McKay's writings in the immediate postwar period often paralleled and echoed the sentiments of the Brotherhood. The Brotherhood abandoned its secrecy during the violent summer of 1919, and formally became the "African Blood Brotherhood for African Liberation and Redemption." McKay's poem "If We Must Die" appeared on three occasions in the *Crusader* to exhort blacks to organize for self-defense.[39]

McKay also supported the Irish Republican Brotherhood. This legendary clandestine organization served as the model for the political organization of the African Blood Brotherhood. Founded simultaneously in Dublin and New York in 1858 with the avowed purpose of overthrowing British rule in Ireland, the Sein Finn achieved its greatest notoriety as the body responsible for planning and coordinating the insurrection that exploded into the Easter Rising of 1916.[40] Cyril Briggs perceived a link between black radicalism and Irish nationalism. Under the headline "The Irish Fight for Liberty the Greatest Epic of Modern Times and a Sight to Inspire to Emulation All Oppressed Groups," Briggs paid a lofty tribute to the Irish struggle and its significance for the liberation of black people in the February 1921 issue of the *Crusader*.[41] McKay shared Briggs's appreciation of the Sein Finn and its importance to the black struggle. In an article describing his impressions of the Irish revolutionary movement, published only a few months after Briggs's piece, McKay wrote that he felt a certain sympathy with the Irish rebels. "I suffer with the Irish," McKay declared, "I think I understand the Irish. My belonging to a subject race entitles me to some understanding of them."[42]

McKay was well suited to be host to this meeting of the Brotherhood and Robert Minor, ostensibly convened in the hope of finding some way to make Marcus Garvey's Universal Negro Improvement Association more class-conscious. "If We Must Die" had become the anthem of the New Negro radical movement. His association with Sylvia Pankhurst and her *Workers' Dreadnought*, "the nest of extreme radicalism in England," had increased his reputation among whites in America and abroad.[43] His stature in the radical community was not lost on the African Blood Brotherhood; Briggs had noted in the *Crusader* that the "*Liberator*, America's foremost white radical monthly, has reorganized its editorial staff, making Max Eastman, Floyd Dell, Robert Minor and Claude McKay co-editors."[44]

Initially, the Brotherhood found reason to support the Garvey movement, advising its members that they were "free to join any other purely Negro organization, and there is no other we can so highly recommend as the Universal Negro Improvement Association." As late as March 1921 Briggs was exhorting readers of the *Crusader* to "join the U.N.I.A. and the ABB."[45] But support for Garvey, given the Brotherhood's own radical orientation, was always more utilitarian than ideological, and by the latter part of the year Briggs, McKay, and the African Brotherhood had launched an all-out attack on Garvey. Writing of his experience with the Brotherhood, Harry Haywood recollected that the Brotherhood had rejected Garvey's racial separatism. They knew that blacks needed allies and therefore they tried to build ideological bridges between their own movement for black rights and the progressive section of the white labor movement.[46]

The relationship between most of the Brotherhood and white radicalism went deeper than merely pragmatism. Most black radicals had been profoundly affected by the Bolshevik Revolution of 1917 and by the subsequent development of the Bolshevik's national policy, including the anti-imperialist orientation of the new Soviet state.[47] "The *Crusader* and the African Blood Brotherhood were ardent supporters of the Russian Revolution," Haywood recalled. "They saw it as an opportunity for blacks to identify with a powerful international revolutionary movement. It enabled them to overcome the isolation inherent in their position as a minority people in the midst of a powerful and hostile white oppressor nation."[48] Although there was no immediate attempt by either the international Communist movement or oppressed blacks in America to forge a link, a muted and subtle new historical process was nonetheless unfolding. Once the Third International announced as its goal the worldwide emancipation of oppressed workers and invited men of all races to join in this crusade, a segment of the New Negro movement recognized the Communists as their natural allies.[49]

Consequently, the African Blood Brotherhood evolved from an independent body emphasizing race consciousness, to a still-independent body that stressed the goal of increasing class consciousness, to becoming something like a black auxiliary of the American Communist party—a process historian Robert Hill describes as a "simultaneous and organic process of political radicalization."[50] This evolution revealed the basic incompatibility of the Brotherhood and the Garvey movement.

While planning for battle against Garvey, Briggs and other members of the African Blood Brotherhood were being wooed by agents of the two American Communist factions that had split in 1919 and were fighting for Comintern support in their internal battle over party organization. McKay's role as host of the mid-1921 meeting and the presence of Robert Minor suggest that the Garvey question was not the only item on the agenda. Minor, considered one of the few white Communist leaders who grasped the importance of the Negro question and recognized the revolutionary import of race consciousness among an oppressed people, may have attended the meeting to advance the interests of the underground faction of the Communist party.[51] McKay's membership in the Brotherhood and his relationship with white radicals like Minor enabled him to act as a political intermediary between the two warring factions and the black radicals. He was also present at a second meeting of "black Reds," this time sponsored by Rose Pastor Stokes, another member of the underground wing of the Communist party.[52]

McKay's position on the editorial staff had also given him the opportunity to meet blacks whom he considered the "more conservative of the Negro leaders," principally officials of the National Association for the Advancement of Colored People. His opinion of African Americans from "polite Negro Society" was mixed. Following a luncheon with W. E. B. Du Bois, McKay wrote that Du Bois deserved his accolades as one of the nation's great polemicists, but he also noted that his own meeting with him was "something of a personal disappointment. He seemed possessed of a cold, acid hauteur of spirit, which did not lessen even when he vouchsafed a smile."[53]

Walter White, then secretary of the NAACP, struck McKay as a "charming personality, ingratiating as a Y.M.C.A. secretary." White's extremely fair complexion made it virtually impossible for McKay to see White as anything other than a "friendly so-called white man." His favorite among the NAACP crowd was James Weldon Johnson, whose "poise, suavity, diplomacy and gentlemanliness," placed him, in McKay's opinion, "among the best the Afro-American race had produced."[54]

McKay's impression of African Americans, and especially of the members of the NAACP, would progressively deteriorate. After all, these were some of the same people he had criticized in the *Workers' Dreadnought* for retarding the economic and social progress of the Negro masses. In 1922, he privately commented to Hubert Harrison in the *Liberator's* office that he was "being lionized at lunch by pseudo-intellectuals," meaning NAACP blacks. Harrison reported the comment in the *Negro World*, prompting McKay's denial and anger. He wrote White, "I could not dream of referring to people who had me as their private guest in such an indecent and uncalled for public way."[55] Of course, as we have seen, McKay's personal opinions and public professions were often in conflict.

Aside from an occasional chiding from Eastman regarding Mc-Kay's "slow and indifferent" manner about coming to work and his tendency to make the *Liberator* read like the *Nation,* life at the *Liberator* from 1921 until the middle of 1922 seems to have been a pleasant experience for McKay.[56] It was made even more rewarding with the publication of *Harlem Shadows* in the spring of 1922. Published with assistance from Joel Spingarn, board member of the NAACP, by Harcourt and Brace, *Harlem Shadows* marked a milestone in McKay's career as a poet. "The publication of my first American book," he wrote, "uplifted me with the greatest joy in my life."[57]

Actually, *Harlem Shadows* was an expanded version of his English *Spring in New Hampshire,* containing almost all the poems in the previous book and the best of those he had written since 1912.[58] The seventy-poem volume received acclaim from conservative and liberal critics alike, and significantly enhanced Mc-Kay's reputation as a poet.[59] Black literary conservative Benjamin Brawley considered McKay's book "outstanding." Allison Davis, equally conservative, declared that *Harlem Shadows* "touched on a nobility and a higher imaginative view than most American realistic poetry ever reaches." Walter White, who had accepted the truth of McKay's denial of Harrison's printed comment, called McKay "without doubt the most talented and versatile of the new school of imaginative, emotional Negro poets." James Weldon Johnson perhaps best captured the significance of McKay's achievement: "Mr. McKay is a real poet and a great poet. . . . No Negro has sung more beautifully of his race than McKay and no poet has ever equalled the power with which he expresses the bitterness that so often rises in the heart of the race. . . . The race ought to be proud of a poet capable of voicing it so fully. Such a voice is not found every day. . . . What he has achieved in this little volume sheds honor upon the whole race."[60]

The poems in *Harlem Shadows* were, in the words of Arna Bontemps, "fragrant and fresh."[61] The following poem, "Harlem Shadows," the volume's title poem, is representative of McKay's craft in 1922:

I hear the halting footsteps of a lass
In Negro Harlem when the night lets fall
Its veil. I see the shapes of girls who pass
To bend and barter at desire's call.
Ah, little dark girls who in slippered feet
Go prowling through the night from street to street!
Through the long night until the silver break
Of day the little gray feet know no rest;
Through the lone night until the last snowflake
Has dropped from heaven upon the earth's white breast,
The dusky, half-clad girls of tired feet
Are trudging, thinly shod, from street to street.
Ah, stern harsh world, that in the wretched way
Of poverty, dishonor and disgrace,
Has pushed the timid little feet of clay,
The sacred brown feet of my fallen race
Ah, heart of me, the weary, weary feet
In Harlem wandering from street to street.[62]

But McKay's halycon days were to come to an abrupt end in May of the same year. An incident occurred that forced him to recognize that even successful black intellectuals could not ignore and escape the burden of race. Furthermore, it accentuated what McKay had experienced in Jamaica: the cruel duality of being *in* but not *of* two cultures. The incident forced him to reconsider his position on the relationship between blacks, socialism, and white radicalism.

The *Liberator* received an invitation extended by the Theatre Guild's publicity agent to send its drama critic to review Leonid Andreyev's play *He Who Gets Slapped*. Since the regular drama critic was away, McKay as coeditor decided to assume the role of theater critic. In the company of William Gropper, the *Liberator's* artist, McKay went to the theater, where he discovered that the management had intended the "first row" tickets to be used only by whites. While the white Gropper was offered a seat near the stage, McKay, who was functioning as the official drama critic, was shunted upstairs to the balcony. Gropper declined to sit alone and accompanied the outraged and terribly hurt McKay to the balcony. "Suddenly," McKay recalled, "the realization came to me, I had come here as a dramatic critic, a lover of the theater, and a free soul. But—I was abruptly reminded—those things did not matter. The important fact, with which I was suddenly slapped in the face, was my color—I am a Negro."[63] Outside the safety of the *Liberator*'s office the world of bigotry and color conflict that he had tried to avoid and intellectually deny rushed in to crush McKay.

He had been hurt, perhaps more than at any other time in his life. His armament of viewing questions of race from the perspective of an artist and an intellectual had failed to shield him from the prejudice he usually had viewed from a distance. He had been aware of Jim Crow laws in Alabama and antiblack prejudice in England, but he had managed to stay one step ahead of being personally affected. His reaction at the theater, however, was one of outrage, hurt, and a "sense of helplessness." "I sat there," he remembered:

> Apart, alone, black and shrouded in blackness, quivering in every fiber, my heart denying itself and hiding from every gesture of kindliness, hard in its belief that kindliness is to be found in no nation or race. I sat inwardly groaning through what seemed a childish caricature of tragedy. Ah! if the accident of birth had made Andreyev a Negro, if he had been slapped, kicked, buffeted, pounded, niggered, ridiculed, sneered at, exquisitely tortured, near-lynched and trampled underfoot by the merry White horde, and if he still preserved through the terrible agony a sound body and mind sensitive to perceive the qualities of life, he might have written a real play about being Slapped.[64]

The rebuff McKay received affected him far more than any of his colleagues on the *Liberator* staff suspected. McKay had hoped the incident at the theater would be a test of the true "colors" of his radical comrades. He expected his fellow staffers to rally to his defense; instead, they simply dismissed the incident. In their commitment to nonracialism, McKay's white comrades missed the full importance of what had happened at the theater. "There the matter stopped," Freeman later recalled, "no boycott or demonstration was organized against the theater which humiliated a gifted Negro poet and through him his entire people."[65]

But the matter was not closed for McKay. His disillusionment over the inaction of the *Liberator* group instigated a reevaluation of his ideas on the relationship between blacks and white radicals. He was no longer content to accept the theoretical premise that the Negro constituted only an extreme form of exploitation by capitalism. Using his review of T. S. Stribling's play *Birthright* as a forum, McKay admonished his white friends for "believing that the pretty parlor talk of international brotherhood or the radical shibboleth of the class-struggle was sufficient to cure the Negro cancer."[66] White radicals, he suggested, were content with an intellectual recognition of the Negro's place in the class struggle, while ignoring the fact that the disabilities of black workers were heavier than those of whites. As a Negro it was his proud "birthright" to put the special case of the Negro proletarian before the white members of the movement.

Unmistakably, McKay indicated that racial considerations would have to be addressed before white radicals could hope to enlist the masses of blacks into any revolutionary effort, whether Socialist or Communist. In fact, he concluded that the ability of white radicals to address the special problems of the darker races would be the most crucial test American radicalism faced—a position already reached by such other black radicals as Owen Chandler, fellow Jamaican Wilfred A. Domingo, and most notably Hubert Harrison.[67] If white radicals were unable to differentiate themselves from capitalists on racial issues, black leaders would be in no position to convince black workers they should organize and work alongside their white counterparts.[68]

McKay's criticism was not lost on his *Liberator* friends, some of whom thought them "excessive." Responding to his chief critic, Eastman, McKay accused him of being a "nice opportunist" always in search of the safe path and never striking out for new and uncharted territory if there were any danger signs ahead. "The fact is," he wrote Eastman, "I received letters of encouragement and appreciation from working class leaders and *Liberator* readers as soon as I began printing those articles."[69] He also had been quick to point out that the article "He Who Gets Slapped" had been reprinted and syndicated all over the United States.

Although McKay later maintained that he had written additional articles on the problems of black-white relationships within the class movement, no further article on the subject appears in the pages of the *Liberator*. Perhaps McKay misremembered, or perhaps he was retrospectively exaggerating his role in the race versus class debate. There is no disputing, however, that after the theater incident, McKay found his position as a member of the *Liberator* staff more and more uncomfortable. Within two months, he resigned as coeditor; he published his last article for the magazine in August 1922. During this time, McKay said little publicly about his growing disenchantment with his "friendly critics" on the *Liberator* staff, a situation that has since given rise to a number of conflicting views surrounding the actual circumstances of his abrupt departure.

The view held by most of the *Liberator* members was that McKay's withdrawal had been the result of a personality conflict between McKay and Mike Gold. Both Gold and McKay had been acting as coeditors in Eastman's absence at the time of the theater incident. From the beginning a coeditorship between them had seemed unlikely. Gold was considered the "proletarian" of the *Liberator* group. As Freeman recalled, "He affected dirty shirts, a big black uncleaned Stetson with the brim of a sombrero; smoked stinking, twisted Italian three cent cigars and spat frequently and vigorously on the floor!"[70] Gold had had a terrible childhood in the poverty-stricken section of New York's Lower East Side, and later, as his friends have suggested, he sought to solve his personal conflicts through rage against capitalism. Eastman once considered him psychologically unbalanced, a man who "became a zealot, a being alien to the basic temper of the magazine. He wanted us to go out into the farms and factories, not omitting the slums and gutters, and find talented working men and women who could produce a really proletarian art."[71]

McKay was generally thought of by his contemporaries as the aristocrat of the group, a warm, sensuous, romantic, and affectionate man. Yet he could suddenly become a "knot of tangled impulses, out of which fits of unaccountably spiteful behavior would at times burst." He had disliked Gold from the start and looked down upon Gold's tobacco-stained teeth, and his idea of printing doggerel from lumberjacks and stevedores and the true revelations of chambermaids as opposed to "serious art."[72] However, it was not until Gold personally attacked McKay for printing a submitted article about a lynching in the June 1922 issue that their incompatibility became apparent to the board of editors. Gold had become irritated with McKay's continued publication of material focusing on race, which was clearly not in keeping with the class-struggle critique.[73] After near fisticuffs, both demanded that the board choose between them. According to Eastman, "it was not an easy choice and the result was fatal, but a choice made entirely upon the intrinsic fitness for that particular job."[74] Thus McKay resigned and Gold continued as editor.

McKay left the *Liberator* and departed for Moscow late in the fall of 1922 (this trip is discussed in detail later in this chapter). While there, he wrote Eastman informing him that he was in the process of writing a book for the Russian government on "blacks in America." In it, he intended to elaborate on his reasons for leaving the *Liberator*. The book, McKay insinuated, would reveal that racial matters more than anything else had prompted his withdrawal from the *Liberator*. Specifically, he charged that the *Liberator* group did not possess a comprehensive grasp of the special problems of the black worker, and that the lack of support for his determination to place the problem before the readers had forced his resignation. Neither Eastman nor any of the group ever seriously discussed the race question. According to McKay, the general atmosphere of the *Liberator* did not encourage serious discussions of any of the real problems of a capitalist society, much less the Negro problem. McKay cited an incident in which he and Eastman, unable to find a decent restaurant on Sixth Avenue that would seat McKay, had finally been forced to lunch in a dirty place, whereupon Eastman jokingly remarked, "If I were a Negro I couldn't be anything but a revolutionist."[75]

Nothing more clearly illustrated McKay's problems at the *Liberator* than Eastman's stance on how much of the magazine should be devoted to the problems of blacks. McKay maintained that a revolutionary magazine advocating the issues associated with the class struggle in America should direct most of its attention to the Negro problem, arguing that the use of blacks to break strikes during the last decade was dramatic proof that the success or failure of the revolution depended on its resolution. Eastman's position was that introducing too much material on blacks in a magazine whose circulation consisted of a majority of "Whites, full of peculiar ignorance and intolerance, of the Negro" would frighten away potential white sympathizers. Eastman further responded to McKay by expressing the opinion that such a policy would not only be inaccurate, but "unwise."[76]

McKay dismissed Eastman's comments and concluded that it was impossible to attempt a serious discussion of black problems with the *Liberator* staff. The staff's attitude forced him to discuss the racial problem only with the radical Negro group in New York. And even this, according to McKay, brought Eastman's disapproval. Eastman expressed fear that a congregation of black men and women at the *Liberator*'s office would bring harassment from the Justice Department.[77]

McKay's Russian book appeared late in 1923 under the title *Negry v Amerike* (The Negroes in America). Despite his threats to Eastman, the book makes little specific allusion to the *Liberator*. However, it does suggest that McKay had not forgotten his experience on the *Liberator*. McKay remarked in the book's introduction:

> Some comrades may think that I am too harsh and too imbued with race consciousness. I would reply to that for the Negro in America it is very useful to be imbued with race consciousness, but it is still more useful for him to look at the problem which disturbs him from a class point of view and to join the class struggle as an "internationalist." The Negro in America is not permitted for one minute to forget his color, his skin, or his race. The American Negro who is not imbued with race consciousness would constitute a strange phenomenon.

In a more explicit statement, McKay declared that it was not easy or pleasant to approach the Negro question. "Some white comrades," he remarked, "would sooner agree to go to the barricades than look squarely at the reality of the Negro question in America." To make certain that his *Liberator* friends did not miss the message, McKay included a reprint of the lynching article that had angered Gold and forced McKay's departure from the *Liberator*.[78]

Actually, McKay's withdrawal from the *Liberator* reflected his strong ambivalence as a black radical. At the start, he was comfortable with the *Liberator*'s carefree and iconoclastic approach to serious issues. Before his experience at the theater, McKay had frequently exhibited a similar attitude regarding racial matters. As coeditor he had the responsibility of securing articles for the magazine. Since the magazine was experiencing difficulty getting acceptable material, he prevailed upon H. L. Mencken to send anything of a "muckraking" nature. If Mencken could not think of anything offhand, perhaps he could suggest something. For example, McKay remarked, "Boardman Robinson recently told us of a barbecue that a millionaire gave H. G. Wells, to which all the correspondents were invited and where a sort of historical pageant of America was pulled off. And he mentioned your saying something like this, 'Everything was fine, all that was needed was a little lynching scene.'" McKay suggested he might title the article "The Nigger in the Woodpile."[79]

Moreover, it must be noted that members of the *Liberator* staff had good reasons to be surprised by McKay's shift on the race question, and even to judge this shift as hypocritical. None of McKay's earlier articles had suggested any tactical or philosophical differences on the role of blacks in the class struggle.[80] In his first article on the Sinn Fein, McKay mirrored the *Liberator*'s attitude on the race question. As a member of an oppressed minority, he supported the nationalist movement, but his spirit was with the proletarian revolutionists of the world. It did not matter, McKay declared, "that I am pitied even by my white fellow workers who are conscious of the fact besides being an economic slave as they, I am what they are not—a social leper, of a race outcast from an outcast class."[81]

Though McKay had alluded to the special problems black workers faced, he had not argued for special recognition of their problems within the working-class movement. At this point in his life, his acknowledgment of the Negro problem was more an intellectual recognition than the emotional recognition he experienced later.

McKay's only other reference to blacks and the working-class movement before the incident at the theater had been his attack on Marcus Garvey. He had denounced Garvey for muddying the waters of the Negro movement for freedom, by advocating racially chauvinistic, bourgeois capitalism, and by repudiating the fundamentals of the black worker's economic struggle.[82] But again, McKay's criticism of Garvey was in keeping with the principles of the *Liberator* group and the African Blood Brotherhood.

The incident at the theater hurt McKay not only because he had been racially insulted, but also because he finally became aware of his white friends' inability to fully understand and share his pain.

Perhaps V. F. Calverton had been correct when he wrote that though white radicals and bohemians might become the Negro's friend, they were in no position to aid the black man in his struggle for recognition as a human being, on the basis of merit, quality, or distinction.[83] Yet, McKay could not turn to African Americans or even to fellow West Indian radicals for solace because his greater intellectual identification with whites prohibited any such refuge. The theater incident had forced him to abandon the traditional class struggle approach of his *Liberator* colleagues and had prompted him to insist that the *Liberator* make an effort to place the special problems of blacks before the radical world. It was no "perverse whim," but an enormous hurt that now prompted McKay to once again leave the United States even at the moment he was finally beginning to achieve literary success. At a farewell party given by James Weldon Johnson and his wife, Grace, McKay bid goodby to America and departed for Russia.[84]

He arrived in Russia late in 1922, determined to place a discussion of race and its relationship to the class struggle before the Fourth Congress of the Third International. Though he achieved a personal triumph, he was unable to influence a change in the Communist position on blacks within the class struggle. Also, for the first time, McKay faced a challenge concerning his fitness as a radical spokesman for black America.

The *Liberator* incident had provided the impetus to travel abroad, but events in Russia determined McKay's choice of destination. Since the Russian Revolution in 1917, McKay had been attracted to the Soviet Union. He had praised the Bolshevik revolution as a "great experiment" that should be studied and communicated to the masses of black people by its leadership. He had found the teachings of Marx prophetic, and though Lenin had modified these teachings to fit Russian conditions, the Russian revolution could justifiably claim to be a legitimate child of the *Communist Manifesto*.[85] Russia had become the vanguard of revolutionary action in Europe and the hope for proletarian revolutionary action throughout the world.[86] McKay hoped to influence the radical community's thinking on the importance of race in the class struggle, and Russia offered him an international forum.

That McKay had not gone to Russia earlier attests to his original satisfaction with his job on the *Liberator* and with his life in general. In 1919 John Reed, a founder of the American Communist movement, had extended an invitation to McKay to visit the Soviet Union. The invitation was a reflection of Russia's often ambivalent, but genuine belief in the importance of involving black revolutionaries in the world revolution. McKay had declined Reed's offer, later recalling that at the time he did not feel qualified enough to speak on the Negro question.[87] But in 1922 he decided to accept the "long-standing invitation" and travel to Russia to write a series of articles on the new regime. He wished to examine the current status of the peasantry of Russia and of the Jews, to compare their present status to their former life under the tsar, and to contrast life for Russian peasants and Jews with life for blacks in the American South.[88]

It is not clear whether McKay's passage was actually paid by the Russian government. Some years later he remarked to James Weldon Johnson that he had worked his way to Europe, and that once there he was aided by Edgar Whitehead, a friend and British Communist who acted as a liaison and interpreter for the Russian Communists in Berlin.[89] Earlier that year McKay had appeared before a board of special inquiry at Ellis Island as a character witness on behalf of Whitehead.[90] According to McKay, he did not wish to go to the Soviet Union as an official member of the Communist party. He had expressed this sentiment at a screening of prospective travelers to Russia conducted by Russian party officials in Berlin. He informed them that while he sympathized with the purpose of the "great Russian revolution," he intended to go as a writer for the American Negro press.[91]

McKay's response satisfied the Russian interviewers but was immediately challenged by the recently arrived delegation of American Communists. According to McKay, the delegation did not want him in Russia representing America unless he was endorsed by the American Communist delegation, which had its own black spokesman. The delegation would not endorse McKay and insisted that he be sent back home. However, with the aid of Sen Katayama, a Japanese revolutionary and member of the Third International, McKay overcame their objections and attended the congress.[92]

His arrival in Russia was an immediate personal success. His dark complexion fascinated the Russian people, who greeted him with unbounded enthusiasm. "Never in my life," he recalled, "did I feel prouder of being an African, a black." At times he was physically lifted into the air by the crowds of Russian people. "From Moscow to Petrograd and Petrograd to Moscow I went triumphantly from surprise to surprise, extravagantly feted over every side. I was carried along on a crest of sweet excitement. I was like a black ikon in the flesh."[93] He was treated as a celebrity and his black face was photographed and posted everywhere in Moscow.

The unbounded enthusiasm with which McKay was received by the Russian people, in contrast to the vast, vicious, and crushing system of discrimination he had experienced in America and England, made Russia seem like "Greener Pastures."[94] Russia appeared a "Canaan," a land free of color oppression. Here, McKay desperately wanted to believe, a Negro might be better off as a poet than as a pugilist, reversing the fate G. B. Shaw had once suggested.[95] "They were curious with me," he wrote, "all sundry, young and old, in a friendly, refreshing manner. Their curiosity had none of the intolerable impertinence and often downright affront that any very dark colored man, be he Negro, Indian or Arab, would experience in Germany or England."[96]

In Petrograd, Moscow, and countless small villages, McKay detected no race snobbiness: "It was so beautifully naive; for them I was only a black member of the world of humanity." But most important, he exclaimed, "There were no overdoing of the correct thing, no vulgar wonderment and bounderish superiority over a Negro's being a poet. I was a poet, that was all, and their keen questions showed that they were much more interested in the technique of my poetry, my views on and my position regarding the modern literary movements than in the difference of my color."[97]

Intoxicated by the attention, McKay lost his objectivity and found that Russia and the Bolsheviks could do little wrong. To H. L. Mencken he wrote, "The flexibility of the people and government in adapting themselves to lightning changes is a stimulating thing to see." He was much impressed with the newly established Department of National Minorities, which adapted new laws to fit the peculiar needs of the minorities. That policy, he declared, was the greatest asset to the political strength and unity of the USSR.[98]

McKay also confided to Mencken that before he went to Russia he had presumed the existence of a rigid censorship. But, having been there for a while, he claimed to have found intellectual freedom. He had seen anarchists, critical of the Communists, selling their papers in the streets of Moscow; he had noticed copies of Russian counterrevolutionary papers, published in Germany, lying around homes in Petrograd; and he had noted as wide a variety of literary movements in Moscow and Petrograd as one would find in New York and Chicago.[99]

The longer McKay stayed, the more intensely pro-Bolshevik he became. What was happening in Russia, he asserted to Mencken, was a process of disintegration and growth of a new system of international cooperation. With all its wonderful natural resources and the new system of collective labor, Russia had already begun to challenge the bourgeois competitive system of the Western world. Using Marxist analysis, he concluded that though the American economic system was efficient, the forces of social disintegration interwoven in the fabric of America were far greater than the present-day problem of Europe. America could not avoid the consequences of "Its Plutocracy, its Southern Oligarchy, its Western Farming interests, its Labor Aristocracy, Proletarian masses, a great body of unassimilated Foreign born Labor in its Basic industries, acute immigration problems, and a great body of unassimilable Negroes." It was just a question of time, he predicted, before America would succumb to the forces that had destroyed old Russia: "The outlook for America is certainly not all Utopian. Its future is rosey as hell fire!"[100] McKay's observations helped to strengthen his belief that Bolshevism was a practical means of social reform. The recent overtures by the Communist party offered him encouragement that his analysis of blacks and the revolution would find a sympathetic audience during the Fourth Congress.

In 1921 the Third International proudly declared that it had broken with the traditions of the Second International, which had recognized only the white race. It was determined to involve workers of all colors, white, yellow, and black, in the emancipation of the world's working class. Unlike the Socialists McKay had known, the Communists he met in Russia appeared to be willing to do more than mouth platitudes about the glories of white and black labor solidarity. The International looked upon American blacks as an important link in its program of world proletarian revolutions. Under the Leninized version of Marx, American blacks were viewed as an asset because they fit neatly into Lenin's theory on the role racial and national minorities were to play in the revolution.[101]

The postwar black American had greatly impressed the Communists. The great black migration during the war had brought hundreds of thousands of blacks to the industrial centers of the East and Midwest, giving them an economic and political base they had not previously possessed. The racial unrest in the postwar period announced the growing race-consciousness of blacks, many of whom were now more inclined to *demand* rights than to *request* privileges. This militance, the Communists believed, could be rechanneled, and American blacks could be trained to assume an important role not only in the proletarian revolution of the United States, but in the national liberation struggles of backward imperialist colonies throughout the world.[102]

McKay's recognition as one of the most militant of race poets and of black radicals of the postwar period ensured that his participation at the Third International would be welcomed. At the opening session, McKay was seated on the platform beside Max Eastman and Gregory Zinoviev, president of the International. Addressing the Congress, McKay remarked that, once he heard the Negro question was to be discussed at the Congress, he had felt a moral obligation to speak on behalf of African Americans, especially since he had published "If We Must Die" and had become a spokesman for Negro radicalism.[103]

He warned the Congress that the international bourgeoisie might try to use blacks as a trump card in their fight against world revolution. Great Britain and France had used black troops to build their colonial empires. The United States had used black troops in the Spanish-American War. More important, American capitalists used blacks to fight organized labor, and utilized a tactic of setting white against black workers. He pointed out that American blacks faced a life more terrible and fraught with dangers than that endured by the Jews in Russia under the tsar.[104] Despite those conditions, blacks in the United States were still only race-conscious and rebellious, and not as yet class-conscious and revolutionary. Whether blacks would continue to be pawns of the bourgeois and capitalists in their fight against white labor depended upon the tactics adopted by the Communists to meet their special needs. It was useless to expect blacks to become class-conscious or to "close ranks" with the Communists as long as blacks considered white workers their greatest enemy.[105]

A more serious problem than tactics that faced the Communists was the deep-seated prejudice manifested by white comrades themselves. "In associating with the comrades of America," McKay commented, "I have found demonstrations of prejudice on the various occasions when black and white comrades had to get together: and this is the greatest difficulty that the Communists of America have to overcome—the fact is that they first have to emancipate themselves before they can be able to reach the Negroes with any kind of propaganda."[106] Their refusal to face squarely this issue only compounded the problem.

McKay's criticism was accurate and extremely difficult for Russian officialdom to answer. But Leon Trotsky made an effort to respond to McKay's critique. The commissar advised McKay that whether it involved the employment of Negro troops on the European continent, the capitalist exploitation of Africans and Asians, or the Negro slaves of American capitalism, there could be only one correct approach to their liberation. It would be through the number of enlightened, young, self-sacrificing Negroes, filled with enthusiasm for raising the material and moral level of the great mass of Negroes, and at the same time grasping the convergence of interests of the Negro masses with those of the masses of the whole world. Trotsky assured McKay that he knew the North American "situation" had been complicated by the abominable obtuseness and caste presumption of the privileged upper strata of the working class itself, who refused to recognize Negroes as fellow workers and fighting comrades. Unfortunately, the American Federation of Labor, led by Samuel Gompers, was founded on the exploitation of such despicable prejudices, and constituted the most effective guarantee for the successful subjugation of white and colored workers alike. While Trotsky had no idea how to fight this policy or what organizations would be most suitable for the American Negroes, Negro chauvinism must be rejected. Any program would have to be carried out in the spirit of solidarity of all exploited people without consideration of color.[107]

McKay had also attracted the attention of Zinoviev, who wrote McKay, in an argument only slightly more convincing than that of Trotsky, that the Russian government was making a sincere effort to eradicate the racial problem. The Communist International, Zinoviev wrote, was uncompromisingly putting into practice the policy of equality and fraternity of all workers, regardless of color or race. He confessed that the Third International intended to fully address and indicate solutions for the race problem. The Comintern did not forget for a minute the persecutions to which Negro workers were subjected, but the best solution was for Negro workers to organize their own mass organization and link up with other divisions of the fighting proletariat.[108]

McKay's pithy analysis had been candid, accurate, and to the point. But his pleadings had little impact except for influencing the establishment of a commission that eventually produced "Theses on the Negro Question." As indicated by Zinoviev's and Trotsky's comments, the Comintern, like the Socialists, continued to see the American black as part of an international and "minorities" question, rather than as a special American problem. Furthermore, it continued to place the Negro question within the context of the whole colonial question.[109]

In spite of the Comintern's failure to address itself adequately to the race issue, McKay regarded his visit to Russia as "an individual triumph." Yet, a month following Zinoviev's letter, in June 1923, McKay left Russia. His reason for this abrupt departure, less than a year after his arrival, and his subsequent denial that he had ever been a Communist have never been adequately explained. McKay had been taken to virtually every place in Russia to present lectures on "Blacks in America." He had met Trotsky, had traveled to major Red Army camps where he delivered readings of "If We Must Die," and had been toasted by the Red Fleet at Kronstadt. Perhaps, after he was thus displayed, McKay had no more propaganda value for Russian officialdom, and he himself gradually grew disillusioned with his use as a symbol of black support for the Communist cause. But McKay's own autobiography and Federal Bureau of Investigation records also offer several other contrasting possibilities.

Repeatedly in McKay's *A Long Way from Home* he notes that he told Communist officials in the Soviet Union that he could never be a disciplined member of the Communist party, and that he could not undertake or guarantee any practical work as an agitator or party organizer. But, he was quick to point out, his unwillingness to serve in these capacities did not prevent him from seeing what was needed to organize American Negroes. This practical work, however, was precisely what the Communists needed and desired from McKay. Indeed, Trotsky had already proposed the training of a group of Negroes as officers in the Red Army with young self-sacrificing blacks like McKay to lead them.[110]

The Federal Bureau of Investigation believed that McKay had actually assumed the position of "President of the Negro Section of the Executive Committee of the Third International." The Bureau was concerned that McKay might have left the Soviet Union carrying documents and a considerable sum of money from the Communist International with instructions to set up a "colored soviet" in America. Orders were issued by FBI director William Burns that, should McKay attempt to enter the United States, he and any of the other "Negro Delegates to the Fourth Congress be held together with all their baggage, documents, etc." so that a thorough examination could be conducted.[111]

The FBI had taken a serious interest in McKay since publication of his "If We Must Die" and had developed a significant file on McKay's activities both in America and abroad. A series of memorandums, including an eighteen-page document, scrutinized his radical activities and his writings. For a number of years the agency had been aware of McKay's membership in both the Industrial Workers of the World and the African Blood Brotherhood. While at the *Liberator* McKay unsuspectingly told a Bureau agent that though he was a year behind in dues he continued to desire membership in the IWW. His close relationship with Cyril Briggs was well known to the FBI. In one memorandum the agency recounted an interview with Briggs's wife; during the interview Mrs. Briggs purportedly promised that as soon as she obtained information on McKay's return to America from her husband she would contact the agent. Reference was also made to McKay's relationship with Sylvia Pankhurst. The FBI claimed that McKay was a "confidential man" for Pankhurst.[112]

McKay's writings left no doubt in the minds of officials at the FBI that he was both a Bolshevik and a member of the

Communist party. Excerpts from a number of his poems and articles were included in FBI memorandums to demonstrate McKay's views, principles, and beliefs—among them McKay's "Enslaved," "America," and, not surprisingly, "If We Must Die." "Enslaved" called for the oppressed, enslaved, lynched, and long-suffering black race to be liberated by the "avenging angel" that would swallow up the white man's world of wonders in the earth's vast womb. McKay's "America" struck a somewhat different note, one of racial indignation at America's "cultural hell," and noted his determination to stand "erect against her hate," without "terror, malice nor even a word of jeer."[113]

But it was McKay's appearance at the Third International and his subsequent articles that moved the FBI to initiate an elaborate and sometimes seriocomical network of communications both within the Bureau and with outside agencies to report on McKay's activities and whereabouts.[114] Informants in contact with the American Communist party and informants on Negro activities were instructed to watch for McKay and the other black delegates to the Fourth Congress. Even before his trip to the Soviet Union FBI agents had observed McKay sponsoring several meetings of Communists in his New York apartment.[115]

The FBI frequently mentioned the relationship between McKay and Rose Pastor Stokes. Stokes had attended the Fourth Congress and had praised the Comintern's establishment of a Negro Commission and the adoption of the "Commission's Theses on the Negro Question." During the Fourth Congress an enthusiastic Stokes enjoined her American comrades to carry on not only for the benefit of foreign-born workers, but also on behalf of the American workers whose black skin was a greater bar to full fellowship with white American workers than the lack of an American birth certificate. Addressing the racist tendencies of white comrades, she argued that Communists had nothing to fear from the liberation of black peoples. Common oppression ultimately placed all workers in one camp for the struggle against the oppressor.[116] Such enthusiasm contributed to Stokes's appointment as the first American Communist assigned to work among the masses of blacks in America.[117]

While the FBI recognized McKay's and Stokes's agreement on the basic principles of communism, they were also aware of their differences over party organization. In contradistinction to Stokes, McKay was opposed to the idea of the Communist party functioning underground: he felt that to arouse the masses the party should have a legal organization.[118] McKay had expressed this idea in the *Bolshevik*, the organ of the Fourth Congress of the Third International. His comment had come in response to the impression he had given that he was not a Communist. McKay wrote, "Actually I am a Communist, and my request to transfer me from the illegal [underground] party in the United States to the legal one was dictated by purely practical considerations." It was much less dangerous to be a Communist, he went on, than to be a Negro in America, and he noted that the only practical way to spread revolutionary ideas among the ignorant black masses would be through an aboveground Communist party.[119]

McKay's recollection years later regarding his differences with Stokes was consistent with his comment in the *Bolshevik* in 1922 and the FBI report. I must note, however, that McKay's remarks concerning his former comrade were marked by condescension and sarcasm. In *A Long Way from Home* he described Stokes as the main prop of James Cannon, chairman of the American Communist delegation, and as "sly as a puss" in her effort to keep the American party illegal and underground.[120]

Judging from the statements in McKay's autobiography and those in the FBI files, it appears likely that McKay probably left Russia because he had gotten all he could from his visit to the Soviet Union and was unwilling or unable to give the Communist party what it needed most: a commitment to toil among the masses. By his own admission, he was far better at giving advice than at working in the fields. Writing from the Soviet Union, he informed fellow comrade Grace Campbell, then secretary of the African Blood Brotherhood, that the Communist party of Russia had much faith in the colored people of America and believed that "they should organize and show some spirit," and form Communist groups.[121] Or, as he put it to James W. Johnson, "I went into Russia as a writer and a free spirit and left the same, because I was convinced that however far I was advanced in social ideas, if I could do something significantly creative as a Negro it would mean more to my group and the world than being merely a social agitator."[122]

71

McKay's willingness to represent the oppressed masses of black workers in America, while at the same time refusing to get involved in the work necessary to create a strong Communist black wing undoubtedly contributed to growing resentment against him by the official American Communist party delegates. They considered the combination of McKay's personal popularity and his criticism of American Communists as a threat. Writing to Walter White following his departure from Russia, McKay noted, "I am back of Russia after a great triumphal trip there. The more because I went in unofficially and met with opposition from the American comrades. It was not race prejudice though. It was graft and bad tactics and because although I am a Communist, I am a fearless champion of race rights even when that championship should reflect on American comrades."[123]

Finally, McKay's departure may have been influenced by his realization that though his trip was an "individual triumph," it did little to change one of the paradoxes of American radicalism. According to Mark Solomon, a scholar concerned with American blacks and communism, the very attachment of the Communist left to Lenin and the experience of the Russian Revolution provided the framework for a political shock of recognition for the American Negro. Both the strengths and the limitations of the relationship between black and radical whites in the Communist movement were based in the European roots of the party's view of the Negro question. The strength grew out of Lenin's injunctions that oppressed national minorities were necessary to proletarian revolution—"an injunction applied to the American Negro with prayerful devotion." The weakness was reflected in an inflexible and often grotesque application of party theory to a unique American phenomenon. The tragic result was a pattern of contradictory elements of attraction and repulsion, of success and failure.[124]

Thus, increasing pressure by the Russian Communists to personally involve himself in the movement, the opposition of his American comrades, the realization of his failure to achieve any fundamental change on the Negro question—all these things combined to influence McKay's decision to leave the Soviet Union. Moreover, immediate health problems also played a part in McKay's decision: he had syphilis and believed that he would find better medical treatment outside the Soviet Union.[125]

McKay's participation in the Third International had not gone unnoticed by the black community in New York. The *Messenger* applauded McKay's efforts to plead for his race and was pleased to report that resolutions were adopted in the interest of Negro emancipation. The *Messenger* regarded the mere presence of blacks at this "great deliberative body" an important example of the monistic behavior of races, morally and physically.[126] The *New York Amsterdam News* took positive note of McKay's comments before the Congress, reporting on how blacks, victims of American barbarism and mob spirit, were denied the right of free assembly. McKay, the *News* continued, told how American capitalism incited hatred in an attempt to turn the minds of the workers from the irrepressible conflict to race war.[127] Abram Harris, a black Socialist and scholar from Howard University, praised McKay as one of a group of intrepid Negro Marxists who were the latest development in racial leadership.[128]

Not all commentary was so favorable. The *Opportunity*, the organ of the National Urban League, complained that McKay had published an explanation of the American race problem that rivaled in misstatement the worst that had been said about the Negro by his most annoying enemies. McKay had claimed that the education of blacks depended entirely on a small cadre of northern white philanthropists. He also charged that the *Urban League Bulletin* disseminated propaganda among blacks to prepare them to become strikebreakers. For this task the League had established schools. The *Opportunity* concluded that neither blacks, socialism, nor truth were served by McKay's erroneous comments.[129]

The *Opportunity*'s criticism of McKay was undoubtedly motivated in part by McKay's obvious attack on its integrity, but other blacks were also rankled over McKay's sometimes excessive enthusiasm for Russia and his repeated criticism of American blacks for their lack of class consciousness and their lukewarm reception of communism. In 1921, he had criticized Du Bois for what he considered a sneer at the Russian Revolution. During the course of an NAACP membership drive, Du Bois had flippantly referred to those who supported the revolution in Russia as the "horde of scoundrels and bubble-blowers, ready to conquer Africa, join the Russian Revolution, and vote in the Kingdom of God tomorrow."[130]

Stung by McKay's remarks, Du Bois redefined his position, denying he had intentionally sneered at the Russian Revolution: "It might be the greatest event of two centuries and its leaders the most unselfish prophets." Yet he could not be sure what the revolution and the Russian brand of socialism would mean for American blacks—only time would tell. The energies of blacks, Du Bois responded to McKay, could best be spent in America working for the American Negro. Du Bois considered McKay's attitude naive; he himself did not believe that all race problems would be solved once blacks embraced the working-class program. Could blacks trust the white working class? Du Bois asked, especially when history gave so little assurance that blacks would be welcomed by their white counterparts. Until that time it would be foolish for blacks and associations like the NAACP to join a revolution that they did not at present understand.[131]

Gradually, Du Bois's doubts were resolved in favor of the Soviet Union, and he allowed McKay to use the *Crisis* to answer critics who charged that he had lost his integrity as a writer and become a propagandist for Russia. Responding to those critics, McKay declared that, as a result of the things he had seen and learned from the "Greatest event in the history of mankind," he was proud to be known as a propagandist for Soviet Communism. McKay expressed his belief that Negroes should join with other oppressed minorities to resist American capitalist propaganda and counter with a propaganda movement of their own. Looking to Russia as an example of what a handful of people could do, the Negro should use this period of ferment in international affairs to lift his cause out of national obscurity and forward it as a prime issue for the world.[132]

McKay's urgings persuaded few blacks to join the Communist cause. Even the more radical among blacks, the West Indians, did not rush to join the Communist party. Though Du Bois himself called the Russian Revolution "the most amazing and most hopeful phenomenon" in the postwar period, four decades passed before he said, "I seek a world where the ideals of communism will triumph."[133]

For the majority of blacks, attraction to communism was an intellectual attachment. Even McKay, who had been one of communism's most vocal supporters, exhibited a considerable amount of ambivalence about communism. Eventually, he even denied his Communist affiliation. While it is clear McKay was a member of the Communist party, over the years he would argue that he had refused during his visit to Russia to allow himself to be identified as a member of the party and had remained a "guest" of the Soviet government. Upon his departure he proudly proclaimed he left Russia with no radical affiliations and at no time considered himself under any special obligations.[134]

McKay's ambivalence about his membership in, and identification with, the Communist party should not be surprising. In spite of the passion and emotion he spent espousing and celebrating the Russian experiment, his reasons for attending the Congress always remained more personal and narrow. His insistence on placing the special problems of blacks before the radical world had been motivated more by his own deep personal hurt than from a desire to become an integral part of any collective organized revolutionary endeavor.[135] And while McKay's very presence at the Third International served to widen the choices oppressed blacks had in a country that seemed totally committed to their oppression, he was—as with most things in his life—still unable to commit himself to this particular cause.

Furthermore, McKay's problems with the American Communist delegation in Moscow may have affected him more than he admitted in his autobiography. The internecine warfare raging between partisans of legal and underground work within the American Communist party in Moscow did not permit McKay the luxury of remaining an "outside observer" or a "guest" without any special obligations. Pressed for his opinion on the question by American comrades, McKay infuriated fellow comrades with his support of a legal organization, his unwillingness to personally involve himself in the movement, and his public criticism of the racial ambivalences of white Communists. McKay's disagreement with party members and his tendency to personalize issues possibly account for the rancor so apparent in his recollection of fellow comrades in *A Long Way from Home*.

McKay left the Soviet Union convinced that his personal integrity on the issues of race and the international working-class struggle had caused him to become the target of Communist attacks. It was the beginning of a bitter and vituperative exchange that lasted until McKay's death.

4

"How Shall the Negro
Be Portrayed?" and
Home to Harlem

*A*S MCKAY prepared to leave Russia, back in the United States the Harlem Renaissance was gradually gaining momentum. "If We Must Die" had established McKay as one of the pioneers of the infant literary movement. With the publication of *Harlem Shadows* in 1922, African Americans eagerly awaited more from the gifted poet. However, they would have to wait six years before McKay again made literary headlines. His preoccupation with Negro radicalism had, in his words, "become a detriment to his poetical temperament."[1] During the interim, his reputation suffered, and many thought him well on his way to early literary oblivion.[2]

But in 1928 he published *Home to Harlem*, which became the first novel written by a black author to make the best-seller list. The novel also marked a departure from McKay's poetic literary style and earned him the reputation as a leader among a group of emerging young black writers who were in revolt against the traditional, genteel treatment of black life in African-American fiction.[3] The genesis of *Home to Harlem* reveals much about the motives for McKay's literary change of direction, and also illuminates the Harlem Renaissance.

McKay arrived in Germany early in 1923 to seek medical aid for his syphilis. After three months of medical attention, but without much improvement, he left Germany and went to France for additional treatment. In Paris physicians informed him that such an advanced stage of syphilis normally required two to three years of treatment but, because of his excellent overall health, he would require medication for only a year.[4] He convalesced, but the "dreadful disease" in combination with the long period of literary inactivity in Russia sapped much of his creative vitality. However, he did compose the following poems, which vividly reflect his state of mind at the time:

"How Shall the Negro Be Portrayed?"

Pageant

The blind, the almost dumb and the insane,
The lame with crutches, bandages everywhere,
The epileptic foaming where he fell,
The deaf, the paralytic crossed with care,

All congregated in this place of pain,
Like lepers kept together in a pale!
It seems a harsh romance of ancient times,
A modern version of a scripture tale.

Here is the fast of Romance, where disease
Holds court in regal form, hurling defiance
At all the victims humbled by his theme,
Contemptuous of the golden age of science.

A mother brings her bare kneed student boy,
Timidly standing firm the hardened rest,
Who spent, perhaps, his meagre dole to buy
A night of pleasure at a cheap whore's breast.

Another mere girl-mother walks aloof,
Bewilderingly, troubled and forlorn,
Bossoming, lullabying in her grief,
Her baby in disease conceived and born.

A strip of youth, moist lipped and lolling tongued,
Goes at a never changing trotting pace,
Companioned and holding guardian hands,
Each afternoon round his alloted space.

The pageant passes like a great nightmare
Of loathsome life, a lost soul's carnival
Of sin-damned mortale gathered here to win
Salvation through a fearful ritual.

Here breeds disease, the green eyed priest of death,
Unmoved by human woe or wile or ire,
Casting his long and heavy shadow fan
Over the bondaged victims of desire.

The Needle

My body quivers to the needle's sting
Meeting its point as tempers steel to steel;
But afterwards my cells in frenzy sing
The sharp incisive agony they feel.

Convalescing

When I go out from here, the doctors say,
At intervals I must return again,
For purifying treatment till that day
When no vile demons in my blood remain.[5]

As these poems suggest, the effects of the disease profoundly disturbed him. Even as he recovered, McKay feared that syphilis would do him permanent harm and would someday combine with tuberculosis (to which he felt West Indians were especially susceptible) to kill him.[6] Eventually this fear became an obsession that worried McKay until he died. However, it was most acute in the six years preceding the publication of *Home to Harlem*. The disease caused McKay, feeling abandoned and unable to share his fears with even his most intimate friends, to wonder about his future and the practicality of his chosen profession.[7]

Expenses for his extended treatment and convalescence constantly forced McKay to seek financial assistance. Initially, he tried to raise needed money by selling poetry to the magazines. Poetry was not only difficult to sell but brought very little financial reward: no twentieth-century American poet has managed to earn a living solely by writing poetry. Even his much-praised *Harlem Shadows* was returning little in royalties.[8] Ultimately, friends such as Walter White had to organize drives to solicit money in McKay's behalf. White approached a number of publishing houses, inquiring whether they would be interested in helping McKay. As a result of his effort he had been able to send McKay a check for $106.[9] Other friends made individual gifts of money. Louise Bryant Bullitt, the widow of John Reed, repeatedly sent money. She even offered to give McKay Reed's typewriter.[10] Pressed by his need, McKay resorted to contacts in the Communist party to solicit funds. Writing to "Comarade" Grace Campbell, he suggested she go in the name of the black Socialists and see if she could secure help from fellow Socialists. He urged her to convince fellow radicals that he had not been an idle comrade, pleading, "My life here is very unsatisfactory for a propagandist. . . . There is so much work to be done if I'm helped a little, but no one can work against such odds single-handed, especially when he is not even guaranteed a little food and a bed."[11]

McKay's shift away from poetry was motivated by practical necessity: he realized that he needed to make his creative work pay. His misery during his period of medical care gradually undermined McKay's romantic view of writing, and eventually caused him to reject the notion that a writer should write merely for the love of writing.[12] Some years later, shortly after the publication of

Home to Harlem, he assailed Nancy Cunard, heiress to the steamship line and author of the anthology *Negro* (1934), for suggesting that "for art's sake" he *donate* an article he had written. Responding to her suggestion, he remarked, "For the past six years I have been existing by my writings solely and everything I have written has been done for pecuniary consideration. I could never afford to write for nothing." He had promised himself that he would no longer allow his creative work to be exploited.[13]

Though strongly motivated by economic necessity, McKay found writing prose a formidable task. He had little experience writing fiction, and he was totally ignorant of modern prose techniques. Since childhood he had enjoyed all forms of poetry, and he believed that he possessed a natural feeling for rhythm. But prose he had read only haphazardly for his own pleasure. He had, on occasion, tried to write fiction, but his efforts were not encouraged by his friends. Jekyll had always considered McKay a poet; during his *Liberator* days, Max Eastman actively discouraged him from writing prose—warning McKay that he would never do it well, for poetry was his forte.[14]

Disregarding past advice, McKay now planned to write a full-scale novel about "Harlem society," as well as a number of short stories to pay for his daily living expenses. By late 1924 McKay had completed the first of his short stories, but he encountered great difficulty getting them published. In desperation, he enlisted the assistance of Walter White, asking him to try to sell a story about Jamaica.[15] Some months later he again wrote to White, requesting that he try to place a new series of stories he had just completed. One concerned the difficulties of an "Octoroon girl in Harlem." This story, McKay felt, was his best effort to date, and he hoped White would have no problem finding a publisher willing to buy it.[16]

White tried to sell McKay's stories, but could not find a publisher willing to buy even one. Most publishers believed that only the best short stories sold well.[17] McKay's first efforts were probably not very well written. Indeed, even White and Langston Hughes thought that McKay's stories were uniformly "third rate."[18] McKay's problems were compounded by his refusal to seek a professional agent. White and other people McKay imposed on to sell his stories were pursuing their own literary careers and could not afford the time necessary to promote Mc-Kay's work. And though McKay quickly realized that selling short stories long-distance by means of amateur agents was not the most efficient way to ensure the widest placement, he refused to return to America to promote his work himself.[19]

While McKay struggled to get some of his short stories published, he continued to work on his novel of "Negro Society." As with his short stories, his inexperience as a fiction writer made the going rough. He sought the technical assistance of established white writers such as H. L. Mencken and Sinclair Lewis. Although he also sought advice from blacks, he turned to them for information about practical matters, such as marketing assistance or financial aid. Seldom did he value black opinion regarding matters of style or content.[20]

McKay added to his marketing problems by rushing the manuscript of his novel to completion because he had heard a rumor that Carl Van Vechten, a white novelist of some distinction, was also working on a novel about Harlem Negroes. As McKay wrote to White, "I hear by a roundabout way that your friend Carl Van Vechten is doing a novel on Harlem Negro life and I don't want him to get ahead of me because he would hurt my chances, being a white man and a popular novelist known to all the gaudy crop of bleating reviewers, who are all log-rollers, hoping someday to kindly be reviewed for the novels they intend to write."[21]

He pleaded with White to try to secure him an advance on the novel he was currently writing so he could afford to return to New York without appealing to friends and associates for charity or being reduced to working as a stoker in the engine room of a passenger liner to pay for the Atlantic crossing. By December 1924 McKay still had not managed to get his novel manuscript into publishable form. White still had not been able to place any of his stories. Frustrated and discouraged, he wrote to White, indirectly criticizing him for not doing more to get some of his stories published.[22]

In reply, White urged McKay to be more optimistic and to have more faith, for things were certainly moving with rapidity as far as the Negro artist was concerned. "Countee Cullen," White wrote, "has had a book of verse accepted by Harper to be published in September and just a day or two ago Knopf accepted a volume by

Langston Hughes; Rudolph Fisher of Baltimore has had excellent short stories in the *Atlantic Monthly*. James Weldon [Johnson] is working on a book on Negro spirituals and the field of creative writers seems to be growing daily." "The Negro artist is really in ascendency just now," White declared. "There is unlimited opportunity and I think you would be amazed at the eagerness of magazine editors and book publishers to get hold of promising writers." He advised McKay to get his book ready as soon as possible and suggested that three or four publishers were looking for likely material. He assured McKay that he would continue to do all he could to secure him a publisher.[23]

Buoyed by White's comments, McKay forged ahead with his novel. A few weeks later he wrote to White, exclaiming, "I am so happy about the aroused interest in the creative life of the Negro. It is for Negro aspirants to do creative life themselves, to make the best of it—to discipline themselves and do work that will hold ground besides the very highest White standard." Nothing less than the highest standards, McKay believed, would help Negro art to survive and prosper after its current vogue passed.[24]

McKay surprised White by informing him that he had already finished his novel, but had sent the manuscript to Arthur Schomburg, the black Harlem bibliophile, implying that White's lack of effort on his behalf left him no choice.[25] White, who had aroused Viking Press's interest in McKay's work, was irritated—and rightly so—to discover that McKay had treated him in this shabby manner. He was even more irritated when he learned that McKay did not intend to try Viking Press except as a last resort, because he preferred to publish with a more established firm, like Knopf.[26] In the end, White conceded that it was McKay's manuscript and his decision to make regarding publication. But White clearly resented McKay's ingratitude and confided to Schomburg that he would have little time to assist McKay any further.[27]

White's resignation from his thankless role as McKay's unpaid agent came on the heels of a setback for McKay's novel. By now the manuscript, which seemed to change form like a chameleon, had shifted its emphasis away from "Harlem society." The latest version was a "realistic comedy of life" as McKay had experienced it among blacks on the railroads and in Harlem. Of course, McKay was far more familiar with the life of porters than with the life of

Harlem's middle-class blacks. [28] However, Knopf, the publisher to whom McKay insisted the manuscript be sent, rejected it on the grounds that its candid sexual references made it unsuitable for publication. [29] McKay reacted with confusion and disappointment. Writing to Mencken, he indicated that he had tried to be artistically sincere. He went on to suggest that perhaps he was out of touch with the American literary marketplace. Because he was living and writing in Europe, with its more open environment, he may have included certain phrases too raw for the American public. [30] Yet he confessed that he was puzzled and unsure just what publishers were looking for. The first version of his novel, the one about "Harlem society," had not aroused any interest, and now the second version about "blacks on the railroad" had been rejected as too vulgar for American tastes.

Dejected, McKay spent the remainder of 1925 and most of 1926 living from hand to mouth. He worked as a servant for 200 francs a month in Menton; quit after a month to work on a construction job; then gave up the construction job because he had no time to think. McKay confessed in a letter to Bryant that the waiting, hoping, existing, trying to write, in the midst of flies, bugs, filth, and disappointment were almost unbearable. Bryant continued to encourage McKay not to despair, pointing out that his experience would someday provide wonderful material for his writing. She also set about finding McKay an agent, eventually prevailing upon William Aspenwall Bradley, agent of Ford Madox Ford, and considered one of the foremost literary agents in Paris, to accept Claude as a client. [31]

Louise Bryant's support of McKay at this critical juncture in his life—sending financial aid, procuring agents, arranging for publishers to see his work, and enlisting readers and editors to help get McKay's manuscript in publishable form—went far beyond mere professional courtesy extended by one writer to another. According to Bryant's biographer, her correspondence with McKay reveals Bryant as someone selfless in her concern for his progress as an artist and human being, generous, yet retaining her critic's eye—all while her own personal life was rapidly unraveling. Bryant was already suffering from Dercum's disease, an incurable illness marked by obesity at the time of onset, then by weight loss and asthenia as the disease progressed. Other symptoms included "non-inflammatory, painful, subcutaneous tumors" that appeared all over the body, except the face and head.[32]

Although Bryant usually did not mention her disease to correspondents, she did reveal her condition to McKay. But always the manuscript that eventually evolved into *Home to Harlem* dominated her discussion. In 1930 McKay saw Bryant in Paris and was shocked by her appearance. It had been four years since he had last seen her and the meeting was a nerve-tearing ordeal. Bryant, he wrote, "had undergone radical treatment. The last time I had seen her she was plump and buxom. Now she was shrunken and thin and fragile like a dried up reed. Her pretty face had fallen like a mummy's and nothing was left of her startling attractiveness but her eyebrows." In 1936, Bryant finally succumbed to the debilitating disease.[33]

Despite the help of friends like Bryant and others who implored him to return to America, McKay, having left on such a triumphant note soon after the publication of *Harlem Shadows*, refused to return to America a failure.[34] But finally things began to look up for McKay. In 1925 Harper published Carl Van Vechten's *Nigger Heaven*, a novel that legitimized the "vogue of Negro primitivism." Van Vechten's credentials as a novelist and music, art, and drama critic gave his "Negro" work a degree of literary respectability. Despite protests from the more conservative elements of black and white society, *Nigger Heaven* was praised as a realistic portrayal of black life.[35] *Nigger Heaven's* acceptance was probably the most important factor in creating a milieu receptive to McKay's candid portrait of black life in Harlem. Late in 1926 the publishing firms of Boni and Harcourt expressed interest in McKay's "new" manuscript "Back to Harlem," a novel about a Negro doughboy who returns home to Harlem. Moreover, Harper expressed vague interest in publishing some of McKay's short stories. Then Harper informed McKay that it, too, desired to see his novel or even part of it. If they decided to publish his novel, they would hold the short stories and print them in book form later.[36] McKay hastily revised his novel, incorporated characters from his earlier railroad manuscript, and sent the manuscript off to Harper.

Harper immediately sent McKay a contract, along with a $100

cash advance. McKay's joy was undercut by his discovery that the contract ignored his novel entirely and did not commit Harper to a specific date of publication for the short stories. McKay refused to sign this contract because it was clearly not based on his finished work but on his potential marketability. Indeed, Harper had not been satisfied with McKay's manuscript novel, but the publisher did not want to risk the loss of another possible *Nigger Heaven*.[37] The original contract secured McKay's work with little risk to Harper, and guaranteed McKay neither publication of his novel or his short stories nor much in the way of desperately needed advance money. McKay's insistence on a new contract covering the new manuscript paid off. Harper sent him a revised contract covering the novel and the short stories they already had accepted. The novel was published as *Home to Harlem* in 1928; the short stories were published as *Gingertown* in 1932.[38]

In *Home to Harlem* McKay had come a long way from his first abortive attempt at writing about Harlem society in 1923. The earlier manuscript had so focused on the middle class that both McKay and his friends were afraid that it would be construed as simply another "race problem" novel. He remarked to Josephine Herbst in 1924 that he hoped his "novel wouldn't be puffed up as a race problem novel, for it isn't merely that."[39] This is not to suggest that McKay was originally opposed to using material from lower-class black life, for as early as 1923, when he began his novel on Harlem society, he indicated to H. L. Mencken that he was planning a series of prose sketches in which he would leave no subject, however degraded, untouched. These sketches were to be based on his experience between 1914 and 1919 in the semi-underworld of Harlem.[40] Initially, then, McKay considered black lower-class life as a subject more suitable for short stories than for a novel. Gradually, as the consequence of complex influences and motives, the lower-class world reserved for stories began to infiltrate the middle-class world of McKay's ongoing novel, and eventually to become its principal focus.

In its final form, the novel centered upon the exploits of two major characters, Jake and Ray. Jake, the central character, goes AWOL during World War I and returns "home to Harlem." His first night back he picks up a "tantalizing brown prostitute" for $50, but she returns his money as a gift after leaving him during the night. The plot, which is little more than a skeletal device upon which to hang a variety of episodes, involves his efforts to find her again. The reader is picaresquely carried into house parties, cabarets, and dives. Jake takes a job with the railroad crews, so one sees the dining-car life, the dormitories of the black railroad crews, and the brothels that serve these men. According to literary scholar Robert Bone and historian Nathan Huggins, Jake represents pure primordial instinct. His values are based on a free, unfettered confrontation with life. His life is driven by the desires for love and enjoyment. Living is drink, food, dance, and sex. Evil for Jake is what threatens his pleasures or his friends. The other character, Ray, is a young Haitian consumed with a desire to write, whom Jake befriends. Ray personifies the dilemma of the inhibited, overcivilized intellectual. He is the classical "marginal" man, a misfit in the white's civilization, and yet unable to accept the hedonistic life-style of the black world's Jakes. Contrasting Ray with Jake, the primitive black untouched by the decay of Occidental civilization, McKay attempts to convey modern man's rebellion against Western civilization.[41]

On another level, *Home to Harlem* can be viewed as a biographical statement about McKay's own inner conflicts. Through Jake and Ray, McKay expresses his own ambivalences, tensions, and status as a marginal man. McKay had lived both a Jake-like life and a Ray-like life, though never completely comfortable with either. McKay's Jake side offers the reader a tour of black cabarets, house parties and life as a Pullman porter. Jake's bout with venereal disease and his unsuccessful attempt to make light of it are drawn from McKay's real life. Because Jake is McKay, he is never quite as uncomplicated as Bone and Huggins suggest. Though Jake boasts after spending all of his money on a night of lovemaking that "I ain't got a cent to my name, but ahm as happy as a prince all the same," he is not completely liberated from the problems that taunt Ray. As Jake expresses it on the eve of Ray's ocean-bound departure,

> Ef I was edjucated, I could understand things better and be proper-speaking like you is. . . . And I mighta helped mah li'l sister to get edjucated, too (she must be a li'l woman, now), and she would be nice-speaking like you, sweet brown, good enough foh you to hitch up with. Then we could all settle down

and make money like edjucated people do, instead a you gwine
off to throw you'self away on some lousy dinghy and me chasing
around all the time lak a hungry dawg.

Jake assures the reader that "Sure Ise human," and not simply a
creature of passion and savage instinct.[42]
In contrast, Ray represents that part of McKay that under
Jekyll's influence learned to distrust the promises of capitalism.
Ray also embodies the "keen observer" who lived in Harlem, but
who was separated from its people by his different cultural background and his intellectual temperament. Ray is also the McKay
who, in spite of his increasing race consciousness, still clings to the
hope for a world of universal brotherhood. Ray expresses these
beliefs clearly. He declares that all aspects of white civilization are
anachronisms for the black man. Education for Negroes, Ray
suggests, is "like our houses. When the whites move out, we
move in and take possession of the old dead stuff." Civilization,
Ray warns, is rotten, and "we are all rotten who are touched by
it."[43]
But despite his rage against white civilization, Ray cannot fully
repudiate it. He had been weaned on the writings of Bernard
Shaw, Henrik Ibsen, Anatole France, and H. G. Wells. Regarding
race, Ray knows that the best human traits do not belong to any
special class or nation or race of people—black or white. Commenting on the kinship of race, the author writes: "These men
claimed kinship with him. They were black like him. Man and
nature had put them in the same race. He ought to love them and
feel them (if they felt anything). He ought to if he had a shred of
social morality in him. They were all chain-ganged together and
he was counted as one link. Yet he loathed every soul in that great
barrack-room, except Jake. Race . . . Why should he have and
love a race?[44]
McKay ends *Home to Harlem* on a note consistent with his own
life: the book, like his life, is full of unresolved dilemmas. Jake
finds his elusive brown girl and embarks upon a new life. While
the exact nature of this new life is not clear, it must involve some
measure of the responsibility Jake has so far refused to accept.
Whether Jake, whose life had been "truant and undomesticated,"
can accept this responsibility remains for the reader to ponder.

Ray has already decided that he is not suited to a life of marriage and domestication and has set off in search of answers he hopes someday to put down on paper.

Unfortunately for McKay, the publication of *Home to Harlem* came at a time when one controversy after another arose concerning the Harlem Renaissance. These controversies revealed sharp divisions within the black community about the nature of the literary movement. Many questions were hotly debated in newspapers, magazines, and private correspondence about the purpose of the Renaissance and who should portray the Negro. But the question that stimulated the most bitter and acrimonious discussion was "How shall the Negro be portrayed?" This issue struck at the heart of one of the fundamental themes of the Renaissance: the relationship between art and society, and most particularly at the problem of defining a writer's obligation—if any—to society.[45]

Because he had chosen to write about the lower class of Harlem's black community, *Home to Harlem* placed McKay directly in the center of the controversy. Some viewed his treatment of lower-class black life as a slanderous attempt to glorify the lowest class of Negro life. McKay was accused of peddling sensationalism and surrendering to the influence of white bohemia. Because the novel was published at the height of this debate, it forms an excellent backdrop against which McKay's philosophy and his relationship to the Renaissance may be viewed.

Reviews of *Home to Harlem* clearly exhibited cultural splits within the literary community. After reading *Home to Harlem*, W. E. B. Du Bois remarked that the novel had nauseated him.[46] Mary Fleming Labaree, columnist for *Opportunity*, while reviewing *Passing*, included a reference to her disgust with *Home to Harlem*, declaring, "The pity of it, *Walls of Jericho* and *Home to Harlem* perched on our bookshelves with *Plum Bun* and *Passing* nowhere to be seen."[47] The most vituperative comment came from fellow West Indian and nationalist Marcus Garvey. In a full-page attack on McKay's novel, he declared,

> Our race, within recent years, has developed a new group of writers who have been prostituting their intelligence under the direction of the White man, to bring out and show up the worst traits of our people. Several of these writers are American and

West Indian Negroes. They have been writing books, novels and poems, under the advice of White publishers to portray to the world the looseness, laxity and immorality that are peculiar to our group; for the purpose of these publishers circulating the libel against us among the White peoples of the world, is to hold us up to ridicule and contempt and universal prejudice.

McKay's novel, according to Garvey, was a "damnable libel against the Negro."[48]

Harvey Wickersham, author of *The Impuritans*, wrote that McKay had written *Home to Harlem* in much the same exotic and primitive manner used by Carl Van Vechten in his *Nigger Heaven*. Furthermore, Wickersham questioned whether McKay could have really been at home in the Harlem he depicted. Instead of writing a valuable social document about living conditions in Harlem, Wickersham charged, McKay had chosen to conduct a slumming party for the entertainment of "buckra-jig chasers" anxious for an excuse to be base.[49]

However, other reviewers took a decidedly sympathetic view of *Home to Harlem*. The *New York World* praised McKay as a writer of "calm accustomed authority, too proud for apologetics, too proud even to remind ignorant readers that it is not of the respectable Negro that he writes." Only a superior mind, the paper continued, could have fathered *Home to Harlem*.[50] Like the *World*, *Opportunity* lauded McKay's absolute candor and the book's complete freedom from attempts to apologize for, explain, or gloss over the realities of Harlem life. *Opportunity* felt that *Home to Harlem* offered a true love story, somewhat crude, but not without a genuine element of romance.[51] Having finished *Home to Harlem*, Langston Hughes excitedly wrote to Alain Locke, exclaiming "It ought to be named Nigger Hell," and suggested it was the best low-life novel he had ever read. He was sure *Home to Harlem* "must be the flower of the Negro Renaissance, even if it is no lovely lily."[52]

Other reviewers regarded the novel as a significant social document. For example, Burton Rascoe, writing for *Bookman*, felt *Home to Harlem* was a book to invoke pity and terror, a story of the lives led by the "lost generation" of blacks in the teeming metropolis north of 110th Street, and a tale about those who compensated for their defeats in life in a white man's world by living a life of savage intensity among themselves at night.[53] Agreeing with Rascoe, T. S. Matthews in the *New Republic* commented that in *Home to Harlem* you meet the "nigger again," but this time he has the breath of life in him: he is neither the black-faced minstrel of a white man's plantation nor the stilted creature of a white man's culture, but the haphazard and lively spawning of a city street. *Home to Harlem*, Matthews concluded, was a novel of documentary interest, for it offered a true picture of the crude and violent life of the "jungle nigger" in the jungle city.[54]

Such criticism, though specifically aimed at McKay, underscored the problem common to most blacks attempting a definition of the Renaissance's nature and purpose. From its inception, the Renaissance had involved a complex set of impulses, needs, aspirations, and definitions. However, few would deny that a consensus of opinion existed as to the "sense of mission" that permeated any discussion of the New Negro and the Negro Renaissance. As far back as 1915, when the Renaissance was in its embryonic stage, William Pickens, dean of Morgan College, had spoken for the optimism of the movement by announcing that blacks finally stood on the threshold of a renaissance of civilization and culture after four hundred years of interruption by captivity, slavery, and oppression.[55] As the Renaissance evolved, two phases of New Negroism became distinct. The first was defined by economic radicals such as A. Philip Randolph, Cyril Briggs, and others who promoted self-defense and political militancy. Randolph believed the African American had entered a "Second Reconstruction." He predicted that a new culture and civilization would be created by a new class of black intellectuals he designated the "New Negro."[56] During the period running roughly from the time of America's entry into World War I to early in 1923, Randolph and others sought to change social relations directly and qualitatively.

These black leaders envisioned a new economic and political order in the United States based on the political solidarity of the working class, both black and white. The more conservative elements of this group, such as Randolph and Owen of *Messenger*, hoped to achieve social transformation politically, through the power of votes. Those farther to the left, such as Briggs, Moore, and Huiswood, tended to believe that transformation would require strikes and clandestine political activity. Political New Negroes generally agreed that notions of black inferiority were products of a social order used by capitalists to divide, and hence better rule, workers, and that once the social structure of America was reformed, notions of white supremacy/black inferiority would lose their fundamental economic rationale and disappear.

The second phase of the Renaissance was characterized by the emergence of the New Negro culturalists around 1924. They tended to ignore politics and to define New Negroism in spiritual terms; they stressed the importance of self-confidence, called for a new artistic emphasis on the inward search, and sought to anchor black art in black folk culture. As Alain Locke, a representative of this group, expressed it, "In the last decade something beyond the watch and guard of statistics has happened in the life of the American Negro and the three Norns who have traditionally presided over the Negro problem have a changeling in their laps. The Sociologist, the Philanthropist, the Race leader are not unaware of the New Negro but they are at a loss to account for him."[57]

Unlike the political New Negroes, cultural New Negroes such as Locke, Du Bois, and, to a lesser extent, James Weldon Johnson, felt that widespread recognition of the artistic abilities of blacks would naturally lead to the reformation of the American social order. They also tended to view white notions of black intellectual and artistic inferiority as the cause of black oppression. Destroy the claims of black inferiority and black social equality would eventually follow.

The New Negro of the twenties, whether political or cultural, was the product of years of evolution within the confines of a racist society. As William Pickens observed, "The New Negro is not really new: he is the same Negro under new conditions and subject to new demands. Those who regret the passing of the 'old Negro' and picture the new as something very different, must remember that there is no sharp line of demarcation between the old and the new in any growing organism like a germ, a plant, or a race."[58]

The New Negro arose from the disillusionment blacks felt after World War I. Blacks took part in "the war to make the world safe for democracy" because they believed that Wilson's idealistic crusade abroad would lead to better conditions for blacks at home.

But the armistice only brought forth Harding, a "return to nor-malcy," renewed discrimination, Jim Crowism, and mob violence against blacks. The Great Migration of the war period, which brought hundreds of thousands of blacks out of the rural South into the urban North, created new problems for blacks: unemployment, squalor, the necessity of obtaining relief, and a continuation of the ravishes of a racist society. The death of Booker T. Washington in the midst of this period of war and migration created a leadership vacuum. Out of this chaos and confusion, the New Negro would bring order, hope, and a new direction. In short, as Countee Cullen eloquently described it, "There is such a thing as working out one's own soul salvation. And that is what the Negro intends to do."[59]

The political New Negro phase faded during the postwar recession. Thereafter, the dominant group within the New Negro movement was the Negro culturalists. The culturalists promoted "cultural nationalism." They constantly argued that the Negro needed to reassess his past and use it as a guide for the future. Some culturalists urged the establishment of a black metropolis or Negro mecca. Such powerful rhetorical terms as militant self-respect, the willingness to assert one's manhood even at the risk of physical harm, and a positive group psychology were used to give the black man strength to endure the uncertainty and flux that characterized life in the postwar period.

A new literary movement was envisioned as the instrument that would direct the effort by blacks to redefine themselves and help reshape American society. Culturalists believed that black artists and intellectuals would lead the effort to transform society by creating new images of life for black Americans. Intellectuals and creative artists would not only foster the development of a new culture but also provide the means for repairing a damaged group psychology and reshaping a warped social perspective.[60]

No one understood this better than Alain Locke, one of the founders of the New Negro literary movement. Locke asserted that "if modern America could leap through its self-imposed barriers, and if it could find or make an open door, it would pass on a voyage of social exploration and discovery. Such a voyage would not only shed more light on the Negro, but a new vision and practical faith in democracy might also be discovered." The movement, like the New Negro, was not to be an imitator or assimilator of American civilization but an active and creative contributor to it. [61]

Beneath the glittering purposes attributed to the Renaissance, there were some practical realities that could not be separated from any effort by blacks to create a culture that reflected their own experience. The New Negro culturalists believed that the Renaissance would further the solution of the race problem. Writing to Walter White, James Weldon Johnson, who is considered one of the more progressive Renaissance advocates, remarked in reference to a proposal for the establishment of a Negro Art Institute that it had been a cherished belief of his that the development of Negro art would not only mean a great deal for the literary aspirations of blacks, but would provide the easiest and most effective approach to the race question. [62] A black writers' group, whose membership included Countee Cullen, Eric Walrond, Jessie Fauset, Langston Hughes, and Alain Locke expressed similar sentiments. Locke summarized the feeling of the group by commenting that the Negro group possessed a spiritual wealth that, if properly expounded, would be ample for a new judgment and reappraisal of the race. [63]

The notion that literature could foster improved race relations was supported by a wide spectrum of blacks and repeatedly found its way into discussions of the cultural Renaissance in the twenties. The numerous literary contests held to encourage the Renaissance attest to this fact. *Opportunity,* one of the most influential black journals, sponsored contests for this purpose; its editors explained that they wanted to encourage writers because literature had always been a great liaison between the races. [64] Others, such as Du Bois, expressed such sentiments in more militant terms. Literature constituted a weapon to counter the Darwinian belief that African Americans were congenitally incapable of creating and expressing their own culture. Or, as Du Bois characterized it, "until recently the Negro in literature while always present, has been passive—used as a source of material for white writers—normally represented as sub-normal, congenitally incapable, and represented as the unfit survivor of Darwinian natural selection." [65]

It was virtually impossible for either the writers or the critics to ignore the importance of race to the Renaissance movement; nor was there any serious attempt to do so. Perhaps Locke best expressed both the potential and the intrinsic limitations of the movement in his article "The New Negro." The New Negro, Locke discerned, represented a forced attempt to build Americanism on race values. Through race cooperation, race literature, and cultural nationalism, the Negro would forge a new era in race relations. Having weaned himself from traditional paternalism, the Negro would pursue a new course to his objectives. These objectives were the ageless ones of attaining the goal of American ideals and democracy. Naturally, this would involve a new mentality for the American Negro, which at first would be negative and iconoclastic, and then positive and constructive.[66]

Since race was the mainspring of black life, blacks could use cultural nationalism to turn a defensive posture into an offensive one, a handicap into an incentive. Though the New Negro's tone seemed radical, his purpose remained the same. As Locke put it, "the thinking Negro has shifted a little toward the left with the world trend, and there is an increasing group who affiliate with radical and liberal movements, but fundamentally for the present, the Negro is radical on race matters, conservative on others, in other words, a forced radical, a social protestant rather than a genuine radical."[67]

No statement expresses more accurately the paradoxical essence of the Harlem Renaissance than Locke's assessment of the Renaissance's cultural nationalism. It also indicates the concern Locke and other blacks felt about the possible abuses of some black writers and critics. Thus the New Negro and the cultural nationalism of the Renaissance period were products of the American race scene, whose view of the world had been shaped and molded by the "shoots and suckers" of the racism deeply imbedded in the American experience. From 1619 to the 1920s, African Americans, keenly aware both of overt prejudice and discrimination and of their covert nuances, formulated and shaped their ideologies with one eye focused on the limitations imposed on them by a racist society and the other eye turned to their aspirations. In the twenties the principal aspiration for most blacks was the desire for first-class citizenship. The Renaissance represented black hope for the integration into the mainstream of American society. On the whole, the Renaissance did not repudiate American values and ethics. In fact, in some respects, the Renaissance was only one of any number of adjustments blacks had historically developed to cope with the continuing ebb and flow of race relations.[68] It was within this context that McKay's novel ran afoul of the more conservative factions of the Renaissance. Ideologically, he was not able to grasp the full significance or complexity of the Renaissance; his effort at understanding was made all the more difficult because the movement had flowered during the years he lived abroad.[69] What he did understand, he could not sympathize with. In his view, the Negro Renaissance was simply a social uplift movement, a vehicle to accelerate the pace and progress of "smart Negro society." Negroes labored under the delusion that the movement was a success just because a wealthy woman from Park Avenue or a titled European became interested in Negro art and invited Negro artists to their homes. The Negro Renaissance fell short of what McKay felt constituted a "true renaissance": "talented persons of an ethnic or national group working individually or collectively in a common purpose and creating things that would be typical of their group."[70]

Certainly, McKay appreciated the necessity for some kind of black Renaissance, but he insisted it be expressed in pure artistic terms. This, he felt, was the fundamental difference between himself and other African Americans. He refused to allow his work to be deliberately massacred because of the "exigence of false momentary aspirations." "I am a man and artist first of all," he professed, "the imprisoning quality of my complexion has never yet, and never will move me to bend to flunkeyism and intellectual imprisonment with the sorry millions that are likewise tinted."[71] McKay believed that the black proclivity toward viewing art and literature through the distorting lens of New Negro propaganda would seriously stifle the development of a true black literary tradition.

Five years before he published *Home to Harlem*, and long before Harlem had come into vogue, McKay had privately expressed such misgiving to H. L. Mencken. He suggested that a certain segment of the Negro intelligentsia had become too sensitive about its humiliating position, and was no longer excited by the profound aspiration to remain true to itself and realize its artistic ideals as a group: "This is the state of spiritual impotence which Negroes in the United States have been reduced to by capitalist exploitation." The black intelligentsia, imbued with the spirit of propaganda and suffering under the many years of oppression, had ceased to be a reliable and courageous critic of creative work.[72] Three years later McKay intimated to Alain Locke that he would not enter a manuscript in one of the many literary contests designed to help black artists, for he thought that prizes were bad things for any writer who took his work artistically. Moreover, he believed that his work would not be judged fairly because he would not mix art and propaganda.[73]

In an unpublished manuscript written in 1927, McKay wrote, "Between the devil of Negro intellectualism and the deep sea of Negro life stands the Negro artist." According to McKay, the Negro intelligentsia was interlinked by virtue of a single purpose: a racial duty to integrate blacks into the mainstream of American society. Any black artist who attempted to understand and visualize life as it existed, for example, through the portrayal of the "bloodsurging, shining in the darkness, singing and working Negroes," who were part of the rough salt of black life, would invariably bring the wrath of the propagandist intelligentsia down upon his head.[74]

Yet, the difference between propaganda and art was not always clear. It was one thing to support the exclusion of propaganda from art, and another to demarcate where propaganda ended and art began. For some, like Du Bois, there was no necessity to distinguish between the two. Du Bois argued that all art was propaganda and ever must be, despite the wailing of the purists. "I stand in utter shamelessness," he declared, "and say whatever art I have for writing has always been for propaganda, for gaining the right of Black folk to love and enjoy. I do not give a damn for art that is not used for propaganda."[75]

In a somewhat more moderate tone, William Pickens had expressed a similar point of view. Pickens felt that artists were mistaken if they believed that art and propaganda could not coexist in the same work. As far as he was concerned, "Art and propaganda always exist side by side; for in fact propaganda is the subsoil out of which all art is grown. But it is the function of art to conceal the propaganda as to make it more palatable to the average recipient while not destroying it."[76]

Even Walter White, who generally tried to separate art and propaganda, had exhibited the same reasoning in his reply to Eugene Saxton's refusal to publish his book *Fire in the Flint* on the grounds that race was too volatile an issue and would inflame one section of American society against the other. White rebutted Saxon by replying that it was time the defense be heard. For fifty years, White charged, the argument had been all on one side. The Pages, Cables, and Dixons all had painted the Negro as a vicious brute, a rapist, a good old nigger, or a happy-go-lucky, irresponsible, and shiftless type.[77] Aware of the dilemma facing black artists over the question of art versus propaganda, James Weldon Johnson sympathized with those writing "defensive and exculpatory" literature, but believed that ultimately black artists and black art would be best served by rising above propaganda and race, and creating art that reached out to the universal in truth and beauty.[78]

At times McKay himself had difficulty distinguishing between propaganda and art, the line often being very fine. Louise Bryant, returning two of McKay's rejected short stories, added the notation that she was pleased that they did not display the obvious propaganda of the previous year.[79] McKay had admitted to White that every work of art was in reality personal propaganda in that it reflected the way in which the artist saw life and wanted to present it. But he had also noted that there existed a vast chasm between the artist's offering a personal expression of himself and his making himself the instrument of a group, of a body of opinion. The first was art, and the second was prostitution.[80]

Nevertheless, McKay concluded that black literature was being intimidated and emasculated by the fears of minorities.[81] McKay did not believe that a writer's choice of subject matter or his treatment of this subject matter should conform to the dictates of society in general or to any special group within society. In his view, the New Negro culturalists had no right to complain about *Home to Harlem;* indeed, as far as he was concerned, it was his critics, not he, who were impeding the advance of black literature.

McKay did not publicly respond to the criticism of *Home to*

Harlem until well after its publication; he used his next novel, *Banjo*, to answer his critics. In *Banjo* (the novel will be discussed fully in the next chapter), as he had already done in *Home to Harlem*, McKay allows his two major characters to speak for him. Ray, the overcivilized aspirant writer who reappears from the first novel, presents McKay's views on the Harlem Renaissance. Passionately, Ray declares:

> We educated Negroes are talking a lot about a racial renaissance. And I wonder how we're going to get it. On one side we're up against the world's arrogance—a mighty cold hard white stone thing. On the other the great sweating army—our race. It's the common people, you know who furnish the bone and sinew and salt of any race or nation. In the modern race of life we're merely beginners. If this renaissance we're talking about is going to be more than a sporadic and scabby thing, we'll have to get down to our racial roots to create it.[82]

To those blacks who had objected to the suitability of McKay's use of the lower classes in *Home to Harlem*, McKay/Ray responds that Negro intellectuals are unable to appreciate anything truly black. The acquisition of a white man's education has taught them to despise their own people. "You're a lost crowd," Ray concludes, "you educated Negroes, and you will only find yourself in the roots of your own people."

Ray enjoins the educated Negro to realize that until he matures and accepts that he will never belong to the white race, and seeks inspiration in his own roots, the black race will never produce a real renaissance. McKay suggests that if the black literati are sincere in their feelings about racial advancement and supporting a renaissance, they need to study the Irish cultural and social movement, the struggle of the Russian peasants, the story of Ghandi and what he is doing for the common hordes of India, and the simple beauty of the African dialect.[83]

But McKay was not left to defend his position alone: a whole group of literary artists and critics joined in the discussion. In fact, McKay had not been among the first who had publicly expressed their views about the proper portrayal of the character of the Negro. The catalyst for the discussion of the writer's obligation in his choice of subject matter had been a symposium conducted by *Crisis* magazine in 1926 under the title "The Negro in Art: How

Shall He Be Portrayed?"[84] In responding to the question whether an artist, black or white, was under any obligation or limitation as to the sort of character he portrayed, the overwhelming majority had replied no. However, in the wording of their replies, an interesting difference between the white and black respondents appeared.

Almost invariably, the white writers tended to express an unequivocal no. Sherwood Anderson, for example, commented that not only should there be no limitations, but the Negro was making a great mistake by becoming too sensitive about the issue of how Negroes should be portrayed. H. L. Mencken expressed the same view and added that the artist labored under no obligations whatsoever and should be free to depict things as he saw them. Indicating that he was fully aware of the reasons why Negroes were sensitive to portraits of the lower strata of their race, Carl Van Vechten declared that these attitudes were inimical to art. He pointed out that this concern about the proper way to portray blacks had caused more than one of his Negro acquaintances to refrain from using such material. Commenting on the crux of the issue, Van Vechten remarked, "The squalor of Negro life, the vice of life, offer a wealth of novel, exotic, picturesque material to the artist. On the other hand, there is little difference if any between the life of a wealthy or cultured Negro and that of a White man of the same class." In the end, Van Vechten concluded, the question was really whether black writers were going to write about this exotic material while it was still fresh or would they continue to make a free gift of it to white authors who would exploit it until not a drop of vitality remained?[85]

Van Vechten's comment cut clearly to the point and revealed the dilemma facing black artists and critics, which was evidenced in their responses. The black participants noted their wish to allow the artist freedom to express himself without the restraint of racial guidelines. Yet, they also suggested that black history and the continuing problem of race relations would not allow blacks the luxury of such impartiality and detachment. Consequently, black responses were usually more guarded and qualified than those of the white respondents.

Walter White, for one, lamented that, at the very time when black writers were gaining readers, a division had arisen about what subjects were appropriate. White believed that a writer should certainly have the freedom to express the sort of character he wished. But he was troubled by the inordinate amount of attention given to lower-class black life and strongly disagreed with Van Vechten's view that lower-class Negro life provided the writer with interesting, original material, while upper-class Negro life merely provided material already familiar from fictional portraits of upper-class white life. White believed that upper-class blacks, by their very struggle to achieve success, had sharpened their sensitivity to the intense race drama in America. Their sensitivity to pain, insult, and tragedy had its compensation in the keener awareness and appreciation of the rhythmic beauty, color, and joy which were so valuable a part of Negro life. In fact, White declared, it may be harder for a writer to write a good novel about upper-class blacks because of the "subleties" such a portrait would require. White also pointed out that those critics who justified the assertion that only the lower-class Negro be depicted, by claiming the artist has the right to choose his own material, were the same critics who insisted that the Negro artist confine himself to one field.[86]

Jessie Fauset, essentially in agreement with White, expressed the notion that no writer should be limited unless it became evident the artist had consistently chosen the worst types of blacks to portray and painted them with malice.[87] Countee Cullen proclaimed that he would be the last person to vote for the infringement of an author's right to tell a story, to delineate a character, or to transcribe an emotion in his own way and in the light of truth as he sees it. Nevertheless, Cullen went on, because Negroes had not yet built up a sufficient body of "sound, healthy race literature," black authors should not write about abortions and other aberrations that whites were all too prone to accept as true about blacks. Already, for white readers, the Negro of fiction was typically ignorant, burly, bestial, sensual, and loose living.[88]

Abundant evidence existed to support Cullen's fears that literature using the lower strata of black life would only reinforce racist attitudes already held by many whites. White admirers of Van Vechten's *Nigger Heaven*, for example, provided one sort of evidence. Southern writer Ellen Glasgow thought that the book revealed "the best argument in favor of African Slavery that I have ever read." While she was sure Van Vechten intended no propaganda, she found in the book the accent of realism that led her to compare the world of Harlem with the life of blacks as she knew them in the South. Another admirer of Van Vechten was convinced that his book was truthful and comprehensive as well as entertaining.[89]

Regardless of such evidence, black sensitivity concerning the depiction of African Americans in literature was often difficult for whites to understand. Responding to H. L. Mencken's remark that blacks were too sensitive, Du Bois stated that, although no racial hostility was evident in Mencken's remarks, Mencken, like many other Americans, did not understand just where the shoe pinched. He was especially concerned with Mencken's assertion that blacks had just as much opportunity to publish as whites, regardless of the subject matter. Certainly, Du Bois declared, white Americans were willing to read about Negroes, but they preferred to read about blacks who were fools, clowns, or prostitutes, or in despair and contemplating suicide.[90]

More emphatic, Countee Cullen declared that, as far as he was concerned, the opinion of white writers and critics did not matter. "Whites were not under the same obligations to us that we are to ourselves." As members of a group that had created a vast heritage of sound literature, whites could not understand black sensitivity. Whites, Cullen felt, could not appreciate blacks' disinclination as a people toward their racial defamation, even for "art's sake."[91]

It was just this sort of racial obligation and fear that McKay rejected. As an artist, his sentiments closely paralleled those of white writers and critics. He considered himself under no obligation whatsoever and accused African Americans of not facing their problems squarely and discussing them fearlessly. Their restraints continued to paralyze the creative spirit of would-be black artists. And despite the critical reviews in black newspapers and journals, he did not consider *Home to Harlem* or any of his prose an abuse of black subject matter. In defense of his work, he wrote to James W. Johnson, arguing that he had not deviated in any way from his intellectual and artistic ideas of life. He regarded *Home to Harlem* as a real "proletarian novel," but he did not expect the "nice radicals" to see that quality because they knew very little about real proletarian life.[92]

Proclaiming himself a genuine artist interested in creating "imaginative portrayals of life and artistic truth," McKay denounced black Americans for refusing to accept artistic presentation of any and every phase of Negro life. Too many blacks were afraid of the white man's ridicule and hopelessly lost in the white man's prejudice.[93] Better-off blacks had been living their lives behind closed shutters for fear of cracker insults and mud. Responding to Du Bois's criticism of *Home to Harlem*, McKay wrote, "Certainly I sympathize with and even pity you for not understanding my motive, because you have been forced from a normal career to enter a special field of racial propaganda and honorable though that field may be, it has precluded you from contact with real life." McKay claimed that he had never been afraid of the "light" and would continue to love truth as he saw it.[94]

The light, as McKay saw it, was simple: African Americans had a wonderful storehouse of peculiar racial characteristics, which the daring black artist should take hold of and exploit. In the Negro community there were obvious traits, physical and cultural, common to blacks as a whole. Their eyes shined like stars. Their teeth were ivory white. Their laughter sounded like falling water. They were great dancers. Then there were the "homely things" in the Negro's life-style: Maudy's wash tub, Aunt Jemima's stories of white folks, Miss Ann's old clothes for work and wages, George's "Yessah—boss!", dining car and Pullman service, barber and shoeshine shops, chitterling and corn pone joints.[95] To McKay, these were the qualities and characteristics of black life that indicated the vast storehouse of material for the sympathetic black artist.[96]

On the surface, there was nothing wrong with McKay's view that unique material existed in the lower-class black community for artistic use. Other writers expressed the same ideas even more emphatically than McKay. Perhaps the most eloquent advocate of this view was Langston Hughes. Hughes had spearheaded the discussion about the legitimacy of using lower-class black material during the *Crisis* symposium. There, Hughes remarked that he did not see the value of any pronouncement of restriction, for the true literary artist would write about what he chose, regardless of outside opinions. According to Hughes, there was no single correct subject for an artist to write about. "It's the way people look at things," Hughes noted, "not what they look at that needs to be changed."[97]

In response to George Schuyler's denial of the existence of any peculiarly Negro art, Hughes articulated even more strongly his belief in the importance of writing about the masses of black people. Hughes spoke passionately about his disappointment with blacks who were afraid of being themselves. Their tendency to ape white ways of doing things threatened to choke Negro art. This "urge within the race to whiteness, the desire to pour racial individuality into the mold of American standardization and to be as little Negro as possible had precluded the utilization of a wealth of material in the lives of the carefree masses of people who work a little today, rest a little tomorrow, play awhile and sing awhile and don't mind being themselves."[98]

Unlike his earlier statement in *Crisis*, Hughes was even more critical of middle-class blacks and their fear of the "racial mountain." He and other writers of his artistic persuasion intended to express their individual dark-skinned selves without shame or fear: "If White people are pleased we are glad. If they are not, it doesn't matter. We know we are beautiful. And ugly too. The tom-tom cries and the tom-tom laughs. If colored people are pleased we are glad. If they are not, their displeasure doesn't matter either. We build our temples for tomorrow, strong as we know how and we stand on top of the mountain, free within ourselves."[99]

Similarities between the views of Hughes and McKay were more apparent than real. Hughes's point of view was different in many respects. First, even though Hughes criticized the black tendency to ape whites culturally, he recognized that even the "better" classes of blacks, who borrowed so much of their culture from mainstream white society, were still Negro enough to be different from whites—thereby furnishing the black artist with a lifetime of creative work.[100] Second, Hughes never expressed his resentment of black, middle-class conservatism through his literature. Third, Hughes used material associated with the great unwashed of the Negro race in a different way than McKay did. Hughes was concerned with the expression of the folk's rhythm and warmth and the incongruous humor that so often, as in the blues, became ironic laughter mixed with tears.[101] For example,

Hughes's *Not without Laughter* (1930), a novel dealing with the struggle of Sandy, his main character, to reconcile the conflicting forces that divide his family in a small midwestern town, is representative of his efforts at expressing black folk rhythm, warmth, and humor. While filled with aspects of lower-class life that also appear in McKay's novels—Aunt Hager, a humble religious woman who has raised her three daughters by taking in washing; Harriet, the youngest daughter, pleasure-seeking, rebellious, and bitterly resentful of racial injustice; Tempy, a daughter who has married well and is a social climber, careful to avoid anything "niggerish"; and Anjee, Sandy's mother, living from day to day between visits from her wandering husband, a guitar-plucking, blues-singing Jimboy—Hughes is able to paint individuals in which the "tom-tom" both laughs and cries.[102] Indeed, he conveys to the reader the idea that "laughter and achievement" are not incompatible. Consequently, Hughes manages to convey more of the "human" qualities of the Negro in his work than McKay does. McKay's books are characterized by exotic and primitive sensationalism. More often than not, McKay sees a world full of "Jakes," while Hughes celebrates a world filled with Jess B. Semples, a character first introduced in the *Chicago Defender*. Describing Semple, Hughes wrote: "He talks about the wife he used to have, the woman he loves today, and his one-time play-girl, Zarita. Usually over a glass of beer, he tells me his tales, mostly in high humor, but sometimes with a pain in his soul as sharp as the occasional hurt of that bunion on his right foot. Sometimes, as the old blues says, Simple might be 'laughing to keep from crying.'"[103]

McKay, in contrast to Hughes, not only criticized the conservative attitude of middle-class blacks, but accused them of creating an unofficial censorship system to obstruct the efforts of black artists like himself. He criticized black novelists whose works' purpose seemed only to show whites that upper-class blacks actually existed. African Americans like Jessie Fauset, who wrote Sunday-school self-help tracts for good-behaving Negroes, lacked perspective (social, psychological, and even humanitarian) on the Negro question. Such people, according to McKay, had behind them that "awful gang of New England and Quaker philanthropists—the people that read the *Nation*."[104]

McKay was particularly bitter toward black critics because of their influence on black artists. While he found white critics amusing, he regarded black critics as often inept to the point of downright silliness. He hoped that the voice of the black artist and his literary expression would carry farther and be saved from the "brayings" of the black apologists.[105] After the publication of *Home to Harlem*, McKay blamed black critics and middle-class Negroes for the imposition of restraints on black authors and artists. He complained that the race-conscious black middle class controlled hundreds of Negro weekly magazines and newspapers, and used that control to censor what was printed about the Negro. Thus they served as arbiters of life within the Negro world.[106]

While too many African Americans rejected their race's intuitive love and color, wrapping themselves up in respectable gray, whites continued to take literary advantage of the material lower-class blacks provided. As a class, McKay felt, whites enjoyed an advantage over black artists in getting books about blacks published.[107] McKay had said as much about Van Vechten in 1925 and he later pointed to the many white writers exploiting the field during the 1920s. By 1928, works about blacks written by whites included Eugene O'Neill's *Emperor Jones* (1920) and *All God's Chillun Got Wings* (1924); Waldo Frank's *Holiday* (1923); Sherwood Anderson's *Dark Laughter* (1925); and DuBose Heyward's *Porgy*, followed by *Mamba's Daughters*.[108]

To offset the advantages whites held over blacks, the African-American artist would have to dig deeper into the black experience. The Negro artist, declared McKay, had to be more determinedly aggressive in his work because of his minority position. He had to delve further to bring out the ore that would attract the indifferent majority. To win recognition, blacks had to work toward unique and distinctive achievements in the artistic field.[109] Unfortunately, while rebelling against the gentility, decorum, and class snobbery of middle-class blacks and attempting to deal with his fear of white competition, McKay took a creative path that almost produced the equivalent of the plantation Sambo, now dressed in urban garb.[110]

As I mentioned earlier, it would be less than accurate to dismiss McKay as a panderer to the vogue for the exotic and primitive. Yet McKay wanted to achieve popular success, wanted to make money from his writing, and he was certainly aware of white interest in the exotic features of black life. He had mentioned to Joel Spingarn in 1917 that "what whites wanted to see in the Negro was something ragtimy and barbaric."[111] Following the attacks by black critics on his *Home to Harlem,* white friends wrote to assure him that he was on the right track. Typical was Charlotte R. Osgood, white patron of Zora Neale Hurston, Langston Hughes, and sometimes McKay, who praised McKay's novel and reminded him that as far back as she could remember she had always been interested in primitive peoples and their fine living.[112] Another friend and long-time admirer of Negro life and art, in trying to comfort him against attacks by black critics, praised his work and claimed that the black bourgeosie was simply jealous.[113]

McKay steadfastly refused to accept the racial injunctions of black writers and critics. Just as his independence and iconoclasm shaped his economic and political ideas, these characteristics influenced McKay's art and separated him from black Americans. "Thus, it seems," he wrote his critics, "respectable Negro criticism is not ready for artistic or other iconoclasm in Negroes."[114] Ultimately, McKay lamented, "We must leave the real appreciation of what we are doing to the emancipated Negro intelligentsia of the future, while we are sardonically aware that only the intelligentsia of the superior race is developed enough to afford artistic truth."[115] Until then he would have little use for either African Americans or the New Negro movement. "The Negro Renaissance movement in America seems a hopeless mess to me," he confided to Mason in 1930. "If I were in touch with any of the young aspiring Negro artists I'd advise them to get as far away from it as possible."[116]

Like many whites of the period, McKay denied what James Weldon Johnson called the "dilemma of the Negro author." In truth, the black artist had to appeal to both black and white audiences if he hoped to succeed financially, but at the same time he had to navigate between the shoals of a middle-class black audience and a black critical establishment that demanded favorable portraits of blacks and the cliffs of a white audience and a white critical apparatus that preferred demeaning stereotypes or "exotic" portraits. If the black artist decided to "hell with whites" and concentrated on Negro audiences, he then ran afoul of whites as much as blacks.[117] It was this dilemma that urged one black writer to declare that it "would be the final tragedy if after exploiting the Negro's body for two centuries we ended by exploiting his heart and soul."[118] For McKay as a black man to deny this seemed to some nothing less than heresy.

5

Banjo: *Art and Self-Catharsis*

*C*RITICISM FROM blacks of McKay's *Home to Harlem* and of *Banjo*, his next novel, along with the general debate over the black artist's obligation to his race, underscored a difference of philosophy between McKay and other blacks. This criticism and McKay's public and private response to it can also be used to illuminate McKay's general relationship to the American black community. In turn, this relationship sheds light on a bitter intraracial conflict within the American black community.

Banjo, published in 1929, was set in Marseilles, France, 6,000 miles away from the streets of Harlem. Subtitled "the story without a plot," the novel offers a simple series of episodes united more by the presence of a recurring group of characters than by an interlocking and developing plot. The chief character wants to lead a pick-up band. The second leading character, on a quest to find authentic stories for a novel he hopes to write, joins him. The twosome thereafter lead the reader through a maze of mostly unrelated episodes.[1]

Banjo's episodic nature had caused some concern among his friends even before the novel was completed. Louise Bryant Bullitt warned McKay about his habit of rushing a piece of literature to completion. She told McKay that he had lovely ideas, but admonished him for never properly developing them. If he was ever to publish first-rate material, she indicated, he would have to work harder.[2] McKay's life seemed to be marked by a sense of urgency, and his approach to writing often reflected it. His writing career was dotted with a series of "lovely ideas" that somehow never fulfilled their expectations and potential. Before he had polished one piece of writing, McKay would begin another.

McKay's frenzied approach to *Banjo* also vexed his literary agent, William A. Bradley. Bradley had advised McKay to spend a great deal of time developing his story because it was set in a world unfamiliar to most Americans. He was especially concerned about the shotgun manner in which McKay introduced his characters at the start of the novel. He complained to McKay that the effect gave the manuscript an immediate sense of superficiality.[3] But McKay ignored both Bullitt's and his agent's advice.

Banjo received mixed reviews. The book's "exotic" treatment of blacks excited interest, but its casual, even random, form was viewed as a serious flaw. Reviewing *Banjo*, Du Bois commented that it was a better piece of writing than *Home to Harlem*, that it was full of experience, and that it was vivid and colorful. But he went on to remark that "it is described as a story without a plot, but it is hardly even that. It is in no sense a novel, either in the nature of its story or in the development of character. It is on the one hand the description of character. It is on the other hand the description of a series of episodes on the docks of Marseilles and a sort of international philosophy of the Negro race." Du Bois complained about McKay's treatment of blacks in the novel: "Here [are] a lot of people whose chief business in life seems to be sexual experience, getting drunk, and fighting." Du Bois did note that McKay's race philosophy was of great interest, since McKay was an international Negro and a direct descendant of Africa.

Du Bois was profoundly disturbed with McKay's portrayal of African Americans. As he had done in *Home to Harlem*, McKay used his new book to introduce statements critical of black Americans. Du Bois suggested that such statements were characteristic of a West Indian who did not thoroughly know his America.[4] Du Bois's sentiment that West Indians knew little about African Americans was one shared by many black Americans—some of whom felt that West Indians exploited other blacks to further their own schemes and desires. According to Du Bois, Marcus Garvey and Claude McKay were the two most conspicuous West Indians who had failed to understand American blacks. Du Bois went on to complain that British West Indians were trying to settle Jamaica's problems in the United States.[5]

Walter White, usually a steadfast supporter of McKay, wrote an even more critical and uncomplimentary review of *Banjo*. White, like Du Bois, was seriously disturbed with McKay's derogatory references to certain classes of African Americans. Writing to Harry Hausen of the *New York World*, White explained that *Banjo* had narrowly missed being a superb achievement. However, the author had fallen victim to certain of his own biases. White singled out some remarks made by the character Ray about what life had done to certain American blacks as an example of McKay's own prejudiced opinion about African Americans. McKay's philosophizing about race did not spring from his recognition of white oppression, White continued, but was fueled by his own prejudices concerning certain types of his own people. McKay's prejudices, White suggested, stemmed from his being born in the West Indies, where a rigid caste system divided the population into three distinct groups—whites, colored (mixed blood), and blacks—whereas in the United States any person with any amount of Negro blood is classified as a Negro. In the West Indies, both the white and the colored classes look down on blacks, creating an understandable black resentment against both of the other groups. This reality, White concluded, was the foundation for McKay's frequent derisive allusions to people of mixed blood and to the Negro intelligentsia. White also felt that *Banjo* embodied McKay's reaction against the bitter criticism blacks had directed at *Home to Harlem*. White suggested that McKay should have spent more time digesting facts and carefully weaving them into the fabric of his novel. White's critique was not totally negative. He predicted that when McKay achieved greater objectivity, he would create increasingly powerful pictures of the life he knew so well.[6]

Aubrey Browser of the *New York Amsterdam News* was so disturbed about McKay's attack on the African-American middle class that he wrote, "White authors do not need to write against Negroes anymore, the Negroes are writing against themselves."[7]

As both White and Du Bois correctly observed, *Banjo*, despite its French setting, is marked by McKay's contemptuous opinions of middle-class black Americans. Bitter over the raking he had received for *Home to Harlem*, McKay was convinced that the black Babbitts were out to get him.[8] He therefore used *Banjo* to present a clumsy defense of his own literary position. Thus Ray, the West Indian who aspires to a literary career in *Home to Harlem* and who reappears in *Banjo*, defends a writer who utilizes unsavory black experiences. When another character expresses fear that whites would use such a story to further slander black people, Ray obviously speaks for McKay's own view:

Let the crackers go fiddle themselves, and you too. I think about my race as much as you. I hate to see it kicked around and spat on by whites, because it is a good earth-loving race. I'll fight with it if there's a fight on, but if I am writing a story— well, it's like all of us in this place here, black and brown and white, and I am telling a story for the love of it. Some of you will listen, and some won't. If I am a real story teller, I won't worry about the differences in complexion of those who listen and those who don't, I'll just identify myself with those who are really listening, and tell my story.[9]

Through Ray, McKay rejects the argument that a black writer should portray only black successes. Ray points out that he is not a reporter for the Negro press and cannot afford to keep up with black "society folk." Furthermore, he does not think that society folks are setting such a fine example for the race. "I can't see that," Ray explodes:

They say you find the best Negro society in Washington. When I was there the government clerks and school teachers and the wives of the few professional men formed a group and called themselves the "upper class." They were nearly all between your complexion and near white. The women wore rich clothes and I don't know whether it was that or their complexion or their teaching or clerking ability that put them in the upper class. In my home we had an upper class of Negroes, but it had big money and property and power. It wasn't just a moving picture imitation. School teachers and clerks didn't make any ridiculous pretenses of belonging to it. . . . I could write about the society of Negroes you mean if I wrote a farce.

Ray concludes his polemic against middle-class blacks by attacking their class snobbery:

Gee! I remember when I was in college in America how those Negroes getting an education could make me tired talking class and class all the time. It was funny and it was sad. There was hardly one of them with the upper-class bug on the brain who didn't have a near relative—a brother or sister who was an ignorant chauffeur, butler, or maid, or a mother paying their way through college with her washtub. If you think it's fine for the society Negroes to fool themselves on the cheapest of imitations, I don't. I am fed up with that class.[10]

Obviously, McKay intended his arrows to sting "that class" of blacks who had attacked his *Home to Harlem.* But it was McKay himself who felt the sharp sting of an arrow when Walter White's review appeared in print. Enraged by White's critique, McKay wrote to James W. Johnson, describing White's review as "fundamentally malicious and pretentious." "I know and see very deeply into more phases of Afro-American life than Walter White does," McKay declared. Furthermore, McKay wrote:

> He is all wrong about the West Indies too and should take a trip there before rushing into print. He would find the differences between the mulattoes and blacks just as artificial as in the States, if it were not for European encouragement. At any rate I have distant mulatto relatives who pass as white in New York. And all my brothers including myself were married to mulatto women. In my village, I grew up on equal terms with white, mulatto and black children of every race because my father was a big peasant and belonged. The difference on the island is economic, not social.[11]

But Du Bois and White had raised some fundamental questions about McKay. They questioned both his motivation and the sincerity of his portrayal of black Americans. His pronouncement that he understood African-American life better than White, and—by implication—most other African Americans, went to the heart of Du Bois's and White's objections to *Banjo*. For this reason, some found it puzzling that McKay had chosen to follow up his first novel with a book whose story was set in Europe. After all, McKay had been one of the most avid proselytizers for creative writing that used African-American life as its source. In his defense of *Home to Harlem*, McKay had repeatedly stressed the necessity of exploiting the vast material that earthy African-American life offered. Why then had he turned his back on the American scene to write a story set in France?

Unlike *Home to Harlem*, *Banjo* was a financial failure. Technical weaknesses certainly contributed to its lack of success. But the major reason for its poor showing on the market, according to Eugene Saxton, an executive at Harper, had been McKay's choice of an unfamiliar setting, which made the book less attractive than one with a Harlem background.[12] While McKay's exotic-primitive motif was still very evident in *Banjo*, the familiar Harlem background that had attracted many readers to *Home to Harlem* was missing from *Banjo*.

The reason he had chosen Marseilles as his setting and had created such an episodic plot was rooted in the very criticism he challenged. His assertion that he knew more about African-American life than most American-born blacks was an exaggeration. In fact, McKay had little more experience among American blacks than some bohemian and radical whites.[13] His relationship with the ordinary blacks celebrated in his poems and prose always remained perfunctory. He had worked alongside blacks in America only from 1916 to 1920, when he had left the United States to travel to his "spiritual homeland," England. From 1922 until 1934, he spent all of his time abroad. But even during the years when he had worked among lower-class American blacks, McKay managed to remain aloof from his environment.

His association with the black masses had never been voluntary; it had occurred as a result of his own failure to succeed at middle-class pursuits. By McKay's own admission, he had gleaned all he could from his Harlem experiences. Writing to Eastman after the publication of *Home to Harlem*, he had lamented that "all [his] hankering for the United States had disappeared," and, more important, "all of it [Harlem] had gone out in the first novel." Of the future projects he outlined for Eastman, none mentioned Harlem as a background.[14]

The hostile reaction of Du Bois, White, and other blacks to McKay's books stemmed in part from their disappointment with the black settings and characters he chose to depict (low-life instead of middle-class life), in part from hostility to McKay as a West Indian who presumed to be an authority on American blacks, and in part from anger at his assault on middle-class blacks. By 1929, the year of *Banjo's* publication, middle-class blacks had grown even more sensitive to the depiction of black Americans in fiction; the black audience who borrowed books from the library or who bought books for their homes wanted to see positive portraits of blacks. Thus, it is not surprising that the *New York Amsterdam News*, one of the few black newspapers to praise *Home to Harlem*, was outraged at *Banjo*, complaining that it was full of things that would please white readers, "Coon stuff."[15]

Black writers and critics had logical reasons to be sensitive about literature that seemed to perpetuate old stereotypes concerning blacks. McKay tried to argue that the black middle class was offended by his subject matter because it identified more with whites and had no sympathy for the black lower class. But it is not true that the small black middle class turned its back on poorer blacks. Middle-class blacks during the twenties did not lead a life separated from lower-class black life. All blacks, whatever their economic circumstances, lived in the same neighborhoods, attended the same churches, shopped in the same stores, and so on. Even the Harvard-educated Du Bois, who occupied the heights of black society, had what today would seem a surprising amount of contact with lower-class African-Americans. According to George Kent, author of *Blackness and the Adventure of Western Culture*, many of the Renaissance writers and critics brought to their "task" a cosmopolitan range of experiences that protected them from a simple, myopic middle-class perspective.[16]

McKay's suspicions that black intellectuals were out to get him and had criticized him for personal reasons were totally unwarranted. Certainly, tensions existed between African Americans and West Indians. As I mentioned earlier, the twenties were marked by sporadic outbursts of intraracial antagonisms between the two groups. However, from the publication of "The Harlem Dancer" in 1919 to the publication of *Banjo* in 1929, blacks generally praised McKay as a writer of unquestioned talent. Two of the most important black critics, William Stanley Braithwaite and Benjamin Brawley, continued to praise McKay's talents during the late twenties. In 1927, while characterizing Cullen's *Color* as lacking the mechanics of art, and Langston Hughes as a young man of ability who got on the wrong track after falling under the spell of Carl Van Vechten, Brawley praised McKay as a writer of great poetic talent.[17] Even after the publication of *Home to Harlem* and *Banjo*, Brawley, though now convinced that McKay, too, had gone off the right track, still spoke highly of his "genius." In defending himself against a McKay charge that he lacked the necessary breadth of sympathy to fairly judge black artists, Brawley responded that a number of the younger writers, regardless of their school of writing, continually wrote him and sought his advice. But unfortunately, Brawley suggested, some of these younger men, for all their brilliance, lacked poise and spiritual mooring. Of McKay himself, Brawley noted, "Mr. Claude McKay is a writer of unquestioned power and ability. At the same time he has not yet produced the great novel he is capable of writing. When that book does appear I shall be the first to acclaim it."[18] Even the irascible Wallace Thurman praised both McKay's poetry and his prose. McKay was one of the writers, Thurman felt, who should be spared extermination with "those who should have never been born."[19]

Black criticism of McKay's work was largely based on an honest difference of opinion. No personal animosity was involved when Braithwaite, acting as a committee judge, objected when McKay was awarded the Harmon Gold Medal for Literature in 1928. Braithwaite argued that Nella Larsen Ime's *Quicksand* was a better piece of literature than *Home to Harlem*. The committee, Braithwaite protested, had decided to give the award to McKay because of his literary potential, and not because his book was the best of all the works submitted.[20]

Braithwaite was not alone in questioning whether McKay deserved the award. While not on the committee himself, Walter White had been asked to comment on the proposal to name McKay as recipient of the award. Acknowledging that McKay possessed great ability, White noted that he had not used that ability fully. He cited *Home to Harlem* as an example. White remarked, "There are passages in this novel where Mr. McKay forgets himself as a novelist and becomes once again the poet. Those passages are of exceedingly great beauty. The novel as a whole, however, does not greatly impress me. I have no objection with him in what he considers the choice of his material as an author, nor do I quarrel with him in what he considers the form of a novel. *Home to Harlem* does not impress me as fine and as sincere an accomplishment as Mr. McKay is capable of." Ironically, White went on to say, "I happen to know something of a forthcoming book, *Banjo*, upon which Mr. McKay is now working. I have not seen any part of the manuscript but I understand from one who has that it is a much finer piece of work."[21]

Black assessments of McKay's works had mixed both praise and criticism, based on the particular critic's general standards for judging art. But McKay's suspicions and attitudes regarding black Americans were often more personal, rooted in certain prejudices and misconceptions, that he, as a West Indian, held about American blacks, the concomitant frustrations he suffered as a Negro, and the bitterness he directed toward what he believed was an "impotent black American." The only real thread that bound McKay to black Americans was the "veil of color" both shared. As a youth in Jamaica he had accepted the stereotyped notion that American blacks were seriocomical clowns. Contrary to his later protestations, throughout his life he continued to see American blacks as possessing certain "peculiarities" from which fortunately he had been spared.

McKay frequently complained that American blacks lacked "manliness." In discussing the black scholar Alain Locke, McKay criticized Locke because "It's so hard to nail down what he's driving at. It's a fault of many colored writers. I don't know if it can be traced to the long years the black race has lived in America without being allowed to express its own thoughts and feelings."22 McKay believed that the African-American approach to writing and literature revealed a lack of courage. Timidity often led black artists to write in a style that was confusing and habitually evasive.

McKay's criticism of Locke had resulted from the Howard University professor's decision not to include McKay's poem "Mulatto" in the 1924 special Harlem issue of the *Survey Graphic*. This potentially controversial poem described the searing hatred of a bastard offspring for his white father—a hatred so intense that the son waits for the hour to plunge a knife into his white father's heart. Incensed by Locke's decision, McKay lashed out that Locke's attitude toward literature was like that of Booker T. Washington's in social reform: playing it safe. Not only Locke, but all African Americans were dismissed as cowardly by McKay. "I guess if the *Liberator* had not set that example with 'If We Must Die,' " he wrote, "not a Negro publication would have had enough guts to publish it." White people were longing and hoping for Negroes to show that they have guts, McKay reminded Locke. "No wonder," he concluded, "the Negro movement is in such a bad way."23

McKay warned Locke that he did not want any of his poems published in *Survey Graphic* if "Mulatto" was excluded. But Locke ignored McKay's wishes, refused to publish "Mullato," but did include other McKay poems in *Survey Graphic*. Moreover, the following year, when Locke included a selection of McKay poems in his anthology *The New Negro*, he misrepresented Mc-

Kay.[24] Locke purposely changed the title of McKay's poem "The White House" to "White Houses," for fear of possible repercussions.[25] The original title, McKay noted in a letter to publishers Simon and Schuster, "was wholly symbolic. It was a composite picture of the attitude of antagonistic white America as the black poet sees and feels it. It is symbolic of the general public, and not of individual attitudes, that the doctor [Locke], in substituting 'White Houses,' places the poet in the cheap, childish, snarling position of crying out against white houses shut in his face. That may likely be the position of Dr. Locke and the school of Afro-Americans he represents. It is certainly not mine."[26]

Locke's actions just encouraged McKay's belief in African-American literary cowardice. The whole affair, he lamented, forced him once again into the unpleasant position of making comparisons between white gentlemen and black gentlemen, to the disadvantage of the black ones.[27] At least regarding Locke, McKay was not alone in his judgment that this member of the black cultural establishment was a "dyed in the wool pussy-footing professor."[28] Both Langston Hughes and Jessie Fauset were critical of Locke's proclivity to presume that as a doctor of philosophy he knew more about a writer's work than the writer himself. Criticizing Locke for his pretentiousness, Fauset wrote that it had both annoyed and amused her that "you who cannot write, had the arrogance to presume to criticize those who had creative talent." She also accused Locke of having the tendency to play safe with "white folks."[29]

Locke may have deserved McKay's anger, but did every black critic in America deserve McKay's condemnation? For one reason or another McKay found fault with practically every African-American writer or critic. He had already expressed doubts about their ability to criticize capably his work—criticism of *Home to Harlem* and *Banjo* seemed proof enough. They were little men with no ability, he complained, hiding behind the Negro movement in order to exploit Negro artists as much as they could. McKay declared that he thought all "colored editors [and most black writers] were rotten 'bastards.'" He felt about them as "Lasca" had about Negro leaders in Van Vechten's *Nigger Heaven*.[30] Braithwaite, for instance, was a "nice man," but, as a critic, he was hopelessly lost.[31] McKay expressed outrage and contempt for

116

Countee Cullen, who had remarked in his anthology of Negro poets that McKay's hortatory poems were "vituperative," a term Claude considered synonymous with the police-court term "abusive." Even his worst critics, McKay railed, had never used such a contemptible word.[32]

Problems about the publication of some poems was the catalyst for a McKay attack on W. E. B. Du Bois. In 1928 Du Bois published some poems that McKay had submitted earlier, which by then were not characteristic of his style or ability. Writing to Du Bois, McKay thundered, "I think I beseeched you over a year ago not to publish those poems I sent to the *Crisis* towards the end of 1925."[33] McKay reminded Du Bois that the poems were sent for a special purpose: he had been ill and was in need of money. He complained that, having written to a number of other New York publications to state his situation and need, and then asking them to help by purchasing a number of his poems, the only publication that had not bothered to reply was Du Bois's *Crisis*, the only "Negro" publication he had written to. Thus he thought it particularly inexcusable that a year and a half later, the two poems appeared in the *Crisis* without his knowledge or permission.

Du Bois answered McKay, explaining that the poems were published due to a mixup resulting from an oversight by Jessie Fauset, who at the time had been in charge of the literary section. McKay discounted Du Bois's apology and preferred to believe that the whole affair was the *Crisis*'s way of letting him know that they had no time to waste on a "non-influential, down and out fellow writer."[34]

McKay was especially outraged that his poems had been published in the same publication that had castigated his *Home to Harlem*. As Claude vehemently put it, "I particularly resent the publication of my poems in the same number of the *Crisis* which criticizes my novel, the editor steps outside the limits of criticism to become personal. I should think that a publication so holy-clean and righteous pure as the *Crisis* should hesitate about printing anything from the pen of a writer who wallows so much in the dirt, filth, drunkenness, fighting and lascivious sexual promiscuity."[35]

McKay felt that Du Bois had no comprehension of aesthetics and therefore was not competent to pass judgment upon any work of art.[36] Du Bois formulated his own solution to McKay's indignation. He notified McKay that, while he had apparently misunderstood earlier letters in which McKay had clearly given him permission to publish any poems, providing that McKay was paid for their publication, in the future he would not publish any of McKay's poems.[37]

Clearly, Locke could have been more courageous about publishing "Mulatto" and should have sought McKay's permission before changing the title of "The White House." And, perhaps, Du Bois could have been quicker in publishing McKay's poems *and* in sending him payment for publication. But white editors, too, were frequently guilty of lack of courage, interference with an author's manuscript, tardiness in returning or publishing manuscripts, and slow with payment of money owed to authors. Many of the things McKay attributed to the incompetence of black editors were simply endemic in the publishing business, black or white.[38] Yet, when such problems involved black editors, McKay always interpreted the situation in the worst light—and usually as an expression of animus against him personally.

In some respects, he had always demanded more of blacks and irrationally held them accountable for his own failings and shortcomings. For instance, he found it absurd that *Crisis* had turned down a poem he had sent in 1920. When the same poem was published in *Pearson's,* he sent Du Bois a note quoting the poem from *Pearson's* and suggested in the note that black editors exhibited less competence than white editors.[39] After "Mulatto" was published in the *Bookman,* following Locke's refusal to publish it, McKay sent Locke a similar gloating note.[40]

The same attitude was continually reflected in criticism of black writers and editors who dared find fault with his work. Here I must note that McKay, in the years immediately preceding the publication of *Home to Harlem,* had been adamant about the necessity of good, hard, candid criticism by blacks of black artists writing literature. Nothing, he claimed, would be more detrimental to the Negro Renaissance than indiscriminate flattery and praise. However, he himself resented forthright criticism. When blacks criticized his work, their efforts were dismissed as the "hog water of Negro journalism."[41] On the other hand, he was generally deferential in the face of white criticism. Whether from Eastman, Bullitt, Mencken, or even the "dilettante of Negro primitivism," Charlotte Osgood Mason, negative criticism was accepted quietly, if sometimes sullenly. In spite of his formal protests against indiscriminate flattery, McKay felt blacks owed him a "certain racial indulgence" he was unwilling to reciprocate.[42]

Basically, McKay was hypocritical regarding the value of negative criticism, and two-faced regarding its source: he would endure white criticism with little or no complaint, but he responded angrily to all black criticism, choosing to view any negative black opinion either as a sign of incompetence and cowardice on the part of the black critic or as a personal attack.

McKay sought to avoid contact with the American "black bourgeoisie" as much as possible. Writing of his first encounter with Jessie Fauset in 1924, McKay recalled that, having met her twice at a café in Paris, he would not see her again because she was too prim, schoolmarmish, and "stifled" for him.[43] His sense of being an outsider among African Americans had increased to the point that by the time he was attacked for *Home to Harlem*, McKay dreaded the thought of returning to America and facing the black intelligentsia. Of this feeling, McKay remarked, "But the resentment of the Negro intelligentsia against *Home to Harlem* was so general, bitter and violent, that I was hesitant about returning to the great Black Belt. I had learned little about the ways of the Harlem elite during the years I lived there. When I left the railroad and the companionship of the common blacks, my intellectual contacts were limited mainly to white radicals and bohemians."[44]

Contemplating a return to the United States, McKay decided to visit Paris, where many American Negro intellectuals were camping in the summer of 1928. There he met Countee Cullen; John Hope of Atlanta Baptist College, who he decided was even more Nordic-looking than Walter White; and Alain Locke. Attired in a newly purchased suit with gloves and a hat as accessories, McKay felt he had won over the majority of blacks he met. In the end, however, he concluded that "they were nearly all Harlem conscious in a curious synthetic way, it seemed to me—not because they were aware of Harlem's intrinsic values as a unique and popular Negro quarter, but because White folks had discovered black magic there." He doubted that returning to Harlem would be an advantage, especially since he had done his best writing

CLAUDE MCKAY

about Harlem while living abroad. Perhaps it would be better to leave Harlem to the artists who were on the spot and give them their chance to produce something better than *Home to Harlem*.[45] McKay's apparently generous gesture to leave Harlem to the newer group of artists was in fact an admission of his precarious position within the African-American community. He wrote Eastman that he had flirted with the idea of returning to America for a few months to get material on that damned thing called "nigger society," but that he had seen enough of Americans, white and colored, in Paris that summer to know that "if I ever mused the thought of living in America again I was a fool."[46]

McKay's sensitivity to the criticism of *Banjo* was understandable, though unjustified. Indeed, judged as a significant literary work, McKay's *Banjo* was a failure. Sadly, what began as a promising romanticized account of life for an international aggregation of black vagabonds on the Marseilles docks and its main character, Lincoln Agrippa Daily, alias Banjo, ends up a vehicle of catharsis for McKay. During the first part of the novel, we are introduced to Banjo, a transplanted, southern-black, banjo-playing free spirit, who wants nothing more than to form a little band from the international mélange of black and brown men who have settled on the rough-and-tumble waterfront of Marseilles in the 1920s. Men whose names are as colorful as their lives, Malty, Ginger, Dengel, Bugsy, Taloufa, and Goosey, join Banjo in drinking, dancing, loving, playing, and brawling.[47]

It is not until McKay introduces Ray, the young West Indian writer from *Home to Harlem* in part 2 that the novel seems to have any direction or purpose. But once Ray is introduced, *Banjo* becomes simply a sequel to *Home to Harlem* or, more accurately, an autobiographical medium in which McKay continues to sort out his personal view of life, race, class, and his general philosophy of the world. Thereafter Banjo assumes secondary importance as a character and merely serves as an authorial device to present McKay's ideas and philosophy, much as Jake served to do in *Home to Harlem*. The character Ray even informs us that "Banjo's rich Dixie accent went to his head like old wine and reminded him happily of Jake."[48]

When McKay takes up Ray's story, Ray has turned his back on Harlem and has been traveling in Europe, sometimes staying long

periods in places that stirred his imagination. He has not renounced his dream of self-expression as a writer, but he finds it
more difficult to obtain the kind of temporary work conducive to
an artist's work habits in Europe. The Old World lacks the background that young America offers a romantic black youth to indulge his instincts. "In America," Ray informs us, "he had lived
like a vagabond poet, erect in the racket and rush and terror of
that stupendous young creation of cement and steel, determined,
courageous, and proud in his swarthy skin, quitting jobs when he
wanted to go on a dream wish or a love drunk, without being
beholden to anybody." Now it seems he is always beholden to
someone, dependent on the occasional little check from America
for a slight sketch or a letter of encouragement with an enclosed
banknote from a friend.[49]

Increasingly as the novel progresses, each event and situation
acts as a sounding board for McKay. The character Goosey chal-
lenges Ray for considering the waterfront and its black inhabitants
as a fit topic for a book. Goosey fears that the white "crackers"
would use any such portrait against the race. McKay seizes this
opportunity to respond to critics of *Home to Harlem* regarding his
choice of subject matter.

On another occasion he uses a fictional situation to offer his view
on the significance of nationhood, race, and—perhaps uncon-
sciously—his own cultural marginality. Upon listening to two
white men, one British and another French, extol the virtues of
their respective civilizations and especially their treatment of
blacks, Ray in a fit of contemplation muses that he did not possess
the sentiment of patriotism or nationhood because "he was a child
of deracinated ancestry." He views patriotism and nationalism as a
poisonous seed and is happy not to be infected by these ideas. Ray
feels that it is an unnatural thing for a man to love a nation—a
swarming hive of human beings bartering, competing, exploiting,
lying, cheating, battling, suppressing, and killing among themselves. Nations are evil because they organize their villainous
rivalries into a monstrous system for plundering weaker peoples.
The patriotic man loves only *his* nation's individuals, things, and
places. But the vagabond lover of life, unattached to a particular
nation, finds individuals and things to love in many places and not
in any one nation.[50]

CLAUDE MCKAY

But the abandonment of an identification with one race or nation and the attainment of complete cultural universality was always easier said than done, as McKay knew from personal experience. Again, it is Goosey who serves as the mirror in which McKay can view his own ambivalence. Goosey, the resident race chauvinist, chides the group for their continual self-derogatory Negro jokes, and especially for their use of the word *nigger* in the presence of Kid Irish, a white person. "I think we've had enough of colored jokes," Goosey quips. "The weak and comic side of race life can't further race advancement." When Ray tells Goosey to shut up and stop talking like a "nigger newspaper," he expresses profound disappointment. "'Niggah from you, Ray!' exclaimed Goosey, 'and with white folks among us! I expected that from Banjo or Malty, but not from you.'" In a rare show of anger and irritation, Ray lashes out at Goosey and through him at all educated Negroes:

"Yes, nigger," repeated Ray. "I didn't say 'niggah' the way you and the crackers say it, but 'nigger' with the gritty 'r' in it to express exactly what I feel about you and all coons like you. I know you think that a coon is a Negro like Banjo and Ginger, but you're fooling yourself. They are real and you are the coon—a stage thing, a made-up thing. I said nigger newspaper because a nigger newspaper is nothing more than a nigger newspaper. Something like you, half baked, half educated, full of false ideas about Negroes, because it can't hold its head up out of its miserable purgatory."[51]

Not to be outdone, Goosey, much in the same way Du Bois, Locke, and Walter White had criticized McKay for *Home to Harlem* and *Banjo*, explodes:

"Get your monkey-chasing hand out of my face, black nigman," cried Goosey, getting hot. "Because you're a man without a country, you have no race feeling, no race pride. You can't go back to Haiti. You feel there's no place for you in Africa, after you've hung around here, trying to get down into the guts of the life of these Senegalese. You hate America and you despise Europe. You're just a lost sore-head. You pretend you'd like to be a vagabond like Malty and Banjo here, but you know you're a liar and the truth is not in you."[52]

The remainder of *Banjo* continues to be a painful exercise in self-purgation. Toward the end of the novel, McKay unsuccess-

122

fully tries to develop a theme that many literary critics have
identified as the central one of *Banjo* and *Home to Harlem:* the
indictment of Western civilization and the conflict of black vagabondage versus white civilization. It is left for Ray, who has lived
both in the world of the black "imitative" middle class and in the
world of the black vagabond, with its imprudence, freedom from
restraint, spontaneous improvisation, and defiance of everything
drab and respectable, to pose this conflict in favor of the world's
Jakes and Banjoes.[53]
   In a thinly disguised slap at the black brahmin W. E. B. Du-
Bois, McKay through Ray asserts that the Negro is not the "problem" of civilization, but is instead the one significant and challeng-
ing aspect of the human life of the world. Unfortunately, a certain
school of Negro intellectuals had contributed their best to the
"problem" by presenting the race wearing a veil. Negroes were
too fond of the sunny open ways of living to hide behind any kind
of veil. " 'If the Negro had to be defined,' Ray asserted, 'there was
every reason to define him as a challenge rather than a "problem"
to Western civilization.' "[54]
   Apparently reasoning that two Banjo/Jakes were better than
one to drive his point home to the reader, McKay resurrects Jake
for a cameo appearance. Jake informs Ray that several things had
happened to him following their farewell in Harlem. After finding
his "tantalizing sugar brown" Felice, he had married her and they
produced a baby boy whom they named Ray. However, after two
years of matrimony, Jake became dissatisfied. The novelty of
marriage had worn off and it was no longer "joy-making" to go to
work every day and come every night to the same "old pillow."
Though Jake now travels and has himself a "broad," he has not
altogether abandoned Felice. He returns periodically and, he
assures Ray, "Whenevah I come home Ise always happy to be with
her and that Ise doing mah duty by Ray."[55]
   Ray is touched by the revelation that Jake has named his son
after him and hopes to provide his namesake with an education
like his. Ray quickly assures Jake that he has nothing to apologize
for: "You're a thousand times a better man than me, Jake. Finding
a way to carry on with a family and knuckling down to it. I just ran
away from the thing." Even Jake is surprised to learn that Ray had
abandoned his own wife and child. In a line certainly influenced

by McKay's own abandonment of his wife and child in Harlem, Ray laments, "I leave more things than I want to remember."[56]

Banjo ends with an unconvincing appeal to the reader that suggests that blacks worldwide with their primitive innocence should resist assimilation to Western civilization. Jake and Banjo have enabled Ray to see the light:

> That this primitive child, this kinky-headed big-laughing black boy of the world, did not go down and disappear under the serried crush of trampling white feet; that he managed to remain on the scene, not worldly-wise, not "getting there," yet not machine-made, nor poor-in-spirit like the regimented creatures of civilization, was baffling to civilized understanding. Before the grim, pale rider-down of souls he went his careless way with a primitive hoofing and a grin.

Acknowledging that he was not of the humble tribe of humanity, Ray nostalgically looks to Africa to provide him with a "positive feeling of wholesome contact with racial roots." He had not, and could not, feel the same way about African Americans, who "long-deracinated, were still rootless among phantoms and pale shadows and enfeebled by self-effacement before condescending patronage, social negativism, and miscegenation." Ray indicates that never in America and especially among the Negro intelligentsia did he experience any of the simple, natural warmth of a people believing in themselves, such as he had felt among the rugged poor and socially backward blacks of his island home. Nor was black life on the island undermined by hopeless, enervating talk of the chances of "passing white" that was a common topic of discussion among the American Negro intelligentsia.[57]

On the other hand, the Africans made him feel that he was not merely an unfortunate accident of birth, but that he belonged to a race weighed, tested, and poised in the universal scheme. African blacks inspired him with confidence. They were a people protected by their own indigenous culture; their natural defense against Western civilization was the richness of their fundamental racial values. Only when he was among the black boys of the ditch and the black and brown working masses of America did he sense something of that raw-unconscious and the devil-with-them pride in being Negro that was his own natural birthright.

They were the true keepers of the African Negro soul, lifting

Banjo

their kinky heads out of the hot, suffocating ashes, the shadow, the terror of real sorrow to go on gaily grinning in the present. The more he mixed in the rude anarchy of the lives of the black boys, the more he realized how close-linked he was to them in spirit. That identification, along with their "jigaway music," filled Ray's head full and poured hot fire through his veins, tingling and burning.[58]

Yet, ultimately, Ray knew the identification would forever be romantic and incomplete, for he "could not scrap his intellectual life and be entirely like them." The best he could do was to hold on to his intellectual acquirements without losing his instinctive gifts—those of black laughter and melody and simple sensuous feelings and responses. Both for Ray, the fictional character, and McKay, the artist, "to be educated, black and his instinctive self was something of a big job to put over."[59]

In *Banjo*, McKay poured out much of what he was struggling to achieve in his own life: an understanding of his own identity. Too much of the person Claude McKay peered through the pages of *Banjo* for it to succeed as a dramatization of the conflict between the unspoiled folk and Western civilization. The catharsis so evident in *Banjo* represents McKay's personal journey to answer the question "Who am I?" At best, he was only able to respond in the manner of his black characters in *Banjo* who, when foreign officials asked for their papers, were distinguished by the official phrase: "Nationality Doubtful."[60]

6
Back to Harlem

*T*HE BLACK Renaissance of the 1920s was marked by a widespread tendency toward self-analysis. For many of the Renaissance writers, such self-analysis proved to be a painful experience. The debates over the many questions surrounding the literary movement forced many of the writers to struggle with the question of their own identity.[1] Increasingly, following the publication of *Banjo* in 1929, McKay began to ask himself the questions where did he belong and where was his life headed?

From 1924 until 1930, McKay's life had been without any sense of order and stability, as he moved from one place in France to another. In 1924 he lived in Toulon for a year; then he moved to Paris in 1925, where he remained until 1930. All the while, McKay lived a loner's life, finding it difficult if not impossible to relate to other people. "I'm a son of a bitch," he wrote Walter White. "I really like so few people, those I can like, I prize dearly." Yet even these McKay managed to keep at a distance in order to "examine them with the artist's aloofness."[2]

He had virtually severed all contacts with his only child, Rhue Hope, and his family in Jamaica. And aside from Eastman, he had little contact with his white friends from the old *Liberator* staff. The whites he generally wrote to were patrons, whom he privately held in utter contempt. "Most patrons," he wrote, "are typical Americans. I have no sentiment for them, I just take their money. I love it." McKay felt they richly deserved the contempt in which he held them. They were the typical bourgeois that dominated all progressive movements in America. Living in small communities, bound by restrictions, they associated with radical movements, endeavoring to find that license their own society denied them.[3] However, like most artists, McKay was obliged to keep such sentiments to himself.

While his circle of white friends dwindled, his problems with African Americans had grown (at least in McKay's mind), increasing McKay's sense of isolation and ultimately creating tensions that affected his health. During most of 1929, McKay complained to both William Bradley and Max Eastman that he was on the verge of a mental breakdown.[4] A year later, his condition worsened and he wrote to Eastman, confessing that he had not been well for six months, having been troubled by recurring dizzy spells and headaches. The headaches persisted, becoming so severe that he was forced once again to travel to Germany for medical care. Since he had spent much of his money from the sale of *Home to Harlem,* McKay was fearful that the cost would be prohibitive. While preliminary tests, including two for venereal disease, proved negative, McKay continued to experience muscle pains and dizziness. Despite an exhaustive series of diagnostic tests, physicians could not find a physiological cause for the problem.[5]

McKay's health problems were probably psychosomatic. The anxieties over his sense of isolation and tensions resulting from his concern over the criticism of both his books had manifested themselves in his health. Other factors helped to aggravate his condition. One was his unhappiness about his stereotyped reputation of being solely a writer of the "picaresque." McKay, whose concern with literature had always been universal, was now sought after only for his primitive-exotic-picaresque novels—a predicament he desperately sought to change. Frantically, he wrote Eastman, telling him he wanted to publish some short stories that would prove that he was a writer of many moods—so that the way would open for a book on any theme he might choose.[6]

Another factor that had caused McKay much concern had been his misgivings about the future of the literary market. The Great Depression had set in and, like the rest of the marketplace, the literary market had taken a turn for the worse. McKay, who had heard that despite the general depression in the literary market, a great deal of money was still available for advances on new contracts, hoped to secure a few thousand dollars before all the money dried up.[7] But he knew that to be in the best position to receive an advance, he should return to America, where he could promote himself firsthand. But such a return would force a confrontation with many of the blacks who had criticized his work.

Finding the idea of returning to America unattractive, McKay used most of his remaining money to move to Tangiers, Morocco.

He rented a house, the first place that McKay, now thirty-eight, could call his own. In Tangiers McKay tried to emulate the lifestyle of his white literary friends. From his early contacts in Jamaica to his later association with Max Eastman, McKay had admired and envied the kind of life-style he was too poor to afford. He had lived in some of the worst sections of Harlem, surrounded by conditions he found tolerable only until he became a successful writer.[8]

Renting the house in Tangiers gave McKay a sense of achievement. Proudly, he informed Eastman of the details: "The house is just about the size of yours at Antibes."[9] He paid his rent for an entire year in advance, and he hired a Moslem girl to serve as both his companion and servant.

For a while, his change of scene partially alleviated his melancholy. McKay found himself enjoying his small house and wrote that, while he had little money left, he had "faith in the place and myself."[10] The countryside seemed to compensate for the headaches that still recurred from time to time. The Moorish towns and their "living medievalism" appealed to him. Pensively, he related to Eastman, "I suppose for me the feeling is spiritual, since my people were taken out of a primitive tribal stage. It may be that my attachment to the native life here is a sort of spiritual looking backwards."[11]

But the everyday concerns of making a living and the uncertainty of his future as a literary artist constantly intruded and soon destroyed what peace of mind he was able to achieve. The idea that he was known simply as a writer of the picaresque continued to distress him. Yet he found it harder than he had imagined to write in a different style using different materials. He discovered that he could not produce a first-rate book as his ongoing contract with Harper required. Instead, he sent his publisher a series of short stories. This apparent breach of contract stemmed not only from his mounting fear of being restricted by the market, but also by his own shortcomings. McKay attributed the "whole misunderstanding" to his dissatisfaction with the quality of the novel he promised. It was not good enough, he confided to Max. "I had about written myself dry on the picaresque style."[12]

McKay's agent advised him to fulfill the terms of his contract by submitting a long fiction, even if he was unhappy with it. But

McKay felt that submitting inferior work would ruin his career as a novelist. [13] Besides, he felt that the six Harlem stories he substituted should have been sufficient to cover Harper's advances, especially since the stories "went much deeper into the life of Harlem" than had *Home to Harlem.*

McKay's last novel, *Banana Bottom*, published in 1933 at the height of the Depression, reflected his desire to prove that he was an artist of many moods and not simply of the primitive-exotic-picaresque. It also was his last attempt to advance the theme he had unsuccessfully begun in *Home to Harlem* and carried through *Banjo:* that Western civilization was the Negro's cultural hell and should be rejected in favor of the simple values of the "folk." It was his most successful effort at dramatizing the conviction that "neither Puritanism nor the love of money nor the dominance of science had wrung out of its soul the joy which one may get from merely being one's own self." And it presented Negroes who had a special aptitude for "living—merely living" that white people had never had or that they had lost somewhere along the trail to the modern Babylon of commerce, industry, and granite. [14]

By returning to surroundings he was most familiar with—his native Jamaica—McKay succeeds in both the development of form and theme. Relying less on the obvious propaganda of the previous two novels, McKay allows the quiet pastoral ambience of peasant life to sharply define the conflict between "Jamaican native folk values and Western European values." He also departs from his use of black male vagabonds like Jake and Banjo and the overcivilized West Indian writer Ray, and instead chooses Bita, a Jamaican peasant woman, as the protagonist to carry his message. [15]

Bita was raped at twelve by Crazy Bow, a twenty-five-year-old "mixed blood" idiot. Before her father, Jordan Plant, can send her away to a relative in Kingston to spare her public shame, Malcolm and Priscilla Craig, a white missionary couple who embody Anglo-Saxon civilization, offer to take Bita in and educate her, bringing her up as their own child. Bita is taken to Europe where she is exposed to European culture and receives the best European education. The Craigs' motivation for adopting Bita are varied, ranging from their desire to demonstrate the full measure of an old family friendship between the Plants and the Craigs, their sense of fulfilling God's will, and Priscilla Craig's belief that molding Bita will give her the opportunity to demonstrate what such a girl could become by careful training . . . with God's help.[16]

Bita's return to Jamaica after a number of years abroad sets the stage for McKay's conflict of cultures. On one occasion after another, Bita is forced to choose whether she will follow her instincts, the Jamaican heritage that is "bred in the bone," or heed what the Craigs, European education, and "civilized culture" have taught her. When Bita chooses clothes to wear, she acknowledges this dilemma: "She loved bandanna colours, like all the peasant folk of the West Indies. And although she was now too cultivated to riot in them on all occasions like the rest of the country girls (she had to wear a sort of blue uniform as organist at Jubilee), she anticipated with happiness the freedom of going bandanna on a picnic day."[17]

More and more Bita comes to realize that being civilized, cultivated, and cultured means living a life marked by restraint, repression, and self-denial. Slowly Bita rebels against the values instilled in her by the Craigs and yields to the "folk" in her. This realization of the worthiness of the indigenous folk culture, indeed of its superiority to white Anglo-Saxon Western culture, eventually occurs—but, ironically, not without the help of a white man, Squire Gensir, an eccentric Caucasian who has taken up residence near Banana Bottom in search of Jamaican Annancy stories, Jammas, Sheysheys, and Breakdowns.

Gensir has heard about Bita, the native woman who has been educated in his own country, and out of curiosity wants to see her. He mischievously intices Bita to violate an unwritten social taboo of the pretentious middle class—attending Banana Bottom's tea meeting. Tea meetings were discountenanced as low and rowdy affairs by the respectable church elements. When Gensir inquires why Bita will not be attending the tea meeting, she responds, "No, I couldn't go. I've never once been to a tea-meeting." "Because," as she continues, "there are some things you are not always free to do even though you may want to. All depends on your position. And my position is such if I went to a tea-meeting I know Mrs. Craig would be shocked to death." But Gensir finally convinces Bita to attend and she fully enjoys herself.[18]

In the company of Squire Gensir and with his encouragement,

Bita increasingly questions the value of her recently acquired education and culture—especially if it prohibits one from "being one's self." In a confrontation with her arranged fiancé, Hearld Newton Day, product of white Christian missionary schooling, the embodiment of pretentious bourgeois society, and destined for a career in the ministry, Bita declares, "I thank God that although I was brought up and educated among white people, I have never wanted to be anything but myself. I take pride in being coloured and different, just as an intelligent white person does in being white. I can't imagine anything more tragic than people torturing themselves to be different from their natural unchangeable selves." Soon Bita is in a full-scale retreat from Western culture.[19]

Symbolic of Bita's reclamation of her natural birthright is her attendance at a "house party" with Hoping Dick, a fun-loving, irresponsible black male of less-than-reputable character. Although Bita is a natural dancer, it has been years since she has had the opportunity to do "smart dancing." The house party gives her the opportunity to excel in the thing she "loved." And as Bita stands up to Hopping Dick, hands poised in the air and pirouetting around him to the sounds of a native version of the minuet, she returns to the rustic simplicity of Jamaican peasant life.[20] The process culminates with a short-lived infatuation with Hopping Dick, a fine dandy, but not the marrying kind, and finally with the marriage of Bita to Jubban, a sturdy black peasant, whose child she conceives during their courtship.

The formal exorcism of Bita's demon of Western culture takes place during an old-fashioned religious revival. In the midst of beating tom-toms, emotional frenzied dancing women, and intermittent shrieks and moans, Bita becomes mesmerized by the common fetish spirit. The terrible scene evokes memories of an ancient, nearly forgotten spirit of savage rites. Magnetized by the delightful and yet frightening spell, Bita is swept into the vortex, shrieks, and falls down. Her surrender to the past is greeted by a mighty shout from those who celebrate her return.[21]

While McKay managed to maintain more distance between himself and his novel in *Banana Bottom*, his character of Squire Gensir is almost totally autobiographical.[22] Gensir is the reincarnation of his mentor Walter Jekyll. McKay says as much in the preface when he advises the reader that "all the characters, as in my previous novels, are imaginary, excepting perhaps, Squire Gensir." He then proceeds, using Bita, to describe his own relationship with his mentor from the Blue Mountains. McKay leaves little out: Jekyll's desire to collect Jamaican folk tales, his desire to meet an educated black Jamaican who wrote poetry in the Jamaican dialect, his life as an agnostic and free thinker, his disdain for the pretentious middle class. McKay writes of Gensir, "If there was one thing he detested it was that social quality that has been ridden so hard by moderns and bohemians: middle class gentility." When the character Babs asks Squire Gensir how he is able to tolerate the manners of the peasantry, the Squire responds, "easily and with pleasure."[23]

McKay's admiration and respect for Jekyll are evident in his depiction of Squire Gensir. He is careful not to include anything that does not reflect well on his mentor. McKay notes that in a country where sexual relations were the natural uninhibited response of the peasants, Gensir "lived aloof from sexual contact, a happy old bachelor (as Mrs. Craig often remarked), not the slightest blemish upon his character—a character about which nothing was whispered either naturally or otherwise." McKay's creation of Squire Gensir not only allowed him to vividly underscore the folly of the black peasantry who denied their heritage in favor of Western civilization but also enabled him to repay his debt to Walter Jekyll by honoring him through the medium of fiction.[24]

The absence of McKay's tumultuous tirades in *Banana Bottom* permitted contemporary readers to view the novel, in the words of Sterling Brown, as a "quiet story, quietly told."[25] Yet McKay could not, if he intended to write a realistic novel of Jamaican life, avoid treating several subjects that were among his most persistent dislikes: "Yellow Negroes" and religion. While in his personal life he generally avoided the recognition of intracolor conflict in Jamaica, his desire to create a realistic and honest portrayal of Jamaican life forced him to address the problem in *Banana Bottom*—revealing yet another paradox in McKay's life. Through Bita, his dark brown protagonist, McKay explores color consciousness in Jamaica.

Bita's silent objection to her arranged marriage to Hearld Newton Day to please the Craigs opens the door for a discussion of

Jamaica's color stratification. Though Day is repulsive to Bita, the author explains that her dark complexion offers her little hope of finding a more appealing husband. In fact, what could a cultivated Negro woman from the country expect who would be better than a parson. However, had Bita been born light brown or yellow, she might, with her training, easily win a man of a similar complexion—a local functionary of the law courts, perhaps, or a manager of a business in the city. But, the author writes, "She was in the black and dark-brown group and there were no prospects of her breaking into the intimate social circles of the smart light-brown and yellow group."[26]

Moreover, as proud as Bita is of her color, she is infuriated by the presumption of superiority by the near-whites. When Bita forcefully resists a sexual assault by Marsh Arthur, the bastard, near-white son of a wealthy country gentleman, he is surprised and proceeds to upbraid Bita: "Wha' de hell you putting on style. You ought to feel proud a gen'man like me want fer kiss you when youse only a black gal." Bita is momentarily rescued by Jubban, who comments that "De backra [white] men t'ink all black womens them nuttin." Bita replies that "the Glengleys [Marsh's father's family] are not pure backra, but what's the difference? They all have the same mind." While Bita is hurt by Marsh's use of the phrase "only a black girl," a common expression that might be flung at any decent Negro anywhere, the reader is assured that "no sneer, sarcasm, no banal ridicule of a ridiculous world could destroy her confidence and pride in herself and make her feel ashamed of that fine body that was the temple of her high spirit. For she knew that she was a worthy human being. She knew that she was beautiful."[27]

Few, if any, of McKay's light-skinned characters have any redeeming qualities. And since, according to Bita, they "all have the same mind," and are "slimy white hogs," it is not happenstance that Bita's rapist, Crazy Bow, is the result of miscegenation. "The village," McKay writes, "would have been proud if Crazy Bow had been able to make good at books and go into the Civil Service, the place where all the intelligent light-coloured young men went."[28] As McKay's voice Bita denounces this presumption and privilege that Jamaica's mulatto class enjoyed by the mere virtue of the nocturnal activities of "backra" men.

McKay's attack on the privilege of Jamaica's mulatto class is linked with a "quiet" but devastating assault on civilized religion. McKay suggests that, of all the symbols of Western European repression, Christianity is the worst. Its ministers are condescending, pompous, and hypocritical. They unfairly deride and condemn all that comes naturally to the Jamaican peasant:

> If there was anything that Priscilla Craig and her fellow workers in Christ agreed on in discussing the qualities of the natives, their faults and their virtues, it was the lack of restraint among them. Where the law of the land was concerned they were quite docile in obedience. They did not seem to grasp the meaning of the high social significance of existence. Sex was approached too easily. And for that reason some of the most promising men who had been chosen or had chosen the preaching or teaching professions often found themselves halted and worthless in the midst of their career.[29]

However, the Craigs are confident, at least initially, that, "It wasn't because these people were oversexed, but simply because they seemed to lack that check and control that was supposed to be distinguishing of humanity of a higher and more complex social order." But when Priscilla Craig's experiment to demonstrate the transforming power of God fails and Bita embraces her native culture and falls in love with Hopping Dick, Craig dismisses her not only as an ingrate but as a "nymphomaniac."[30]

McKay also makes the case that too much religion, whether Western religion or the native superstitious Obeah, can lead to disastrous consequences. When Tack Tally believes that he is responsible for the death of his girlfriend's father during a fight (he actually dies from a heart attack), he is convinced that the local practitioner of Obeahism has not adequately protected him from evil and commits suicide.[31]

Even more tragic, at least from the point of view of the missionary community, is the fall of Day. The son of the senior deacon at Malcolm Craig's mission in Jubilee, Day is considered the natural successor to Craig. The marriage of Bita to Day, a native, and his succession to one of the finest missions in the colony is thought to be the best possible tribute to the labor of Craig and a fitting fulfillment to the pioneer purpose that lay behind the founding of the mission. Day had prepared himself for his future role with a deadly seriousness, including the sexual restraint so absent in most of the natives. However, shortly before his graduation, the "forced" repression of his natural sexual desires by the demands of the ministry—daily meditation, constant prayer, thinking purely, and maintaining watchful vigilance against corrupting influences—takes its toll, and Day defiles himself with a goat. The goat is killed and Hearld Newton Day is hurried off to the city, from where he embarks for Panama, dashing the hopes of the Craigs for either his marriage to Bita or his succession to the mission. Day's defilement is McKay's warning about the consequences of artificial repression of natural instincts caused by Western culture and religion.[32]

Unfortunately, despite *Banana Bottom*'s strengths, it failed to attract a reading audience, failing miserably on the market. While aware that the financial crisis in the United States hurt the novel, McKay also feared that he had not included enough sensationalism to attract an audience. McKay concluded, "Evidently my readers prefer my realism of rough slum life than of rural life. If so I can supply the need."[33]

Shaped by that appraisal of the book market, McKay's next manuscript illustrated how far he was willing to go to achieve popular success. *Savage Loving*, is the story of "real low down stuff." Jilted by a colored girl, a black boy stows away in the cold storage room of a ship. When the boy's legs freeze and have to be amputated, a New York ambulance chaser gets him several thousand dollars in compensation. The money enables the boy to return home and take up with the same girl who had earlier jilted him.[34] McKay hoped that such hard-hitting realism or sensationalism would be financially successful and enable him to repay Harper the money it had advanced him.

McKay submitted his new novel to several publishers, but they all rejected it. Countee Cullen, who was shown the manuscript by one of the publishers, called the novel "obscene."[35] Clifton Fadiman of Simon and Schuster noted that every once in a while it revealed a grand sensual power but that, on the whole, the book was a failure. Instead of being riotous with African color, the style was dull and unemotional. "I imagine," Fadiman continued, "McKay is trying to work a Hemingway on material to which Hemingway is not adapted. . . . One is never quite sure whether

CLAUDE McKAY

his novel is intended as a literary book or a piece of Macauley sex stuff."³⁶ Another publisher told McKay that he had to reject the manuscript because it was so full of fornication.³⁷

Financial distress caused by the rejection of *Savage Loving* and the failure of his last two novels forced McKay to again consider returning to America. He hoped to survive with the aid of a Guggenheim Fellowship he had applied for and possibly earnings from a lecture tour among those "nice negroes."³⁸ In addition, he began to plan another novel, in which the leading characters would be African Americans. If the book could be completed in time, he could promote it personally during his lecture tour in the United States. Yet, the possibility of writing a novel about the people he held in such contempt and fear naturally engendered some anxiety. He would not be sure how to go about it without arousing opposition from his old enemy, that "class of Negroes" (middle-class American blacks). In a lugubrious mood, he remarked, "They are all so touchy. And if I go back home I'll have to live among them. Fact is I am afraid of the idea of returning for good. For now I can't live like in the days before the *Liberator*. I'll have to find myself among the 'Niggerati' as I hear they call themselves in Harlem."³⁹ Lacking alternatives, McKay would finally have to confront that class of blacks that had always made him feel so uncomfortable. He could not hide with white radicals at another *Liberator*. Any hope of getting "on" in the United States would have to come through the black middle class.

Going back to America under his present circumstances would be humiliating and embarrassing to McKay. He would return as he had left: practically penniless. It was in such a spirit that he wrote Eastman, "Fancy writing like a castrated tom cat creaming and spitting all over the place!"⁴⁰

If the thought of going back to America depressed McKay, the fear that he had waited too long and would never be able to return alarmed him even more. In 1928, he would have had little difficulty reentering America. His friends, black and white, had implored him to return and contribute his genius to the blossoming Harlem Renaissance. Periodically, he had gone through the motions of requesting assistance from the American consuls to return. Each time, however, McKay finally changed his mind and allowed the opportunity to slip away.⁴¹ Actually, he had never

136

intended to return and had only pursued the channels of reentry to keep the door open in the event a situation arose that necessitated his departure.[42]

It was now 1933, and what once would have been relatively easy to accomplish, suddenly seemed almost impossible. Conditions that would have allowed for a smooth reentry had changed drastically between 1928 and 1933. The first, and perhaps the most important, problem was the state of the economy. Despite some restrictions on immigration, U.S. officials during the prosperous 1920s had allowed a steady flow of immigrants to enter the United States. But by 1933, the peak year of the Depression, with much of the population unemployed, officials pursued a policy of discouraging immigration.[43] The American Immigration Department sought every possible way to disquality those they did not consider desirable from entering the country. McKay's controversial association with the Communists in Russia made him easy prey for officials seeking to deny him admission.

Writing to Eastman, McKay described his problems with officialdom:

"I went to the consul today and he had heard from Marseilles and showed me a circular from the American Immigration that I left Russia for Copenhagen with a large sum of money for propaganda in America! Now I know why the Consul at Marseilles was so changed and cold when I went to him a second time after I had written to the Consulate in 1929 asking for the date concerning my entry in the U.S. The Immigration officials replied that the documents were sent to the consul at Marseilles. When I did come to Tangier I gave him (consul) my address, but was never notified about my quota number. I suppose the information put him against me as it did the French authorities at Rabal and Fez. And all because of those dirty British bastards working respectably in the dark.[44]

The intrigues among the various consulates concerning McKay's Communist affiliations were only part of his problem. For instance, McKay had never taken out American citizenship papers. Like many West Indians, he had preferred to keep his British citizenship to distinguish himself from other blacks. America, as far as McKay was concerned, was only the place "where I make my living by writing and selling my production to the American public."[45] He had never expressed any loyalty to, nor interest in, the United States other than as a means of support. Lacking citizenship papers, McKay was forced to apply for admission under the British quota.

By 1933, he indicated he was more than willing to renounce his British citizenship and take out American papers if such actions would facilitate his return to America. Now he was also suggesting that his whole view of the British empire had soured over the years. "Certainly, I should be glad to change to U.S. citizenship if I can," he wrote Eastman. "I am of the New World anyway and although I could exist anywhere there is food and water to get, I've always felt I was legitimately British which I am not after all. Those islands of the New World belonging to European natives are certainly a bastard lot, but always I put it off—and now I am sorry."[46]

Under the immigration requirements, a person desiring entry to the United States had to prove that he would not be a financial burden to the country. McKay would have had no problem with this requirement in 1928, at the height of his fame, but he was a penniless has-been in 1933. McKay was so poor he had to give up his little rented house and beg his friends for financial aid. He had been accurate when he assessed his situation in 1933 by remarking, "The only place I can think of now is America. I could make a living lecturing to Negro audiences, but I am an alien and I am sure they won't let me in on my Russian record without special intervention."[47]

Reluctantly, McKay sought such special intervention from some of the very people he criticized. In response to his request, Walter White spoke on McKay's behalf to Wilbur J. Carr, assistant secretary of state. White managed to secure from Carr a statement that he saw no reason why McKay should have to come in under the British quota. Carr indicated that if McKay presented himself to the U.S. consul in Marseilles, filled out a visa application, and demonstrated that he had a future means of support, he would be allowed entry to the United States. Carr also said, in so many words, that, although he would be questioned in a routine fashion about his connection with the Third International, he would not be refused entry on that score.[48]

While his past association with the Communists proved a relatively easy obstacle to overcome, finding the funds to prove himself self-sufficient was another matter. The Guggenheim Fellowship he had applied for—with some impressive recommendations—did not materialize.[49] Other possible funding sources proved equally elusive. Walter White had indicated that McKay would be an asset to *Crisis*, but the magazine's deepening financial problems closed off that possibility.[50] The possibility of his returning at the invitation of a group or an organization also faded in the next few months.

Even his white friends found it difficult to aid McKay. McKay's race barred him from the kinds of jobs they might have found for a white writer in distress. A friend of Eastman reported that she had been unable to secure McKay a job because she could not think of one that "wasn't specifically Negro." She hastened to add, "It must be infuriating never to be just another human being."[51]

By the end of 1933, it appeared that McKay's ambivalence and hostility toward African Americans, the tensions arising from Harlem Renaissance issues, and his general disdain for America had permanently exiled him in Africa and Europe. Bitterly he wrote Eastman, "Nobody has sent me a penny but you! Johnson never replied—Schomburg writes and suggests all kinds of schemes but not one cent—and the others! I wonder why Johnson didn't try to raise some money the way he told you. But he couldn't I suppose among Negroes, *They love me so much.*"[52]

Unfortunately, McKay sought to place the blame for his own past mistakes, indecisiveness, poor judgment, and political and financial problems on black Americans. Had he returned earlier, he would have avoided the situation he now found himself in. Moreover, he selfishly failed to take into account the problems African Americans were encountering themselves. For most blacks, survival during the depression had become a full-time occupation. Few blacks had money to contribute to any worthwhile cause, and the middle-class blacks who still enjoyed prosperity can be forgiven an unwillingness to help a man who regularly attacked them in his writing. McKay's situation was desperate as he expressed to Eastman the hope a miracle would happen and "save him for arts sake!"[53]

Nothing as spectacular as a miracle occurred but, through the efforts of Eastman, a plan was set in motion to retrieve McKay from his grave situation in Europe. First, through the cooperation of an unnamed consul, McKay was given a visa with the understanding that he had job opportunities awaiting him in New York and would not become a public charge.[54] Vague promises from James W. Johnson that he would be able to secure McKay a lecture tour were accepted as evidence of financial security by the consul as a favor to Eastman and some friends. Eastman himself sent McKay enough money to pay for his passage from Cadiz, Spain, to New York. As he made last-minute preparations to execute the plan, McKay wrote to Eastman, "Funny a man's life seems to work out going round in circles." For McKay, his situation seemed much as it had in 1926,[55] when McKay appeared headed for an early nadir.

McKay's ship docked in New York in February 1934. McKay once again gazed upon the great edifices of New York City. But getting back was only the beginning of a new series of problems for McKay. Many questions remained unanswered. America, the country whose bigotry had appalled McKay and forced him to flee its outstretched arms, still remained unabashedly racist. The restrictions that normally circumscribed the black artist's life had been made worse by the depression. As his white friends had already indicated, he would have to compete for the few jobs that were made available to talented blacks. Most important, what would be his relationship with the African Americans he had reviled so bitterly and whose Harlem Renaissance he had spurned?

The debate over his novels, and the very nature of the Renaissance itself, had exacted a serious toll on his physical and mental health. Undoubtedly, the warning of his friend Gladys Wilson that he should never return to the United States because the country was a "hell for the Black man" echoed through his mind.[56] The following poem, written shortly after arriving, captures much of that confusion and ambivalence:

> But oh, I was reluctant coming back!
> I felt like one expelled from heaven to hell
> To the arena packed of White and Black
> America's heart-breaking spectacle.
>
> Yet, though I feared to face this strange return
> Afraid that I would never again recapture
> These accents for which often I would yearn
> And in my exile dote upon with rapture.

Back to Harlem

Returning I discovered happiness
Though mingled with the thoughts of farewell pain
Yet any pain was good that brought me this;
The thrill of finding voice to sing again.[57]

The poem, which begins on a negative chord, ends with a rather positive affirmation of his future. McKay's return to Harlem elicited little excitement or notice. There were no crowds and few friends to greet the author who had done so much to popularize black Harlem in his novel *Home to Harlem*. Many viewed his return with either indifference or hostility. This was especially true of many radicals, who considered him a traitor and a "hog who had come to root in Harlem." The following poem, written by Bella Gross, white columnist for the Communist *Harlem Liberator,* reflects this sentiment:

Home to Harlem, Claude McKay!
The Blue Eagle's screaming and there's the N.R.A.
To the Scottsboro marchers are shouting and singing
To the tune of the Red Front Band—
They shall not die—they shall be free!
Negro and White, unite and be free:
Welcome, welcome to Harlem, Mother Wright!
and Lenox Avenue in one mighty shout cries
Welcome, welcome to Harlem, Mother Wright!

How does it feel to be back in Harlem in 1934
And see all the red banners flying
And hear all these voices shouting defiance—
And be out of it all—out of it all
Scottsboro is a rock, hewn out of history
We're making history Lenox Avenue in 1934.

Once your works were red flame sweeping the dark horizon:
Once your voice was the clarion calling an oppressed nation to
     freedom
Once you were ours now the I—— have silenced you.
Their golden noose is around your neck.
Why did you come back to Harlem—dead?

Do you know that Angelo Herndon is in Fulton Lower
Engdohl and Cliff James are gone, and so is Gray.
He built the Sharecroppers Union in a mighty hands . . .
Blood red 19 shall never be again, though some must die—
We'll be victorious, remember 1919—the riots in Tulsa
And the poet who cried—'If we must die—Oh let us nobly die

So that our precious blood may not be shed.'
Then you betrayed us—And the poet is dead. [58]

The hostility McKay expected from the African-American community did not surface. Instead, many American blacks greeted him warmly. Indeed, he soon had an opportunity to resume his role as a writer and cultural leader. A number of African Americans, led by Arthur Schomburg, decided to start a literary magazine. They refused to allow the Renaissance to die a premature death. In the prospectus announcing the forthcoming magazine, they noted that ten years earlier the literary world was enlivened by a Negro Renaissance. But, looking back, what then appeared to be a Renaissance seemed today to be nothing more than a mushroom growth, which had sent no roots down into the soil of Negro life. The Negro Renaissance movement had stagnated for a number of reasons. [59] Black writers and their works had been unscrupulously exploited. The movement had been "nipped in the bud" because the white world had assumed it was simply a passing fad. To prevent a repetition of such problems, the founders sought to establish a magazine devoted exclusively to creating a permanent place in American life for the Negro's contributions to literature and art.

The immediate objective of the magazine would be to give expression to the literary and artistic aspirations of the Negro, and to offer an aesthetic interpretation of Negro life. The founders intended to celebrate the Negro's racial background and his racial gifts and accomplishments. Blacks, whatever their degree of color or their creed, would be encouraged to create artistically as an ethnic group. Finally, the founders wanted to help the black artist to free his mind of the shackles imposed upon it both from outside, by the dominant white world, and from inside, within the minority black community. In most respects, the magazine's philosophy seemed to revive the creed expressed ten years earlier when the Renaissance had first begun to flower. However, one important difference distinguished the new magazine's philosophy from earlier black literary outlets: its desire to accommodate writers and artists of all persuasions and to avoid the pernicious debates of the twenties.

Surprisingly, the founders of the new magazine believed that

McKay would be an excellent choice for editor. Although McKay was not the man of ten years earlier, he still brought some impressive credentials to the magazine. As the founders eagerly pointed out, he enjoyed the reputation of having been a Renaissance pioneer. His eleven years abroad had given him an international outlook on the Negro, as well as a storehouse of experience. With his broad outlook and mature experiences, he could forge a keen instrument for the expression of genuine Negro talent.[60]

The opportunity to become editor of a magazine elated McKay, who immediately wrote Eastman about his good fortune and asked the veteran editor for his advice. The advice McKay sought had less to do with the stated objectives of the magazine than with his concern for establishing controlling power over the proposed sheet. With this in mind, he remarked to Eastman, "I do wish you would send me some pointers on the best way to organize it so that if it goes through and is established I'll have the controlling power and not be maneuvered out in case of a schism." "The thing," McKay continued, "is to be built around me and if it is what I want, I want it to be done on a solid basis."[61]

McKay threw all his energy into getting the magazine started. He busied himself attempting to secure sponsorship support from important literary figures.[62] To introduce the first edition, announce its chosen name, *Bambara*, and raise much-needed funds, he organized a cocktail party.[63] McKay managed to convince several literary figures to act as sponsors, but his cocktail party was a fund-raising failure: it garnered only $25. But McKay was optimistic because of the publicity the affair received from the press. The circular describing the magazine had been turned into a news release by an enterprising agency and published in all the Negro magazines. McKay thought the magazine would be successful.[64]

McKay was gratified by the response he received from Harlem's younger artists, many of whom expressed enthusiasm and interest in contributing to it. Redemption seemed close at hand. A successful literary magazine would resurrect McKay from the literary graveyard and reestablish the respect of those who considered him a "hog come to root in Harlem." It would also give new life to one of the most important movements in the history of the African American.

But harsh reality soon crushed McKay's optimistic hopes. Despite McKay's efforts, 1934 was simply the wrong time to try to begin such an ambitious undertaking. Like so many of McKay's endeavors, the magazine was stillborn. Penniless, McKay soon found himself sixty miles away from Harlem, living in one of the camps established for the unemployed.[65]

McKay went to Greycourt on the advice of an official in the State Department, who first had suggested that McKay apply for relief under an alias, since he was not a U.S. citizen and had not lived the required four years in New York. McKay refused this option because he feared possible exposure in the gossip columns of the black Harlem press. If he was exposed as a relief recipient, he could be deported because his visa was contingent on his ability to support himself and on his not becoming a public charge. Greycourt offered an alternative. It had been established as a camp for the down and outs, providing work with a dollar a day as wages. McKay decided this was far better than relief and signed on as a laborer.

Initially, McKay went to the camp with a sense of "optimistic fatalism." In fact, he remarked to Eastman, the place reminded him of his police and railroad days: barracks life, two in a cell, ship plan, lights out at eleven, barracks food, good enough but slovenly served. While the pay was a dollar a day, fifty cents was taken out for maintenance. One got no wages until he had earned $15, which was held as a stake for the worker if he left the camp. Still, McKay felt the place was better than what he had left behind in New York. Besides, he hoped to get a job working on the camp's mimeographed newsletter.

McKay resigned himself to living at the labor camp as a way to vindicate himself to "those" he felt were responsible for his being there. He told Eastman that blacks in New York had not responded to his plea for a job. "Any of those colored places could have found me a place, even to address envelopes, but I have no pull and I guess they are really afraid of me!" Refusing to give up, McKay was determined to complete a book on bohemian life and make it a success.[66]

But conditions at Greycourt soon turned his determination to despair. Greycourt, after all, was an "awful" place. The barracks life, which he had wishfully compared to his police and railroad days, turned out to be more "apparent than real." The men of the barracks were the worst bums of the Bowery. Not intended as punishment or evil by design, the camp was the product of a "people working to clear away a wreck."[67] McKay complained that Greycourt destroyed as many men as it helped. Unintentionally, it assaulted the very dignity it hoped to preserve. Men ceased being individuals and were forced to give up all their rights and privileges. Even excretion had to be performed in public. Individuals lost their identities. Men were often reduced to children, jealous of the slightest favor shown one of their numbers. If a man had once enjoyed a better life, it was best kept a secret for fear of reprisals from other boarders. Simple necessities, such as underwear, were viewed as luxuries. In short, Greycourt destroyed a man's zest for living.[68]

It would have been miraculous if McKay had escaped the effects of Greycourt. A man of his intellect and sensitivity naturally felt its pernicious effects. He felt like a "caged wild animal." Denied the opportunity to accomplish what he had the ability to do, he felt helpless and impotent. In sheer despair, he urged Eastman to seek the aid of Joel Spingarn: "Please don't forget Spingarn, tell him I have exhausted all ways hunting a job and that I am not standing on any dignity, since I haven't any left, and I am willing to fit into anything that can be found for me."[69]

As McKay sat in the dark halls of Greycourt and contemplated his life, he now understood why people committed suicide rather than become paupers.[70] Bemoaning his situation, he declared, "I am paying a penalty for being too naively internationally minded."[71]

The realization that he had been hit by the boomerang return of his youthful radicalism was reflected in an unpublished manuscript written at Greycourt. The story, entitled "The Enigmatic Expatriate," involves the tale of a strange little old man who moves in the circle of intellectual bohemians abroad. Although he is not and cannot be one of them, he nevertheless follows them from place to place. The man is restive, possessing a phobia about the word "insanity." For some undisclosed reason, he does not want to return home to America. Yet upon receiving word of "the Great Smashup" in 1929, he suddenly decides to return home. He then confesses that he had been extremely wealthy before the crash, but had been put in an asylum in America by greedy relatives. He had been able to leave the country and live eccentrically among the radicals and bohemians. Yet all the time, he preferred America and now that he had no money and nothing to fear he could return, happy at last.[72]

McKay himself was that enigmatic expatriate, no longer a young man, moving around in bohemian circles, not really belonging, forced to leave by the restraints of race and class, yet always hoping somehow to return when the milieu changed. "Enigmatic Expatriate" was a caricature of reality at Greycourt. The camp not only compromised his manhood, it filled him with a sense of dread about trying to live again in the outside world. He no longer felt intellectually free or vital. And though living in Greycourt was like "trying to breathe fresh air in a foul latrine," the idea of returning to Harlem, to go knocking from pillar to post, horrified him.[73]

But eventually McKay had to leave Greycourt. In some ways, he was more fortunate than many of his fellow artists. Time after time, when disaster threatened to finally destroy McKay, someone appeared to help him. This time was no exception. Eastman offered McKay the use of his place at Croton-on-Hudson, but then he rescinded the offer. What lay behind Eastman's change of heart never surfaced, but Eastman may have had second thoughts about the presence of a black man at Croton during the summer, when he and his white friends frequently went swimming in the nude.[74] Still, Eastman did help provide the necessary financial means for McKay to leave Greycourt.[75]

As he had done on previous occasions, James Weldon Johnson also interceded on McKay's behalf. Johnson agreed to use his influence at the Garland Fund to secure McKay assistance. Because of the depression and the scarcity of money, Johnson was less than confident that the Garland Fund would be of any help and advised McKay to also make an application to the Rosenwald Fund. Johnson then personally wrote to Edwin R. Embree, chairman of the organization.[76]

Embree initially responded to the request by expressing doubt. The fund generally supported advanced training for young persons of unusual promise; it did not give grants for established artists to work on their own projects.[77] Johnson entreated Embree to consider that, while he understood the limitations of the fund, he was sure it would be making a safe bet in putting out some money on McKay: "I need not tell you he is one of the most gifted and powerful of all the Negro writers."[78]

With Johnson's support of McKay, the fund chose to make an exceptional grant in the amount of $500 to provide the means for McKay to complete his autobiography, *A Long Way from Home*. With an additional $300 from a publisher, McKay resumed his quest for redemption in the literary world.[79]

7

I Have Come to Lead the Renaissance

*T*HE ECONOMIC catastrophe of the 1930s and the outlook and program of the New Deal stimulated changes in the orientation of black thinking. Concern with economic problems became the order of the day. Younger black radicals, such as Ralph Bunche and Abram Harris, attacked the NAACP's gradualist approach and its lack of attention to economic problems, preferring a general reconstruction of American society through an alliance of black and white workers. Hitler's rise to power in Germany also had an effect on the black community. Prompted by fear of Hitler, the Soviet Union changed its international policy in 1935. Instead of its previous practice of denouncing black intellectuals and the black middle class, it courted them with its popular front strategy. Although initially remaining in the background, the Communists exploited the trend toward more radical economic and class activity advocated by a significant number of black intellectuals. But while other black intellectuals were stressing economic conflict, McKay stressed racial chauvinism. McKay had been a Communist in the early twenties, but in the thirties he became a strong anti-Communist. Once again McKay was out of step with many of his fellow black intellectuals.

Upon his departure from Greycourt, McKay noticed that a number of the younger artists seemed to be at loose ends. Many he felt were bitter against "patrons" of Negro art, who had taken them up for a brief while and then dropped them abruptly. He thought such bitterness was especially evident in Langston Hughes's work. The situation, he suggested, was not peculiar to blacks since "faddists" treated artists that way the world over. As he told James W. Johnson, the so-called Negro Renaissance had been a wonderful break. It had helped black writers realize that there was no easy conquest in creative work and that a little success and a chorus of admiration should never produce complacency.[1] He himself hoped that he could yet succeed in redeeming his literary reputation.

"*I Have Come to Lead the Renaissance*"

Early in 1937 McKay had managed to secure a job on the Federal Writers' Project, where he and a number of other blacks were working in the Harlem section of the Federal Writers' Guild. While there, he communicated to Johnson his desire to establish a Negro Writers' Guild. The guild would guarantee financial support for struggling writers. McKay also proposed the establishment of an African-American Book-of-the-Month Club, which would campaign to sell books written by black writers to the Negro public.[2] By April, McKay had joined a number of other blacks in establishing a Negro Writers' Guild, independent of the Federal Writers' Project. The group of journalists and creative writers gathered periodically in a Republican clubhouse on West 136th Street in Harlem.[3] However, within a few months the guild split over the refusal of McKay and several other members to admit Helen Boardman, a white woman, as a member, despite the guild's constitution that specifically prohibited the exclusion of a potential member on the basis of race, color, or creed.[4]

McKay's opposition to Boardman was an expression of a continuing shift in his attitude toward racial chauvinism and of his mounting fear of the domination of black writers and the masses by the Communist party. Writing of this incident in his *Harlem: Negro Metropolis* three years later, McKay described how Boardman, a devoted supporter of Negro uplift and an activist in the NAACP, had been brought to the guild by a Negro Communist who, without first notifying the guild, proposed her membership. Although Boardman denied being a Communist, the guild's officers felt that she was being used by the Communists to disrupt their group. For this reason and the officers' desire to keep the guild all-black, they opposed her candidacy. But the Communists, according to McKay's account, had enough members in the guild to swing the vote in favor of admitting a white person—precipitating a withdrawal by McKay and other key members of the guild. The departure of McKay's group spelled the end to the guild. When the incident was reported in the Negro newspapers, opponents of Boardman's admission came off looking like advocates of Negro segregation.[5]

McKay's shift to racial chauvinism, which began with the incident at the theater back in 1922, had been strengthened during his prolonged stay in Europe and Africa. It had made him less

149

certain about radical theories, especially those related to blacks.[6] His travels had convinced him that those people who best survived exploitation and repression possessed a strong sense of "group consciousness."[7] McKay had employed such reasoning in defense of his opposition to Boardman's membership. Writing to Boardman, he argued that the black population badly needed self-confidence and self-reliance. To achieve this, blacks would have to overcome the fear of segregation and take action to build a group soul, even if it meant the exclusion of white writers. A group soul, he was careful to point out, did not mean the recognition of a common enemy: there were many organizations based on race that did not increase racial barriers, but helped to break them down.[8] A black writers' guild, he contended, "was merely a particularization of a special group, having special problems, like the Jewish Writers' Guild."[9]

McKay expanded his view on the Negro soul in his autobiography, *A Long Way from Home*, published in 1937, the year of the Boardman controversy. He had reached the conclusion that the American Negro, the most advanced black group in the world, possessed very little group spirit. The lack of a group soul was responsible for the failure of black Americans to take advantage of their unique position in assuming world leadership of the Negro race. And the greatest hindrance to the development of this soul was the fear of segregation. Out of fear or lack of understanding, blacks had missed the fundamental distinction between group segregation and group aggregation—a distinction not lost on other ethnic, national, and racial groups. Failure to grasp the importance of group aggregation accounted for the inability of African Americans to fully develop black institutions. They foolishly preferred to patronize white institutions and support white causes in order to demonstrate their opposition to segregation.

Surely, no sane group desired public segregation, McKay noted, but history had proven that different groups won social rights only when they developed a group spirit and strong group organization.[10] McKay was not suggesting the establishment of a separate state. "I can see no hope nor place for a Negro nation within the United States," he wrote James Weldon Johnson, "the idea seems just a waste of intellectual energy to me."[11] But there were a thousand things that Negroes could and should do for

themselves: develop banks, co-operative stores, printing establishments, clubs, theaters, colleges, hotels, hospitals, and even
trade unions. [12] The most obvious example of what blacks could do
was provided by the American Jew. The American Jewish group
was a conglomeration of Jews from different countries, such as
Russia, Poland, Germany, Hungary, and the Balkan states. Sim-
ilarly, the American Negro group had been augmented by blacks
from the various West Indian islands and from South America.
Certainly not all Jews lived in Jewish communities, but the majority of them were socially conscious and aware of the necessity of
aggressive group organization and the development of Jewish
community life. Jews organized Jewish hotels, theaters, clubs,
stores, printing establishments, colleges, and hospitals, without segregating themselves from the nation's other institutions.
Through their group efforts they had practically broken down
barriers of American prejudice and discrimination by building up
institutions inferior to none. [13] Therefore, McKay declared in the
Column Review, "Segregation was a very unfortunate word. It has
done much harm to the colored group by paralyzing constructive
thinking and action."[14]

McKay's stance on segregation versus group aggregation placed
him in the company of W. E. B. Du Bois—a strange pairing
hardly imaginable ten years earlier. In the January 1934 issue of
Crisis Du Bois had announced that "the thinking colored people
of the United States must stop being stampeded by the word
segregation." Du Bois urged blacks to form communities and
farms of their own, to stick to themselves, and to lobby for their
fair share of the capital that FDR was redistributing under the
New Deal. "It is the race conscious black man co-operating together in his own institutions and movements who will eventually
emancipate the colored race," he declared. The "great step"
ahead for the American Negro, Du Bois concluded, was to accomplish his economic emancipation through a voluntary, determined
co-operative effort. [15]

McKay heartily endorsed Du Bois's position and wrote that he
did not see anything wrong in the idea of Negro communities
getting some of the New Deal money, especially since blacks
already had segregated communities. "I mean," he continued, "if
white communities are getting appropriations as such, Negroes

should not just wail against Segregation and not take advantage of their position, and use the profits to fight Segregation, for money is Power and good under all circumstances."[16]

McKay was furious that "passive Uncle Tom and Do Nothing" Negroes continued to plead for integration in spite of the constant discrimination against, and the virtual segregation of, the Negro race. The real issue Negroes had to face, which black and white integrationists obfuscated, was the economic issue upon which integration depended. Negro leaders might profit, McKay instructed, from a comment by a Jewish intellectual: "Today no minority group has the right to consider itself adjusted to the life of the majority unless it is economically assimilated. To be economically differentiated means to be denied protection of one's right to live by leaving one's livelihood at the mercy of the majority group." Negro leaders who continued to evade the practical issue of group organization and development to trumpet the empty slogan of "integration" without being able to demonstrate a practical plan of integration were not only betrayers but "lynchers of the soul of the race."[17]

McKay did not abandon his objective of establishing a Negro Writers' Guild even after the original guild split over the Boardman membership issue. He reorganized the group and prevailed upon James Weldon Johnson to assume the presidency. In attempting to secure Johnson's service, McKay reminded him that in 1928 Johnson had asked McKay to return to America and contribute his share to the developing "Negro Renaissance," which he was now prepared to do.[18] In August 1937 McKay sent out a special form letter to selected people to attend a meeting of the new group.[19] At its first meeting and in a subsequent communication, he outlined his aims for the group and the reasons behind it. It sought to bring together serious Negro writers and journalists concerned about the social and cultural problems facing black people. McKay challenged the "timid and obstreperous" among them to put aside their fear of the "bugbear of segregation" and see the guild not in terms of narrow sectarianism, but in the universal aspect of group culture. If this could be done, it would be possible to establish through their intellectual fellowship something like a living counterpart of the unparalleled Schomburg Collection.[20] He was aware, McKay wrote to Countee Cullen, that members of the Negro group had different points of view as a result of their individual training and experiences, but they all possessed in common their status as a "Negro minority," and as a minority they were desperately in need of a milieu for the free and unfettered exchange of ideas and views.[21] To avoid the unfortunate problem of the earlier guild, McKay inserted into the proposed constitution restrictions limiting membership to blacks and excluding those who opposed democracy or pledged allegiance to any form of dictatorship.[22]

Eventually, the Black Writers' Guild was established with Johnson as president and Jessie Fauset as vice-president. Its members included Sterling Brown, Ellen Tarry, Gwen Bennett, Vincent McHugh, Henry Lee Moon, and Countee Cullen. Meeting at McKay's tiny apartment, stuffed with rugs, statues, tapestries, and paintings brought from Morocco, the group hammered out the organization's structure. They decided to restrict membership to established writers, but projected formation of an auxiliary for younger, less experienced writers. McKay had some reservations about this plan, but in the presence of so many notable black artists, he was hopeful that the Renaissance might be revived with a foundation similar to the salon of Mabel Dodge Luhan.[23]

After weeks of meetings and sometimes heated discussions, McKay's second attempt at achieving "group consciousness" through the establishment of a writers' guild slowly foundered. Egos clashed. While technically the president, Johnson offered too much advice from too great a distance. Fauset never attended any meetings except the first, held at her home.[24] And McKay often failed to share all his plans with other members of the group, including its president. Ellen Tarry recalled that everyone knew that Claude was not a good organizer, but those who were more qualified were afraid he would get angry if they offered their services.[25] Furthermore, the guild made a serious mistake when it decided to exclude younger writers, for they were the only ones who exhibited real enthusiasm for the movement.[26]

Some members of the black literary community resented McKay's self-appointed role as a leader of "group consciousness." No one was more critical than Alain Locke. Locke took the occasion of the publication of McKay's *A Long Way from Home* to launch a devastating attack on McKay's credentials as a leader of "race soul." In an article entitled "Spiritual Truancy," Locke declared that when McKay wrote *Home to Harlem* during his self-imposed exile in Europe, many members of the black literary community had hoped that a prose and verse writer of such stellar talent would come home physically and psychologically to help lead the group of "New Negro" writers. But although McKay was now back on the American scene and attached to Harlem by literary adoption, he was still spiritually unmoored, and, by the testimony of his latest book, was a "longer way from home than ever."[27]

Locke accused McKay of failing to exhibit the most essential qualities necessary for a real spokesman for the "Negro Renaissance": acceptance of group loyalty, and the intent as well as the ability to express mass sentiment. McKay was a "spiritual truant" who blew hot and cold with the same breath. Locke traced McKay's intellectual wanderings from his days of flirtation with white bohemians at the *Liberator*, to his dalliance with Russian communism, to his present claim of racialism, and declared, "One may not dictate a man's loyalties, but must, at all events, expect him to have some. For a genius maturing in a decade of racial self-expression and enjoying the fruits of it all and living in a decade of social issues and conflict and aware of all that, to have repudiated all possible loyalties amounts to self-imposed apostasy."[28]

Locke concluded that McKay was the "enfant terrible" of the Negro Renaissance and unsuited for the role as a cultural race leader. He implied that McKay, like some other black writers, had never made a serious commitment to using racial materials, and that he had merely exploited a literary fad for his own purposes. Locke claimed that McKay was the supreme example of the generation of black writers who exhibited a lack of purposeful and steady loyalty to their race. He then called upon younger writers to accept the task of approaching the black experience and the folk with high seriousness, deep loyalty, racial reverence of an unspectacular, nonmelodramatic sort, and—when necessary—sacrificial social devotion. They had to purge themselves of writers who had made Negro art their caviar and cake. Negro writers needed to become truer sons of the people, more loyal providers of spiritual bread, and less aesthetic wastrels and "truants" of the streets.[29]

Undoubtedly Locke's opinion of McKay as the "prodigal racialist returning expecting the fatted calf instead of the birch-rod, with a curtain lecture on race salvation" was shared by others, and contributed to the demise of the writers' guild.[30] As the project fell apart, all Johnson could offer McKay was advice to fall back on the idea of enlisting younger writers into the group. McKay, as usual, could not see or refused to accept his part in the failure of the guild. He wrote to Johnson, complaining that the whole affair was an example of the Negro's lack of "group spirit." It seemed to him that the "old group" was too preoccupied with mourning the good old days to create an organization that would serve the needs of today's creative black artists.[31] Though the guild project continued for a short time, McKay had lost his last chance to gain respect as a literary influence in the black community.[32]

McKay had been partially correct in his analysis of why the project failed. Many of the guild's members were "aging creative artists falling back, in a dry season, on the gleanings of memory." Voices exhausted, they fell into various degrees of silence during the depression: Rudolph Fisher and Wallace Thurman died in 1934; Nella Larsen resorted to nursing and virtually vanished into the obscure expanses of Brooklyn; Jean Toomer became a religious mystic, a follower of Gurdjieff; Eric Walrond devoted himself to writing articles and to managing black magazines; Zora Neale Hurston left Harlem for her native South; Countee Cullen, Arna Bontemps, and Jessie Fauset turned predominantly to teaching in high schools and colleges; W. E. B. Du Bois and Alain Locke, the most significant critics of the Harlem Renaissance, continued to deliver high cultural judgments; and James Weldon Johnson, Walter White, and McKay wrote mostly autobiography and social history. The only significant member of the Renaissance twenties to remain as active as ever, both in literary fortune and celebrity, was Langston Hughes.[33]

Programs promoting "group soul" and racial solidarity, which smacked of racial chauvinism, were generally under attack from a younger and more vocal group of black intellectuals who emphasized the context of the class struggle. For them, the primary problem for black Americans was the exploitation of labor by private capital. Black intellectuals who continued to interpret history, social relations, and economic conditions along racial lines were denounced by these younger spokesmen as "anachronisms."[34] Black writers, Richard Wright counseled, should transcend nationalism for the "highest possible pitch of social consciousness."[35] The poet Sterling Brown told a gathering at the 1937 National Negro Congress that "the Negro artist who will be worth his salt, must join with those who are recording a world of injustice and exploitation."[36] Langston Hughes enjoined black writers to end their absorption in the "soul world" and become one of the major instruments in the achievement of working-class goals. In literature they should emphasize the proletarian class in their works. Those who continued to see African Americans in terms of group culture and "race genius" were considered hopelessly outdated and far outside the mainstream of American literature.[37]

This leftist view of literature and art had prompted McKay to establish the black writers' guild and oppose Boardman's membership. He hoped that a professional organization for black writers would encourage younger writers and keep them out of the destructive clutches of the Communists. Politically, McKay had turned 180° since his period of support for and affiliation with the Communist party in the early twenties.[38] By now, he suspected that, under the guise of class consciousness, the Communists had infiltrated groups of black artists, were attempting to seduce all the black writers who were on relief, and ultimately planned to control the black population through such organizations as the National Negro Congress. Only a determined countermovement sponsored by blacks would prevent a Communist triumph.[39]

His fear was not without some basis. During the summer of 1935, frightened by the growing specter of Germany's belligerence under Hitler and the rise of Fascist movements throughout Europe, the Communists called on comrades worldwide to temporarily abandon their goal of world revolution and to join with liberals in a Popular Front to stop the spread of fascism. The American Communist party launched a determined effort to adapt its ideology, tactics, and structure to meet the demands of the new Popular Front strategy. This, according to Mark Naison, was particularly evident in the emergence of the Communist party as an important focal point of political and cultural activity for Harlem intellectuals. The Communists sought to, and indeed did, gain influence over important black writers and artists. One party organizer recalled that 75 percent of the black cultural figures held party membership or maintained regular meaningful contact with the party.[40]

Without a doubt, one of the most notable aspects of the Popular Front had been the ability of a relatively small number of Communists to dominate organizations filled with non-Communists. While there were fewer than 100,000 American Communists at any one time, their energy and commitment caused a host of labor unions, youth groups, peace organizations, civil rights bodies, and a number of miscellaneous clubs, gatherings, and assemblies to faithfully follow the party's political directives.[41]

Among black intellectuals Countee Cullen, for example, accepted an invitation to attend the *Harlem Liberator* banquet in honor of Benjamin Davis, the black Communist councilman in New York City.[42] Langston Hughes, as president of the Communist League of Struggle for Human Rights, greeted the Communist Friends of the Soviet Union Convention. Hughes, the most outspoken of the black artists, traveled to the Soviet Union, associated with Arthur Koestler and Boris Pasternak, contributed to *Izvestia, International Literature, New Masses*, and the Communist party publications for blacks, and founded left-wing Negro theater and literary groups in Chicago, Harlem, and Los Angeles.[43]

Such support among Harlem influentials caused McKay to bitterly complain that Hughes and nearly every black intellectual had become tools of the Communist party. To his literary agent, Carl Cowl, he wrote, "Mr. Hughes is kept in the public eye by the Commies and certain liberals. I don't care a damn if I am not always in the public eye, for I am not that kind of a writer. But Soviet Russia controls Negro writing, directly or indirectly; the Urban League and even the NAACP are subservient to Soviet Russia."[44]

McKay's invitation to join the League of American Writers in 1937 had strengthened his belief in the necessity of creating a black writers' guild. He had joined the league under the impression that it was composed of writers of all political persuasions. However, at the opening meeting of the league, McKay was convinced by attacks on certain individuals that the league was being used solely to promote Communist propaganda. In an "Open Letter" to James Rorty, poet and cofounder of the *New Masses*, a

Communist publication, he made public his disappointment with the league. He reiterated his fear of Communist domination of all writers (black and white) and warned that the world had been divided into two camps of people: those who still believed in democracy and people who preferred dictatorship. More disturbing, he continued, was the lack of outrage and any show of protest by intellectuals who supposedly cherished the right to independent thinking, discussion, and criticism.[45]

A year later he was still publicly denouncing the league. He accused certain unnamed writers of lending their prestige and influence to set up a dictatorship of "letters." The league was being run as a political instrument, based on the Stalinist principle of "rule or ruin."[46] McKay may well have exaggerated the influence of the Communists in the League of American Writers. By the time the Second American Writers' Congress met in June 1937, the openly pro-Communist tone of the first 1935 meeting had all but disappeared. In accordance with the new Popular Front strategy of alliances with "progressive" capitalism, not only had the proletarian literary movement been abandoned, but the party's cultural leaders even hailed literary patriotism. Absent from the list of participants at the 1937 congress were party politicians such as Browder and many party intellectuals—among them Michael Gold, Joseph Freeman, and Granville Hicks. Hicks was so upset that he complained to the league's secretary that the Communists had been shoved into the background. Few of the members of the executive committee of the league were now open Communists.[47]

Throughout the latter thirties McKay remained one of the few members of his group to oppose what he termed the "fraudulent International Popular Front." It was impossible, McKay wrote to a friend, to believe that a dictatorship as ruthless and unscrupulous as the Russians could be trusted to lead a combination of democratic forces.[48] They were masters of deceit, appealing to the most primitive human wants: freedom and equality. In 1938 he protested in the *New York Amsterdam News* what he felt was the persecution of non-Communist workers by the Communists, whom he believed controlled unemployed workers and the Works Progress Administration laborers.[49] The Communists' deceitful appeal to unconditional fraternity and equality between white and black workers against social injustice accounted for their success. Moreover, "The launching of the Popular Front simultaneously with the New Deal WPA," he wrote, "gave the Communists . . . vast influence among colored professional groups."[50] McKay felt the Communists with their Popular Front were a greater threat to the free world than Hitler's Nazi Germany. He declared, "I cannot deny the fact that in my opinion Bolshevism is more dangerous to the world than Nazism. I don't think Hitler ever had a chance to make his doctrine international. Whoever wanted to join the Bund in America but Germans? But every sentimentalist of all races wants to join the Communist Party because it is hooked up with the idea of helping the long suffering working class and abused and exploited people."[51] They "skunked" behind the smoke screens of the People's Front and collective security, supporting the indefensible imperialistic interests of European nations and deliberately deceiving the American people. Even more devious, McKay declared, was Communist manipulation of real issues to promote their propaganda, especially that pertaining to blacks.[52] The Communist party thrived by exploiting the poverty and misery, social discrimination and degradation, and insults that people of African descent had to endure.[53]

McKay's personal disdain for the Communists prevented him from acknowledging that many Communists—their commitment to the Comintern and its policies notwithstanding—were sincerely interested in helping blacks. During the thirties Communists frequently challenged the unequal system of justice afforded blacks in America. The Communists were quick to offer assistance to nine black young men when they were arrested and charged with raping two white women on a freight train near Scottsboro, Alabama, in 1931.[54] Not long before, the Communists had fought to free fellow comrade Angelo Herndon, a black worker sent to Atlanta, Georgia, in 1931 to organize biracial unemployment councils. Herndon was arrested shortly after he organized a biracial demonstration at the county courthouse and charged with "inciting to insurrection." Herndon was sentenced to twenty years imprisonment, but the party eventually succeeded in having the insurrection law overturned and Herndon freed. The party had also been active in organizing black sharecroppers crushed under the weight of southern white oppression. The party even attempted to rid itself of "white chauvinism"—one of McKay's most frequent and long-held criticisms of the Communist party.[55]

McKay's critique of the Soviets proved to be partially accurate. In 1939 the Popular Front period came to an abrupt end with the Hitler-Stalin pact, the invasion of Poland by German and Russian armies, Poland's subsequent division and absorption by the two countries, and the start of World War II.[56] "Just as I believed would happen," McKay wrote, "after loosing confusion among Democratic peoples, the Russian dictatorship betrayed them to the Nazis." He denounced those sentimental idiots who had insisted that the Russian dictatorship was better than the Nazi dictatorship because it did not publicly persecute Jews and other minorities. "I believe the Russian brand is worse," he wrote, "for the Nazis from the first informed the world that they were opposed to international brotherhood."[57]

The Comintern immediately demanded that the American Communist party drop antifacism as a political goal. American Communists were now ordered to work to keep America out of the "imperialist war" and to direct their energies against social democratic leaders, including Roosevelt, who attempted to mobilize American aid for Britain and France.[58] The American Communists, forced to abandon goals that linked African Americans and America's destiny in a forceful and persuasive way, now began to focus more on international issues and to deemphasize mobilizing community protest for increased home and work relief. Following Soviet orders, the party devoted most of its energy to promoting Communist-desired changes in American foreign policy and downplayed efforts to achieve domestic, economic and social reforms.[59]

Following the Nazi–Soviet pact, a chorus of black voices joined McKay's continued denunciation of the Soviet Union. Harlem nationalists claimed that the pact exposed the treachery behind Communist internationalism. Influential black liberals who had soft-pedaled their criticism of the Soviet Union during the Popular Front period now argued that the pact proved that Soviet idealism was an elaborate sham and that the Russians practiced power politics in "exactly the same manner as Hitler, the Japanese, Italians, the British and French." Even long-time radical allies of the Left, such as Adam Clayton Powell, Jr., criticized the Communist party for betraying antifacism.[60]

McKay's appraisal of the Communists following the Hitler–Stalin treaty echoed the general sentiment of most Americans. But the Russian decision to enter into an alliance with Hitler was not nearly so Machiavellian or manipulative as McKay had charged. For American Communists the Soviet agreement with Hitler and such subsequent events as the dismemberment of Poland and the Russian invasion of Finland marked a major division in American Communist history. Before the Hitler–Stalin agreement the Communist party had enjoyed a period of significant growth and influence in the United States, but thereafter the party went into decline. Al Richmond, a party member, has described his shock and confusion about the Soviet "volte face." He also noted that the party's troubles "essentially stemmed from a compulsion to turn Soviet diplomatic necessity into an American political virtue."[61] From the Soviet point of view, the treaty with Hitler was a diplomatic necessity. The refusal of the Western powers to enter into any effective collective security arrangement had forced the Soviets into unilateral action to ensure that they were not the first target of Nazi attack. As Harry Haywood recollected, "The Soviet policy had consistently urged joint action against facist aggression, but the capitalist governments were not interested."[62]

At any rate, no American black, with perhaps the exception of A. Philip Randolph (who made militant anti-Communism a central tenet of his political credo following his resignation from the Communist-infiltrated National Negro Congress), could match the intensity and relentlessness with which McKay attacked the Communists. His vision of communism by 1944 stood in stark contrast to his Soviet apologetics of 1923: "I had a romantic hope that Communism would usher in a classless society and make human beings happier. All I saw in Russia was that Communism was using one class to destroy the other and making people more miserable, which was contrary to what my idea of Communism was." McKay not only reversed himself regarding the Soviet

Union, he also repudiated Marxism in its entirety: "The idea of a fratricidal class war 'is contrary to the ideal of humanity.'"[63]

Although he was criticized for exaggerating Communist influence among blacks, especially in Harlem, McKay took every opportunity to attack the Communists. Much of his *Harlem: Negro Metropolis*, a nonfiction work on Harlem published in 1940, was devoted to describing the extent of Communist influence among black people.[64] His preoccupation with the Communists sometimes became extreme. Writing to Eastman, he predicted that the United States and England would get their just deserts for allowing the German people to be crushed by the Russians, a nation inferior in culture and government.[65] He appeared before the Dies Committee, an anti–New Deal precursor of HUAC, and was questioned about Communist propaganda among Harlemites. His scathing denunciation of the Communists delighted Congressman Martin Dies, who lectured McKay on the need for blacks to seek honest leaders.[66] As late as 1947, McKay was still waging his personal war against the Communist party. FBI agents questioned him about the Soviet Union. At the time McKay was working on a book about Russia and Stalin, which was never completed or published. McKay amazed the FBI agents with the intensity of his denunciation of the Communists.[67] His attitude toward the Communists is best summed up in a comment he made to a friend in 1947: he remarked that he would not care if every Communist was "spiked in the behind and left to die on a pole."[68]

McKay was convinced that the Communists were out to get him—and had used their influence to hurt him since 1923. Early in March 1939 McKay was dismissed from the Writers' Project of the Works Progress Administration after a new rule barred aliens from such employment. By this time McKay was practically a citizen: he had the right to travel on an American passport, and he was waiting for the call to take the oath of allegiance. He unsuccessfully tried to receive an exemption from the new rule, or, as an alternative, to be allowed to take a leave of absence and return when his papers were in order.[69] He attributed both his dismissal and his failure to be granted special consideration to Communist animosity: "I think my recent article in the *New Leader*, attacking the Popular Front Press and blaming the debacle of the Spanish Republic on its native Moroccan policy, is what decided them to get me finally."[70]

In the article, McKay had criticized the newly proclaimed Spanish Republic for its suppression of incipient nationalism in Spanish Morocco. He also accused the French Popular Front of failing to defend the social rights and aspirations of the North African native nationalists against French-colonial aggression. Instead, they supported the side of reaction and attempted to cover up their shameful policy by claiming that the nationalists had been inspired by Fascist agents and were Fascist-minded.[71]

At times, McKay's preoccupation with the Reds was obsessive. "The Reds," he once shouted to Ellen Tarry, "they've gotten control. But I'm going to get them out somehow."[72] In his mind, the Communists were responsible for his failure to get manuscripts published; for initiating a whispering campaign that he was a racist chauvinist and therefore a Fascist, also a Moslem and pro-Arab, and therefore anti-Semitic; and for commissioning Roi Ottley to write *New World a Coming,* which—McKay felt—was published to draw attention away from and to hurt the sales of McKay's own *Harlem: Negro Metropolis.*[73] But McKay refused to "cringe and whine to that slimy gang," even if it meant sleeping in the gutter. However, he was not opposed to relocating out of Harlem to Washington, D.C., or to some other city where the Communists were not so powerful.[74]

That the "Reds" were responsible for all of McKay's problems is patently absurd. During the last years of his life he simply added "Communists" to his list of hates, which already included light-skinned Negroes, black American intellectuals, and the black middle class. Throughout his life, rather than accept personal responsibility for poor judgments, problems arising from his own character flaws, or mistaken life choices, McKay placed blame on external agents: mulattoes in Jamaica, the black middle class or Communists in the United States. McKay had an exaggerated opinion of his own impact and influence on the world around him, and a matching exaggerated opinion of society's interest in him. He credited only himself when he achieved a success; he blamed everyone but himself when he suffered a failure.

McKay's fixation with the Communists profoundly influenced the remainder of his life. In 1914, he had gravitated naturally toward radical philosophies but by 1944, McKay wanted to escape the burden of "isms."[75] But his hatred and fear of the Communists pushed him to embrace one more "ism," the only one he thought powerful enough to protect him from their shadowy omnipresence: Catholicism.

8

A Long Way from Home

BY THE 1930S McKay had finally realized the inevitable influence of race. It had been evident both in his attempts at reviving a literary movement among blacks and in his opposition to the Communists. With even greater determination and amidst public controversy, he extended his racial nationalism to economics.

Throughout the Depression era, strong nationalist tendencies were clearly visible in the economic realm, notwithstanding the popularity of the economic radicals. Exponents of bourgeois economic nationalism found a degree of success through their advocacy of "Double Duty Dollar" movements and the more popular "Don't Buy Where You Can't Work" campaigns.[1] The Double Duty Dollar movements urged blacks to buy from Negroes—making the dollar do double duty by purchasing both a commodity and "advancing the race."[2] At least thirty-five cities witnessed pickets and boycotts by "Don't Buy Where You Can't Work" campaigns struggling to get employment for African Americans in white-owned businesses. Some, for example, those in Cleveland and New York, lasted for years, often engaging large segments of the black community and securing significant numbers of jobs for blacks.[3] The "Don't Buy Where You Can't Work" campaigns were embraced by a diverse spectrum of organizations concerned with black economic advancement, from the nationally based National Association for the Advancement of Colored People to the purely local, nationalist street-corner speakers such as Sufi Abdul Hamid.[4] McKay's defense of Hamid underscores his continuing retreat to racial chauvinism.

During the early thirties Hamid, a former Garveyite, had gained some fame for his fairly successful "More Jobs for Negroes: Buy Where You Work" campaign against Chicago's white merchants. In 1933, Hamid decided to take his campaign to New York's Harlem. There Hamid organized the Negro Industrial and Clerical Alliance to protest the refusal of white merchants to hire black clerks in their stores.[5] From atop soapboxes and on the picket lines, Hamid, dressed in a brightly colored cape, Russian long boots, and a Hindu-style turban, denounced white merchants and called for racial solidarity among blacks to exact jobs from white businesses. Hamid's group experienced some success in the smaller stores on 135th Street, but on the main thoroughfare, 125th Street, his group met determined resistance from the larger white merchants.[6] In May 1934, Hamid moved against Woolworth's 125th Street store after the manager refused to hire members of his group as sales clerks. He appealed to Harlemites to boycott the store.[7] Eventually, some of the stores capitulated and agreed to hire some blacks as clerks. However, in the midst of the campaign that had widened to include other groups, such as the Citizens League (an alliance of Harlem's churches, newspapers, social and political clubs), Hamid was arrested on charges of spreading "anti-Semitism." The arrest followed a meeting between the mayor of New York and a committee of Jewish Minute Men. Hamid was dubbed the "Black Hitler in Harlem" by the Jewish newspapers, the *Day* and the *Bulletin.* After several days of court testimony, Hamid was acquitted, but his effectiveness as an organizer to secure jobs for blacks thereafter diminished.[8]

McKay, who had been following the Sufi affair, became increasingly alarmed at its implications for black self-help and race consciousness. McKay now wrote of a Harlem very different from the one he had described in *Home to Harlem:* a grim Harlem, devastated by a depression that had broken the facade of the Harlem masses' happy-go-lucky, hand-to-mouth existence. The depression only added to white exploitation of black Harlem. Jobs once conceded as "Negro" jobs disappeared, and black white-collar workers, cut off from the opportunity of downtown employment, sullenly watched whites come into the black belt to find jobs when they could not find work anywhere else. And as if to add insult to injury, McKay wrote, "Wherever an ethnologically related group of people is exploited, the exploiters operate on the principle of granting certain concessions as sops. In Harlem the exploiting group is overwhelmingly white. And it gives no sops."[9]

McKay felt that "Don't Buy Where You Can't Work" campaigns of 1933–34 were a natural and justified response to discrimination. He wrote that the label of "Black Hitler" had been calculatingly placed on Hamid by "certain gangsters of opportunism." And in doing so, they tragically discredited any attempts blacks made to organize consumers and tenants to win concessions from merchants and landlords.[10] The difficulty between blacks and Jews, McKay explained to a Jewish acquaintance, was an expression not of anti-Semitism but of the employer-employee relationship. The fact was that most of the landlords and employers in Harlem were Jews. Black opposition would have been the same toward the Anglo-Saxon, the German, or the Irish.[11] McKay went out of his way to indicate that Jewish middlemen were not directly responsible for the deplorable conditions existing in Harlem or any other black belt: "Such conditions are the heritage of the system of Negro slavery; they are the by-product of the policy of special economic discrimination and prejudice which the ruling majority has perpetuated against the colored minority."[12] More emphatically he remarked that "Anti-Semitism is a disease of Europe and white Christianity. And Afro-American victims of the fiery cross must not be dragged into the vortex of anti-Semitism."[13]

McKay's staunch support of Hamid's efforts to provide better jobs in the community, his denunciation of "those" who even after he died continued to brand Sufi anti-Semitic, and his unwavering belief that Negroes should organize among themselves, invited insinuations that he, too, was anti-Semitic. Tom Poston, a Negro reviewer for the *New Leader,* had not only suggested this, but also charged McKay with espousing economic segregation for the African American in his critical review of *Harlem: Negro Metropolis.* In replying to Poston, McKay aggressively denied any anti-Semitism and emotionally declared:

> What I do advocate is the greater social and cultural development of the sprawling, backward Negro community-breeding place of crime and disease, mumbo-jumbo jungle of cultists and occulists, paradise of policy players. I advocate the uplifting of the Negro community to American standards—that encouragement and aid be given to the development of more community enterprises, that Negro workers be permitted to organize with or without white workers.[14]

McKay did not consider himself anti-Semitic, but he resented the Jewish claim that Jews were "brother-sufferers" with the Negro, when the truth was that some Jews economically oppressed blacks. Unlike most black intellectuals, who, as Harold Cruse has argued, "either have been uncritically pro-Jewish or critically tongue-tied," McKay took a forthright position (at least privately) on the domestic implication of Jews vis-à-vis blacks. [15] McKay wrote to Eastman that he was sure the Jews were angry at him about his *Harlem: Negro Metropolis* for its criticism of Jewish groups like the Minutemen for their attacks against Hamid. It was silly of the Jews or anyone else to believe he had "race prejudice" against them. But he felt morally obligated to show what he considered to be Jewish intrigue in Harlem against Sufi. Jews were wrong to label Hamid a Black Hitler: "the whole thing," McKay concluded, "lies in the fact that the Jews, now persecuted by Hitler, want to pretend to the Negro people that the Jewish people are better than other white people. But there is no such thing as one people being better than the other." The *New Leader*, which had published Tom Poston's negative review, and the *Jewish Frontier*, McKay charged, functioned less as social magazines than Jewish propaganda organs, obsessed with Hitler's attitude toward them; they wanted the United States to enter the war against Germany and used the Negro as a "cat's paw."[16]

In spite of McKay's eagerness to "get away and stay away from the Jewish problem," he continued to rail privately at what he considered their self-righteous hypocrisy. He believed that the Jewish claim to "oppressed status" was seriously compromised by Jewish hypocrisy in international relations. The *Jewish Frontier*, McKay wrote to Eastman, was the most bigoted minority journal he had ever read—an organ of Palestine Zionists. Indeed, the Zionists had set up a colonial system in Palestine just like the French in Morocco or the British in the West Indies. This "anachronism" of a Zionist Palestine set up with American dollars and British bayonets was one of the most detestable forms of modern capitalism in existence. [17] McKay did not deny that Jews had suffered and were suffering under Nazism. "Certainly," McKay wrote to Eastman in 1945, "what Hitler is trying to do to the Jews in Europe, denying them political and social rights, taking their money, etc., is just what has been done to the Negro in the South."[18]

Undeterred by charges of anti-Semitism, McKay continued to

support groups and organizations advocating economic nationalism. He was convinced that the depression had ushered in a new era in relations between labor and capital. Soon labor would constitute the only countervailing force against the unbridled power of capital, and the Negro had to ally himself with one or be crushed between the two.[19] And as long as white labor unions remained prejudiced, selfish, and bigoted, black workers should organize separate unions to fight for greater economic advantages, even if blacks had to become scabs to achieve improvements in their status.[20]

It was for this reason that in 1937 McKay supported the all-black Harlem Labor Union. Organized by Ira Kemp in 1936, the Harlem Labor Union was not a genuine labor union, but a nationalist organization that grew out of the "Don't-Buy-Where-You-Can't-Work" campaigns and competed with several other groups in trying to get jobs for blacks in stores on 125th Street.[21] In the early thirties, Kemp, along with Arthur Reid of the African Patriotic League, a spin-off of the Universal Negro Improvement Association, argued for the development of black businesses and the creation of economically self-sufficient black communities. Kemp and Reid tried to organize a boycott of Italian icemen in Harlem. Kemp argued that money given to Italian icemen went directly to Mussolini to defeat black Ethiopia, and that blacks should instead advance black interest at home and abroad by supporting Negro businesses.[22]

The Harlem Labor Union attempted to place unemployed blacks in jobs in Harlem stores and to become the sole bargaining agent for Harlem's black workers. The Harlem Labor Union greeted CIO trade union activism with growing skepticism and outright hostility. Committed to winning black control of Harlem's economy, the union regarded CIO unionization drives in Harlem's retail sector as a threat to its efforts to force Harlem storeowners to hire black workers and to make "race consciousness" the guiding principle in black economic life. Because of their success in securing jobs for black workers, Kemp and Reid represented a formidable threat to the American Federation of Labor and the Congress of Industrial Organizations unions trying to organize Harlem.[23] Kemp, a Republican nominee for assemblyman, denounced white discrimination against black workers in the nation's trade unions, charging that both the AFL and the CIO were indifferent to black workers. Kemp charged that the CIO was even more dangerous than the AFL because its rhetoric concerning the goal of racial equality was used to disguise the unions' own discrimination against blacks.[24]

The Harlem Labor Union's activities provoked considerable opposition from Harlem's intellectuals, liberals as well as radicals; from Italian Americans, because of their attempted boycott of Italian-American merchants; from Jewish Americans who took exception to Kemp's and Reid's speeches against Jewish store-owners and landlords; and from the Communists, for their opposition to interracial labor solidarity as a principle, and their encouragement of black workers to serve as strikebreakers in industrial disputes. Labor organizations criticized the Harlem Labor Union for offering Harlem employers contracts that provided lower wages than industrial "union scale" and a promise of industrial peace, thereby aiding and abetting employer resistance to the activities of established unions. Despite opposition, Kemp and Reid succeeded in creating a place for themselves in Harlem's retail sector and commanded a sizable following among the unemployed and marginal workers of Harlem. The Harlem Labor Union's success resulted, according to Mark Naison, from "their appeals to black solidarity which struck a responsive chord among the Harlemites who had been left out of the New Deal programs and remained divorced from organized labor, and their capacity to win jobs, however low paying."[25]

McKay was not troubled by the Harlem Labor Union's dubious claim to being a genuine union, and agreed in principle with Kemp's assessment of the major unions. But he also recognized that in the long run the future of the black worker rested with the general labor movement. The idea of an independent black union was not supported by the majority of blacks, despite their dissatisfaction with the national unions. McKay felt that Negro organizers had to promote black interests by agitating for more and better positions within the national unions, against the intrigues of reactionary workers and "Machiavellian" employers.

But McKay also felt that such organizations as the Harlem Labor Union did serve a useful function for the black worker. Black workers, angered that white workers continually got the

best positions within the national unions, would join the independent black labor organizations and constitute an indictment and
challenge to the general labor movement.[26]

Appearing in the 1937 issue of the *Nation,* McKay's analysis of
the labor situation drew sharp comments from Adam Clayton
Powell, Jr., assistant minister of the Abyssinian Baptist Church
and columnist for the *New York Amsterdam News.* Powell charged
that the *Nation's* "fair haired boy" had distorted the labor situation in Harlem and advocated the dangerous philosophy of
"nationalism." Powell felt that the Harlem Labor Union could
never achieve any success for the Negro worker. Its success was
predicated on underselling the national labor unions by accepting
wages for its members lower than wages demanded by the American Federation of Labor and the Congress of Industrial Organizations. Powell believed that out of necessity the majority of blacks
would have to find jobs in job markets outside of Harlem, and
consequently the Harlem Labor Union's tactics might actually
boomerang.

Besides being impractical, nationalism was dangerous because
its appeal and success could only be temporary, as with any
nationalistic movement. Powell did not deny that nationalism
always had an appeal, but for the black man in America, such a
movement would be tantamount to committing racial suicide. The
only hope of any minority group in a democracy lay through
assimilation, especially in the field of labor. The future of the black
working masses was tied up with the great trade movements that
were sweeping across America. Therefore, the task before the
black man was to fight his way into the unions and to expand union
strength and power. For Powell, this constituted the only hope for
the black masses to achieve economic freedom.[27]

In some respects, Powell's criticism of McKay had been unfair
and slanted, as McKay pointed out in a rebuttal published in the
New York Amsterdam News. At no time did he use the word
"nationalism" in his article, and it was shamefully inconsistent
that a man who shepherded the largest flock of blacks in the world
should decry the efforts of Negro communities to build themselves up socially and politically to the American standard of living
by labeling such social aspiration "nationalism." Furthermore,
McKay retorted, "None has ever been asinine enough to imagine

that all the Negroes in New York could find jobs in Harlem. No leader, however chauvinistic, could advocate the driving out of white businessmen from the Negro community and in the same breath demand better jobs in their community." Powell and other would-be-intellectuals confused nationalism with racialism, a confusion he felt manifest in Powell's blessing of Kemp's independent labor movement from the pulpit of the Abyssinian Baptist Church, where he had exhorted his congregation to support Kemp.[28]

Powell had also chosen to distort McKay's intent by casting doubt on his credibility, captiously remarking on McKay's sociopolitical beliefs: "We saw him run the entire gamut from liberal to Communist and then limp the rest of the way from Trotskyite to Nationalist. We were told that he had drunk deeply of the heady wine that flowed from Lenin and Marx but was returning to the good old corn of Nationalism."[29] Such aspersion was not easy for McKay to dismiss, for his life had been characterized by flirtations with many of the things Powell alluded to. Yet McKay had not, as Powell intimated, advocated nationalism in its extreme form. His racialism, or race chauvinism, was black nationalism of the simplest expression: he advocated racial solidarity, which had no ideological or programmatic implications beyond his desire that black people organize themselves on the basis of their common color and oppressed condition to move in some way to alleviate their situation. His support of the Harlem Labor Union constituted such an attempt. At no time did he exclude the necessity of working with and in the white national trade unions.[30]

But McKay's "racialism" continued to bring him into conflict with other spokesmen in the black community. Columnist George Schuyler, for example, called McKay a black Fascist and anti-Semite. Schuyler maintained that all schemes for racial organization of Negroes implied segregation and isolation. McKay defended himself against Schuyler's charges by first pointing out that his article on black labor unions dealt only with blacks in Harlem, where many were excluded from white unions and forced to work secretly. It seemed only logical to McKay that this bootleg labor be organized into black unions to fight such restrictions.[31]

That blacks as a group had to make special efforts to lift and protect themselves had been made clear to him during his three

years living in Africa, which he thought were like "three generations of experience." In Africa McKay learned that it was possible
for different groups to exist side by side in social competition
without any group surrendering its soul and advocating its own
extinction.[32] It was regrettable that whenever the Negro took
measures to protect and strengthen his precarious economic position through group solidarity he became the object of such epi-
thets as "anti-Semitic."

McKay steadfastly refused to abandon his emphasis on "race"
and leadership, even though his efforts tended to be viewed by
many as black nationalism.[33] In the face of complaints that his
ideas would lead to segregation, he reiterated his position that
fear of segregation paralyzed the black community, retarding its
progress in politics, culture, business, and labor. The black community was ever agitated and divided over segregation, producing
a form of paranoia. McKay complained that the Negro community
would refuse the building of a hospital for blacks, believing a
blacks-only hospital might lead to the total exclusion of black
doctors and patients from white hospitals. But such concern
would be derided as foolish in an Italian, Irish, or Jewish community.[34]

McKay deplored the reality that 95 percent of the businesses
in Harlem were owned by whites, while capable and educated
blacks had to suffer quietly without work. In most American
communities, businesses recognized their responsibility to give
employment to local people, but in black communities businesses
ignored potential black workers. Meanwhile, the black community, overly concerned about racial chauvinism, abrogated its
social responsibility for such deplorable conditions. The Kemps
and Sufis who advocated racial solidarity were not the ones who
posed a danger to the black community. The danger came from
the Powells and Schuylers who "had made a league with death and
a covenant with hell for the extermination of the Negro group."[35]

McKay's concern for the problems facing the black community,
including Communism and the exploitation of black workers by
national labor unions, continued into the 1940s, though not with
the same vigor. With the publication of *Harlem: Negro Metropolis*
in 1940, he began the final phase of what had been a hectic life. He
was not any less the fighter he had been in 1920, but his battles

over literature, class, radical politics, and race had understandably taken something out of him. His personality, passionate and tempestuous, had prevented him from forming many close personal friendships. The one African American with whom McKay had developed a close relationship, James Weldon Johnson, had died in June 1938. It had been Johnson who had given McKay a farewell party on the eve of his departure for the Soviet Union, and it was Johnson whom McKay felt came closest to approaching his appreciation of the nature of the Harlem Renaissance. Both Johnson and McKay had agreed that the Renaissance had not come into being as a "deformed sport fathered by white publishers; rather, it existed as part of the continuum of black creativity." On June 30, at Salem Methodist Church in Harlem, McKay joined Countee Cullen, Langston Hughes, Carl Van Vechten, Walter White, W. E. B. Du Bois and over a thousand other mourners to say goodbye to Johnson.[36] In 1924 McKay had remarked to Walter White that he was a "son of a bitch," when it came to personal relationships. Now, in 1940, little had changed: he continued to like "so few people."[37]

Yet, he was pained not to receive an invitation to the inauguration of Charles S. Johnson as president of Fisk University in 1947. Hughes, Van Vechten, and other writers had been invited. Whether the omission was intentional cannot be determined, but McKay—of course—assumed an intentional insult.[38] He also felt slighted by an article written by Arna Bontemps a few months later. The article on black poets mentioned Langston Hughes and Countee Cullen, but did not include even a brief reference to McKay. Though hurt by his omission, McKay typically turned disappointment into accusation, claiming that he had no desire to be used by "spineless and spiteful Negro Intellectuals."[39]

In spite of McKay's race consciousness, his feelings about African Americans remained tortured, or at best ambivalent. Even as he promoted his literary and economic programs, he continued to disparage African Americans, claiming that most American Negroes were insincere sycophants, wanting to obtain a free mess of pottage from white people. Shortly before he died, McKay refused to allow an African American to write the preface to a new edition of *Harlem Shadows:* "I don't want any American Negro hand to soil my work. . . . There isn't one who is fit." McKay preferred to have his poems introduced by Dr. John Dewey, a white Englishman.[40]

Despair characterized the final years of Claude's life. While he reviled African Americans, the idea of being a "problem," something he refused to accept during the earlier years, now played havoc with his self-esteem. The acceptance of the consequences of race was a painful admission for McKay in 1937: "It is hell to belong to a minority group. For to most members of the powerful majority you are not a person; you are a problem. I think I am a rebel mainly from psychological reasons, which have always been more important than economic. As a member of a weak minority, you are not supposed to criticize your friends of the strong majority. You will be damned mean and ungrateful."[41]

McKay's comment may have referred to Joel Spingarn, a white board member of the NAACP. In 1921 McKay had remarked that Spingarn was "nothing but a bourgeois philanthropist." Spingarn took exception to the remark and wrote Eastman that McKay was "tactless and suspicious, or at any rate a very hard man to help." As Spingarn put it to Eastman, who thoroughly agreed, "I don't mind being called a bourgeois philanthropist, but I don't like it from him when I have just got through helping find him a publisher."[42] Though Spingarn continued to help McKay over the years, he still chaffed over the insult. McKay's financial plight in 1934 had forced him to appeal once again to Spingarn for assistance and, in the process, to apologize for the 1921 remark: "I hate so much unwittingly to do anything to spoil one friendship after all these years and at this awful crisis in my life. I was fearfully hit by the boomerang of my mixed racial and social radicalism."[43] Apparently, McKay's apology was insufficient, because three years later he was again apologizing for the same offense. He implored Spingarn to finally put the issue to rest, adding, "I was sorry and now that you bring it up again, I can add nothing to a sincere apology."[44] That Spingarn had not put the issue to rest reflected his irritation that a "radical could not have his cake and eat it too," and his general discouragement that any problems, national, world, or racial, would be solved in his lifetime.[45] It was surely a tired Spingarn who commented to McKay that he would not be surprised if someday a Negro should stab him in the back after all the work he had done against white hostility.[46]

175

McKay fretted over the white tendency to lump all blacks together and to ignore their individuality. In 1937 he reacted almost violently to having his autobiography, A Long Way from Home, reviewed together with an autobiography by black Communist Angelo Herndon. Describing his own book, McKay noted that it was not intended as a traditional autobiography but as a recollection of his observations made in Europe and in Africa. The book was meant to detail his reactions as a "human being and as a Negro" to different environments. He hoped his book could become sort of a guidebook as to what an intelligent American Negro may gain from traveling. The reader should be able to use McKay's experiences to see and understand more clearly and broadly the social and cultural position of the American Negro in adjusting himself to American life. [47] But whatever his book succeeded in doing, McKay was sure it had nothing at all in common with a book by a Negro Communist: "The boy pulled off a big job and wrote a little about his young life and much about his ideas. But we are so different in everything except being Negroes. If John Lewis and Max Eastman published their autobiographies at the same time, I am sure the critics would not review them together, because both have radical ideas. But if Joe Louis had published his at the same time I did, they would have reviewed him together with me because we are both black!"[48]

A Long Way from Home and Harlem: A Negro Metropolis were both well reviewed but produced practically no sales. In fact, no one seemed interested in publishing any of McKay's manuscripts after 1940. Fourteen publishing companies refused to publish any of his new poetry or to reissue any of his earlier works. [49] Except for an occasional nonfictional piece, McKay's prose met the same fate. Herbert Weinstock, writing for Alfred Knopf, perhaps best expressed the sentiment of most publishers toward McKay's work when, in 1947, he noted, "I have now read the manuscripts by Claude McKay that you left me. I can't tell you how very disappointing I found them. Something, it seems to me has happened to McKay during the last decade or two that has robbed him of self-criticism. The poetry is flat for the most part, and the autobiographical sketch ["My Green Hills of Jamaica"] is fragmentary, superficial and not very interesting."[50]

McKay was just as unsuccessful at finding nonliterary employment. When he did find a job his employment ended in catastrophe. Elmer Carter, administrator of the Unemployment Insurance Appeal Board, sadly told McKay, "It is an awful tragedy that one so gifted as you should at anytime be financially embarrassed and it distresses me to no end."[51] Yet Carter could not procure McKay any employment. Early in 1942 McKay began seeking employment from the federal government. Hoping that the experience and knowledge he had gained from years of traveling would now prove valuable, McKay sought a job with the Office of War Information, in the area of African, West Indian, and American Negro affairs. Failing in this effort, he continued to seek employment in other branches of the government.[52] The exact nature of the other jobs he sought is unclear owing to McKay's penchant for melodrama. In his correspondence, McKay alludes to a series of interviews, preliminary and final examinations, and dark meetings with government officials. On one occasion he wrote Countee Cullen, "I have definite assurance of a job coming through very soon. I can't tell when and where for that must be kept a secret for the present."[53] On another occasion he apologized to Cullen for missing their engagement because he had had to leave Harlem and "drive to Westchester to see a man from Washington."[54] Given McKay's strong anti-Communist sentiment, he may have been seeking employment with some U.S. intelligence agency. Or, of course, he just may have been trying to make himself look significant in Cullen's eyes.

No "cloak and dagger" job materialized, but he did eventually find employment at the Federal Shipbuilding Yard at Newark, New Jersey, in 1943. Soon, however, McKay's health, which had troubled him for years, began to deteriorate rapidly. He had long suffered from hypertension and he now developed dropsy, an affliction involving the abnormal retention of body fluids, affecting the heart and other organs.[55] Three years earlier McKay had become seriously ill in his Harlem roominghouse. Ellen Tarry found him and enlisted the aid of Friendship House, a local Catholic social services agency. Friendship House provided McKay with a doctor, and volunteers from the house nursed McKay to a partial recovery, but he continued to suffer severe headaches. While working at the shipyard, McKay suffered a stroke.[56]

The stroke affected the left side of McKay's face and impaired his vision and ability to walk. From July to December 1943, McKay was in and out of New York hospitals where doctors tried to control his blood pressure. But, according to Eastman, his heart and kidneys were permanently damaged, and though the doctors believed he would survive for a while, they held out little hope for a full recovery.[57] In an attempt to control his blood pressure, one physician introduced McKay to an herb doctor who placed him on a diet restricted to fruits, vegetables, and fish.[58] McKay's fear of hospitals complicated his treatment. At times he refused a doctor's orders to enter the hospital, and on at least one occasion he left the hospital in the middle of treatment. He communicated his fear to Countee Cullen: "I don't think I'd want to go into the hospital again, for I have a clear idea of what's wrong. The stomach trouble is really a cause of the high blood pressure. And if I go to the hospital, they may take it into their heads to cut me open—as I understand they did to Bessye Bearden the wife of artist Romare Bearden [who died following surgery]."[59]

Friends such as Freda Kirchway and Eastman secured a place for McKay to recuperate at Squash Hollow, Connecticut. Squash Hollow rested down in a valley where the Berkshire Hills ended in Connecticut. There McKay recovered in a spacious bungalow in the deep woods five miles from New Milford.[60] But for all its loveliness and tranquillity, Squash Hollow was isolated and cold. Soon McKay began to grow irritable at the prospect of staying there past October into the winter months.[61] His introduction to the Catholic-run Friendship House via Ellen Tarry during his 1941 illness eventually provided him with the means to escape Squash Hollow's solitude.

Following his partial recovery in 1941, McKay occasionally visited Friendship House and established cordial relations with its staff.[62] The relationship quickly bore fruit. McKay was offered a job working for Bishop Bernard Sheil, the senior auxiliary of the archdiocese of Chicago. He moved to Chicago in the spring of 1944 to become Sheil's personal adviser on communism and the Negro and to serve as a lecturer in the Sheil School of Social Studies. McKay was to provide Sheil with information on the Russian Revolution and its subsequent developments.[63] The bishop had attracted considerable attention for his "outspoken" position on fascism, communism, and race relations. In an address before the annual CIO convention in 1945, he issued a ringing demand to oust fascism and establish real democracy in America. He also told the convention that by admitting blacks into membership on a basis of equality, the unions could destroy economic injustice and beat down the barriers of ill will.[64]

McKay had not been in Chicago long before he wrote Eastman that after doing a lot of reading and research on the Communist party and on Catholic work among blacks, he had decided to become a Catholic. His conversion to Catholicism has been generally misunderstood by historians. The frequent assertion that McKay submitted completely to the Catholic church is untrue. At best, McKay's conversion was a marriage of convenience and principle. McKay had never given himself completely to anything or anyone. His credo had always been "each soul must save itself," and his conversion to Catholicism was no exception to that philosophy.

For example, of primary importance in McKay's conversion was his discovery that the Catholic church was anti-Communist. "From the social angle," he wrote Eastman, "I am quite clear and determined: I know that the Catholic Church is the one great organization which can check the Communists and probably lick them."[65] He believed that the Stalinists, having failed to solve the economic problems of the Soviet Union, were now attempting to fool the common people of the world. The world was being threatened by dictators who, returning to a pre-Christian idea of human society, proclaimed that the ruler was God. But McKay also believed that Jesus Christ would save mankind from the Stalins and Hitlers.

McKay believed that the Catholic church's history had demonstrated its unique advantage over other denominations in meeting the threat of communism, fascism, nazism, and all the other "isms" he felt were sweeping the world. "I do believe that the ancient and medieval world had a wonderful asset, which we lack today," he wrote, "when a Pope of Rome, with the authority of Jesus, could say to a stubborn ruler: Stop! For what you do is contrary to the will of God!"[66] He condemned the Protestants as a denomination of jingoists, pushing nationalism even at the expense of trampling millions underfoot. A religion that had created slavery, and in the process brutalized the Negro to the level of a

179

beast, could never hope to provide stability and unity for the world.[67] McKay went as far as to declare in a published article that the Catholic church had always been free of racial prejudice.[68]

There is no intellectual justification for McKay's historically inaccurate description of either the Protestant or the Catholic churches, but his twisted view of religious history helped defend him against friendly critics like Eastman, who implored McKay not to abandon his lifelong agnosticism and become a tool of the Catholic church. Writing to McKay, Eastman pleaded, "All these years, at such cost and with such heroism, you resisted the temptation to warp your mind and morals in order to join the Stalin Church. Why warp it the other way now for the Catholics."[69] McKay had already assured Eastman that while he was determined to become a Catholic for "sincere religious reasons," he would not change his attitudes about life and his way of living.[70]

In truth, McKay's religious convictions are suspect and probably of less importance than his anti-Communism and his practical concerns. With nowhere else to go and little money, he found that his position as personal adviser to a Catholic bishop gave him some significance again after years of semiobscurity. On several occasions, McKay gave talks to other members of the church.[71] The *Extension*, the biggest Catholic magazine, published an article about him.[72] His conversion to Catholicism would increase his chances of being published by a firm that catered to Catholic authors.[73] McKay admitted to a friend the benefits of his conversion: "It was a good thing I hooked up with the Catholics, instinctive I guess, for they have certainly taken good care of me. You see they all want me to live because they expect me to write more which will redound to their credit."[74]

The church did offer McKay much assistance and aid, but it certainly never intended to become his literary patron. No Catholic magazines agreed to publish any of McKay's work. Indeed, except for the *Catholic Worker*, the most radical of Catholic publications, they turned down all of his manuscripts. Attempting to get his last piece of prose, "My Green Hills of Jamaica," published by a Catholic press, he suggested to Bishop Sheil that he write the preface. McKay instructed the bishop to tell how "you heard that I was broken in body and spirit in New York and you read my poems and decided to bring me out to Chicago and work for the Catholic organization." But neither Sheil's preface nor McKay's baptism was enough to get the manuscript published by a Catholic press.[75] If McKay's fierce anticommunism figured significantly in his conversion, so, too, did his ambivalence regarding black Americans. The Catholic church became a refuge from which McKay exploded in a final gasp of anguish and vituperation. Fellow Catholic Betty Britton penned McKay a hasty note expressing her concern over his increasingly pessimistic outlook for the Negro.[76] McKay had written Britton that he believed that the Negro was a "lost group"—a topic he discussed in the unpublished manuscript "Right Turn to Catholicism." According to McKay, the Negro was not merely a lost remnant of a race, but a lost people without a soul of its own—a race whose eyes were turned not within to appraise and strengthen themselves, but without to the white world that despised them. McKay accused black leaders of a willingness to sell the Negro to any group for a price. Returning to the theme that had dominated McKay's thinking during the 1930s, he lashed out again at the pathetic inability of blacks to control their own destiny through self-realization and self-direction. The continued dashing of their heads against the wailing wall of segregation precluded any radical program for change, and especially the improvement of Negro slums. Blacks were the only group whose leaders were responsible to white leadership, instead of to their own people.[77]

By 1947 McKay's voice was touched with a sense of defeat and resignation. He maintained that since in the United States blacks were a special minority amid a majority of whites, the real issue for Negroes was adjustment and not segregation. When it "came to brass tacks," the Negro would finally have to depend on the goodwill of white America. Blacks far more than any other people in the New World needed a "Good Neighbor" policy.

"Right Turn to Catholicism" did not reveal much concerning McKay's decision to become a Catholic. It was a combination of expostulation, eulogy, and diatribe. Eulogistically he wrote, "As a West Indian, I brought my gifts to the United States. And as an American, I enrolled myself on the side of the American Negro." In the process he had met many more highly educated blacks in America than in Jamaica: doctors, lawyers, journalists, social workers, scientists, anthropologists, philosophers, and Rhodes

Scholars. But whoever he met wanted to talk about the Negro problem: "It was maddening. I found escape from it among the common Negroes, in barrooms, dancing halls and cabarets. I indulged in much eclectic reading. Twice I travelled to Europe on a shoestring. The second time I spent many years in Europe and North Africa. There, happily, I was not condemned to thinking and talking Negro all the time." But in the end, McKay wrote, he had managed to live, and would die, as an individual, a man of color, a poet, a writer, and a member of the human race.[78]

McKay's reflections on his life in "Right Turn to Catholicism" served as a fitting commentary on his life. Early the following year, on May 22, 1948, McKay died of heart failure in a Chicago hospital. After a Roman Catholic service, at which Bishop Sheil presided, he was taken back to Harlem for a final service and laid to rest in a Queens cemetery.[79]

Ellen Tarry recalled that Harlem was saddened at the news of his death. Accompanied by Harold Jackman and Countee Cullen, Tarry met and consoled Hope McKay, the daughter McKay had never seen. Like his life, McKay's death was not without an element of drama. According to Tarry, "Boyish mischief would have played around the corners of his eyes and mouth and he would have sworn that the 'Reds' were responsible for his mortal remains arriving in New York late—four hours after the Mass had been said in absentia." She believed, though, that the angry, bitter McKay of past years was at peace when God called him home to that part of Heaven where weary battle-scarred writers go.[80]

When Max Eastman learned that McKay had died, he commented to his wife: "It is sad to think of McKay, but he really stopped living years ago. Too bad, for he had such good brains and so much charm. Perhaps we should have kept him as a cook or a maid."[81] If McKay *had* stopped living years ago, his demise had been the direct result of living in a world dominated by color prejudice. There is something radically wrong, a writer once wrote, with an environment that causes people to think and act purely in terms of race rather than of humanity and country. Even Eastman, McKay's closest friend and associate, could not really understand the terrible agony McKay suffered because of his "blackness." Few whites could, though Bishop Sheil came close to true understanding. "It is impossible for us White Americans," the Bishop noted, "to imagine the effects of our racial practices on Negroes. The effect is highly disastrous where the cultural, sensitive Negro is concerned."[82]

While Sheil had been referring specifically to McKay, he could also have been referring to Du Bois, Schuyler, Toomer, Walrond, or a host of other black writers and intellectuals. In Claude McKay, one saw the extreme manifestation of this tragedy. It is not that McKay had not tried to avoid the opprobrium of race; he had, desperately. McKay had never demonstrated a gift of prophecy, but the following poem, written in 1916, suggests that he sensed that he would never return to the Jamaica of his youth and would die on alien soil:

> When I have passed away and am forgotten,
> And no one living can recall my face,
> When 'neath some alien sod my bones lie rotten
> With not a tree nor stone to mark the place,
> Perchance some pensive youth, with passion burning
> For olden song that smacks of love and wine,
> The musty pages of old volumes turning,
> May light upon a little song of mine.
> And he may softly hum the tune and wonder
> Who wrote the verses in the long ago;
> Or he may sit him down awhile to ponder
> Upon the simple words that touch him so.[83]

Notes

1. In Search of Larger Worlds

1. Max Eastman, ed., *Selected Poems of Claude McKay*, 7. McKay won the Mulgrave Silver Medal for Jamaican literature for *Songs of Jamaica*.
2. For a discussion of the impact of culture on writers, see Horace R. Cayton, "Ideological Forces in the Work of Negro Writers," in Herbert Hill, ed., *Anger and Beyond: The Negro Writer in the United States*, 37.
3. "My Green Hills of Jamaica," 10, 15; "Boyhood in Jamaica," 135.
4. "To Clarendon Hills and H. A. H.," stanza 1, in *Songs of Jamaica*, 106; reprinted in *The Dialect Poetry of Claude McKay*, vol. 2.
5. "Sukee," stanzas 4, 5, in *Constabulary Ballads*; reprinted in *The Dialect Poetry of Claude McKay*, 2:78–79.
6. Given the importance of the actual shades of color among Jamaicans, it should be noted that the word *black* refers literally to actual color and not to a racial generalization.
7. "A Negro Poet," 275–76. Translator's note in Claude McKay, *The Negroes in America*, xv; "Boyhood in Jamaica," 10, 15; Wayne Cooper, *Claude McKay: Rebel Sojourner in the Harlem Renaissance*, 10–11.
8. "My Green Hills," 10, 15.
9. "Boyhood in Jamaica," 141. Some individuals, including Max Eastman, asserted that McKay was a "full-blooded African." The idea is more romantic than accurate.
10. "My Mountain Home," stanzas 1–3, *Constabulary Ballads*, 124.
11. Ibid., stanzas 10 and 11.
12. "Boyhood in Jamaica," 141.
13. "A Negro Poet," 275–76.
14. "Boyhood in Jamaica," 137.
15. *Negroes in America*, xv.
16. "Boyhood in Jamaica," 140.
17. "My Mountain Home," stanza 6, *Constabulary Ballads*, 125.
18. *Negroes in America*, xv; Wayne Cooper, ed., *The Passion of Claude McKay: Selected Poetry and Prose, 1912–1948*, 3.
19. Preface to *Constabulary Ballads*, 1.
20. "To Inspector W. E. Clark," stanzas 1, and 2, *Constabulary Ballads*, 104.
21. "Bennie's Departure," stanza 2, *Constabulary Ballads*, 15.
22. Ibid., stanza 6, p. 63.
23. Ibid., stanza 18, p. 22. Also see, "Consolation," *Constabulary Ballads*, p. 62.
24. "The Heart of a Constab," *Constabulary Ballads*, 62.
25. Ibid., 63.

26. McKay believed that blacks were temperamentally unsuited to the "Force." Racially, they were all impatient of discipline.

27. "Free," *Constabulary Ballads*, 78.

28. "The Heart of a Constab," *Constabulary Ballads*, 62.

29. Eastman, *Selected Poems of Claude McKay*, 7. It is doubtful that Eastman's description of McKay's laughter as "that high, half-wailing falsetto laugh of the recklessly delighted Darky" would have pleased McKay. See "To E. M. E." in *Songs of Jamaica*, 51–52.

30. Cooper, *The Passion of Claude McKay*, 4.

31. "Hard Times," in *Songs of Jamaica*, 53–54.

32. "To E. M. E.," stanza 5, *Songs of Jamaica*, 52.

33. "Whe' Fe Do?" in *Songs of Jamaica*, 27–28.

34. *Songs of Jamaica*, 192.

35. Peter Abrahams, *Jamaica: An Island Mosaic*, 202–7; Kenneth Ramchand, *The West Indian Novel and Its Background*, 51–55. Tom Redcam was the penname for Thomas Henry MacDermont (1870–1933). As editor of the *Jamaican Times* between 1904 and 1923, MacDermont was noted for his comments on public affairs and his efforts in support of "The All Jamaica Library," an abortive project to create a book-buying public in Jamaica.

36. See Jekyll's obituary in the *Daily Gleaner* (19 August 1929) and in the *Handbook of Jamaica* (1930), 557. Also see Cooper, *Passion of Claude McKay*, 318–19.

37. Philip Sherlock, "The Living Roots," introduction to Walter Jekyll, *Jamaican Song and Story: Annancy Stories, Digging Songs, Dancing Tunes, and Ring Tunes*, vii.

38. Jekyll, *Jamaican Song and Story*, 1.

39. "My Green Hills," 63–64.

40. See "My Mountain Home," stanzas 7, 8, and 9, *Constabulary Ballads*, 125; "De Days Dat Are Gone," *Songs of Jamaica*, 59.

41. "The Hermit," *Songs of Jamaica*, 41.

42. "My Green Hills," 63–64.

43. Cooper, *Claude McKay*, 29–32.

44. Josephine Herbst to Harold Cruse, 18 November 1968; Josephine Herbst Papers, Yale University. Aside from her personal experience with McKay, Herbst had been told he was homosexual by a number of Claude's oldest friends on the *Liberator* staff.

45. McKay's transcript from Kansas State Agricultural College, Manhattan, Kansas.

46. "My Green Hills," 64.

47. Ibid., 11.

48. Ibid., 7.

49. Cooper, *Passion of Claude McKay*, 3.

50. Joel A. Rogers, "The West Indies," *Messenger*, November 1922, 526. Traveling through Jamaica in 1911, Bernard Shaw observed, "Jamaica is tropical, but not too tropical. You have no sunstrokes and no snakes and your colored population is neither enslaved or starved. But what is wrong here is that you produce a sort of man who is only a

colonial." He further commented that, if a Jamaican wanted his son to be a civilized man of the world in the best sense and belong to a great intellectual and artistic culture, he would have to send his son to Europe. What Jamaica needed, Shaw concluded, was the development of its own culture: theater, music, and literature. See "Interview with Bernard Shaw," *Daily Gleaner,* 4 September 1911, 12.

51. "My Green Hills," 7.

52. "My Native Land, My Home," stanza 1, *Songs of Jamaica,* 84.

53. Ibid., stanza 2, line 3.

54. "Old England." Stanza 6, line 4, *Songs of Jamaica,* 64. Also see Jean Wagner, *Black Poets of the United States: From Paul Laurence Dunbar to Langston Hughes,* 296.

55. "My Green Hills," 6.

56. Ibid., 8–9.

57. McKay to James W. Johnson, 5 September 1929; McKay Papers, James Weldon Johnson Collection, Yale University.

58. McKay to editor of the *Nation,* 23 May 1947; McKay Papers, Schomburg Collection, New York Public Library. McKay had written this letter in rebuttal to an article by Margret Marshall, who offered a less idyllic picture of Jamaica.

59. Philip D. Curtin, *Two Jamaicas: The Role of Ideas in a Tropical Colony 1830–1865,* 88–101. The emancipation of 1833 did not give unqualified freedom to all slaves. It stipulated that all slaves' children under six years of age be freed immediately. For the remainder, a six-year period of apprenticeship was mandated to acclimate the ex-slave to free wage labor.

60. Fernando Henriques, *Family and Colour in Jamaica,* 42–49.

61. David Cronon, *Black Moses: The Story of Marcus Garvey,* 9–11; Curtin, *Two Jamaicas,* 40; Henriques, *Family and Colour,* 52; Zora Neale Hurston, *Tell My Horse,* 16–18.

62. Henriques, *Family and Colour,* 67.

63. Cronon, *Black Moses,* 18–19, 40. Garvey also believed that because of association with the British Jamaican peasants had little opportunity to develop self-pride. For a discussion of Garvey's ideas concerning race and miscegenation, see Amy Jacques Garvey, ed., *Philosophy and Opinions of Marcus Garvey,* 18–19, 26.

64. Cronon, *Black Moses,* 18–19.

65. *Negroes in America,* 5.

66. "Right Turn to Catholicism."

67. Langston Hughes recalled an incident involving McKay that vivifies the dilemma of color among Jamaicans. While in Paris in 1923, Hughes met a mulatto woman from Jamaica. Hughes commented on McKay and his fine poem "Springtime in New Hampshire." She insinuated that she did not like McKay's work because of his dark complexion. Shocked at such an open display of prejudice, Hughes reminded her that the quality of one's writing had nothing to do with one's color. To this she replied, "But it did have something to do with the quality of one's affection." See Hughes, *The Big Sea: An Autobiography,* 165–66.

68. T. E. McKay to Claude McKay, 1929; McKay Papers, James Weldon Johnson Collection. He informed McKay that there would also be some difficulty getting her away from his wife's parents who resented McKay for his lack of financial support (T. E. McKay to Claude McKay, 26 September 1929; McKay Papers, James Weldon Johnson Collection). Besides color, McKay was concerned about the impact and the limiting influence of the hills on his daughter. However, after McKay spent most of his money from *Home to Harlem*, his interest in Ruth waned.

69. T. E. McKay to Claude McKay, 27 July 1936; McKay Papers, James Weldon Johnson Collection. T. E. wanted McKay to assist him in getting away from Jamaica to New York. Unfortunately, McKay's own poverty prevented him from aiding his brother.

70. Ellen Tarry, *The Third Door: The Autobiography of an American Negro Woman*, 129, 130, 131. Certainly, McKay's friend has offered only a partial explanation, ignoring the deep-rooted intraracial conflict in Jamaica.

71. *A Long Way from Home*, 20. See also the unpublished manuscript "Notebook"; McKay Special Collection, Schomburg Collection, New York Public Library.

72. Ramchand, *The West Indian Novel*, 55, 56, 241. He suggests that this situation for black writers existed well into the 1950s.

73. Actually, McKay had come to the conclusion that agriculture was not his forte. The Jamaican government's desire to encourage young black men to acquire a scientific agricultural education so it could employ them to teach the peasantry modern ways of farming allowed Claude to appease Jekyll and rationalize his departure.

74. Ramchand, *The West Indian Novel*, 241.

75. The reconciliation of these conflicting tendencies would not be easy, as James Hooker writes of George Padmore: "To be a West Indian is an especially difficult task—far easier to stop being one, to escape to London or Halifax or Accra, there to use those powers and skills which in the islands bring so few benefits." See James R. Hooker, *Black Revolutionary: George Padmore's Path From Communism to Pan Africanism*, 1.

2. In Search of Moorings

1. Eastman, *Selected Poems of Claude McKay*, 7.

2. The Booker T. Washington Papers at the Library of Congress are filled with applications from foreigners seeking admission into the institute. Many are written in Spanish, indicating that many black applicants lived in Hispanic America.

3. "A Negro Poet," 275-76.

4. *Daily Gleaner*, 4 March 1913.

5. John Whittaker to Emmett Scott, 9 May 1913; Booker T. Washington Papers, Box 68, Library of Congress. Whittaker to Scott, 8 May 1913. Besides Whittaker, J. H. Palmer had also looked into this matter for Scott. Both acted as Washington's investigatory committee (Memo, Scott to

Washington, n.d.: Booker T. Washington Papers, Library of Congress, Box 68).

6. Unpublished manuscript in the William Stanley Braithwaite Papers, Harvard University. The poem was probably written between 1916 and 1918, since it was signed "Rhonda Hope," the pseudonym McKay used in his correspondence with Braithwaite until September 1918.

7. "A Negro Poet," 275.

8. Ibid.

9. *A Long Way from Home*, 49.

10. *Daily Gleaner*, 9 January 1911.

11. "My Green Hills," 50.

12. McKay's transcript from Kansas State Agricultural College, Manhattan, Kansas. Judging from McKay's curriculum at Kansas, it is not surprising that he left after two years. Most of the courses dealt with agriculture, a career McKay had no desire to pursue.

13. James Weldon Johnson, "Claude McKay" (unpublished manuscript, Harmon Foundation Papers, Library of Congress), 1.

14. Cooper, *Passion of Claude McKay*, 135–36.

15. *A Long Way from Home*, 4.

16. John Hope Franklin, *From Slavery to Freedom*, 372–80.

17. Hughes, *The Big Sea*, 235. According to Hughes, during the Renaissance period, few blacks lived in the Greenwich Village area.

18. James Weldon Johnson, *Black Manhattan*, 153.

19. Roi Ottley and William J. Weatherby, eds., *The Negro in New York: An Informal History*, 191. This manuscript was originally prepared by the Federal Writers' Project under the working title of "Harlem: The Negroes of New York."

20. Ira De A. Reid, *The Negro Immigrant, His Background, Characteristics, and Social Adjustments: 1889–1927*, 35, 106. Also see Harry Robinson, "The Negro Immigrant in New York" (SPA Research Paper, 30 June 1939, Schomburg Branch, New York Public Library), 4–6. According to Robinson, West Indians, especially those from Jamaica, directed their resentment for discrimination against African Americans instead of whites. They blamed American blacks for the sudden drop in their social status, creating tensions and animosity between the two groups.

21. Owen Chandler, "West Indian Problem," *New York Amsterdam News*, 15 September 1926, 20. W. A. Domingo, once a contributor to the *Messenger*, and Edgar Grey, another West Indian writer, responded to the charges of African Americans. See Domingo, "Restricted West Indian Immigration and the American Negro," *Opportunity*, October 1924, 298–99.

22. W. E. B. Du Bois, *The Souls of Black Folk*, 23.

23. Reid, *The Negro Immigrant*, 110.

24. Ottley and Weatherby, *Negro in New York*, 191. It was not uncommon to hear the phrase, "When a West Indian got ten cents above a beggar, he opened a business which ran from a tailor shop to a Wall Street stock firm." See also Gilbert Osofsky, *Harlem: The Making of a Ghetto*, 131.

25. Chandler, "West Indian Problem," 20.

26. Reid, *The Negro Immigrant*, 9–11.

27. Ibid., 14. Cyril Briggs, editor of the *Negro Champion*, and William Bridges, contributor to the short-lived *Challenge*, were among the leaders in advocating intraracial harmony between West Indians and African Americans. See Reid, *The Negro Immigrant*, 122. Also see Cyril Briggs, "We Must Unite for the Struggle," *Negro Champion*, 27 October 1928, 4.

28. Columbia University Oral History Project, Interview with George S. Schuyler, 1960, 72–74.

29. James Weldon Johnson to McKay, 26 January 1928, and McKay to Johnson, 10 March 1928; McKay Papers, James Weldon Johnson Collection.

30. "A Negro Poet," 276.

31. *A Long Way from Home*, 150–51.

32. One one occasion he asked Max Eastman's advice about the necessity of including the fact that he was married in an application for a scholarship. He preferred not to include the information.

33. "A Negro Poet," 276.

34. "A Negro Writer to His Critics," *New York Herald-Tribune Books*, 6 March 1932; reprinted in Cooper, *Passion of Claude McKay*, 135–36.

35. *A Long Way from Home*, 46.

36. James Burkhart Gilbert, *Writers and Partisans: A History of Literary Radicalism in America*, 12–19.

37. Joyce B. Ross, *J. E. Spingarn and the Rise of the NAACP, 1911–1939*, 28.

38. McKay to Joel E. Spingarn, 9 January 1917; Spingarn Papers, New York Public Library.

39. McKay to Joel E. Spingarn, 8 June 1917; Spingarn Papers, New York Public Library.

40. Rhonda Hope [Claude McKay] to William Stanley Braithwaite, 11 January 1916; Braithwaite Papers, Harvard University.

41. Saunders Redding, "The Negro Renaissance: Jean Toomer and the Harlem Writers of the 1920's," in Hill, *Anger and Beyond*, 21–23.

42. *Seven Arts*, October 1917, 742, reprinted in Eastman, *Selected Poems*, 61.

43. *Seven Arts*, October 1917, 741. Reprinted in Cooper, *Passion of Claude McKay*, 117.

44. W. E. B. Du Bois, *The Negro in the Making of America*, 304.

45. William Stanley Braithwaite, "Some Contemporary Poets of the Negro Race," *Crisis*, April 1919, 277.

46. Allison Davis, "Our Negro Intellectuals," *Crisis*, August 1928, 268–69.

47. Rhonda Hope [Claude McKay] to Braithwaite, 15 February 1916; Braithwaite Papers, Harvard University.

48. Jervis Anderson, *This Was Harlem: 1900–1950*, 197; see also *A Long Way from Home*, 27–28.

49. McKay to Spingarn, 9 January 1917; Spingarn Papers, New York Public Library.

50. Ibid.

51. McKay's correspondence with Braithwaite during this period suggests that he was very appreciative of the advice given him by Braithwaite. Braithwaite continued to offer McKay advice after Claude had been published by *Pearson's* and dropped his pseudonyms.

52. McKay to Joel Spingarn, 18 June 1917; Spingarn Papers, New York Public Library.

53. *A Long Way from Home*, 8–9.

54. Ibid., 20–21.

55. Johnson, *Black Manhattan*, 264–65.

56. *A Long Way from Home*, 31.

57. David Levering Lewis, *When Harlem Was in Vogue*, 19.

58. Cooper, *Passion of Claude McKay*, 108. Cooper erroneously asserted that, as a consequence of his freedom in 1917, McKay achieved in his American poetry a more consistent unity of theme and style than had been true in earlier dialect verses. But, in fact, such an occurrence does not come about until after 1919, and even then not completely.

59. "A Negro Poet," 275.

60. *Negroes in America*, xvii.

61. *A Long Way from Home*, 31.

62. For a discussion of the Industrial Workers of the World, see Patrick Renshaw, *The Wobblies: The Story of Syndicalism in the United States* (New York: Anchor, 1968).

63. Claude McKay's introductory remarks at his reading of "If We Must Die," for Arna Bontemps, ed., *Anthology of Negro Poets*, (Folkways Record, FP 91).

64. "If We Must Die," *Liberator*, July 1919, 21.

65. Redding, "The Negro Renaissance," 22.

66. William Stanley Braithwaite, "The Negro Literature," *Crisis*, September 1924, 204.

67. Johnson, *Black Manhattan*, 264; see also Eugene Levy, *James Weldon Johnson: Black Leader, Black Voice*, 311.

68. August Meier and Elliott Rudwick, *From Plantation to Ghetto*, 213–20.

69. W. E. B. Du Bois, "Returning Soldiers," *Crisis*, May 1919, 14; reprinted in Lewis, *When Harlem Was in Vogue*, 15.

70. Bundt Ostendorf, *Black Literature in White America*, 124. Bundt argues that McKay's "If We Must Die" was the first revolutionary poem, expressing the anger of blacks in the postwar period.

71. Eastman, *Selected Poems of Claude McKay*, 7.

72. Cayton, "Ideological Forces in the Work of Negro Writers," in Hill, *Anger and Beyond*, 45.

73. Sterling A. Brown, "A Poet and His Prose," *Opportunity* August 1932, 256.

74. M. Carl Holman, "The Afternoon of a Young Poet," in Hill, *Anger and Beyond*, 139. See also Arna Bontemps, ed., *American Negro Poetry*, 190.

75. *A Long Way from Home*, 31.

3. The Problems of a Black Radical

1. *A Long Way from Home*, 28, 29.
2. Gilbert, *Writers and Partisans*, 8–47.
3. *A Long Way from Home*, 30.
4. Philip Foner, *American Socialism and Black Americans: From the Age of Jackson to World War II*, 254–57.
5. *A Long Way from Home*, 30, 8–9.
6. Gilbert, *Writers and Partisans*, 24.
7. *A Long Way from Home*, 30.
8. McKay to Max Eastman, 28 July 1919; McKay MSS, Indiana University.
9. Max Eastman, *Road to Revolution*, 172.
10. Ibid., 77–88.
11. *A Long Way from Home*, 34.
12. Correspondence cited in Investigative Activities of the Department of Justice, Exhibit no. 10, "Radicalism and Sedition among Negroes as Reflected in Their Publications," 66th Congress, 1st session, Sen. Ex Doc. 153, vol. 12 (1919, serial no. 7707), 161–87.
13. *A Long Way from Home*, 35–44. The offer had come from a rather obscure individual McKay identified only as Mr. Gray. Gray's dream was to establish a utopian society of Europeans of different nationalities. He had originally offered McKay a trip accompanying him and his even obscurer sister to Spain.
14. James Walvin, *Black and White: The Negro and English Society 1555–1945*, 203.
15. Wayne Cooper and Robert C. Reinders, "A Black Briton Comes Home: Claude McKay in England," *Race*, January, 1967, 67. According to Cooper and Reinders, such poems as "Old England" reflected McKay's belief that England and not Africa was his true homeland.
16. *A Long Way from Home*, 76.
17. Cooper and Reinders, "Black Briton Comes Home," 70.
18. *Workers' Dreadnought*, 7 June 1919.
19. *A Long Way from Home*, 76.
20. Cooper, *Claude McKay*, 145.
21. "Socialism and the Negro," 1.
22. Ibid., 2. See also *The Negroes in America*, xvii, 29–33. According to the original translator, McKay joined the Industrial Workers of the World in 1919. He believed that Negro workers who wanted to organize had to turn to the IWW for support. Also included in the volume is McKay's recollection of a conversation he had with William Haywood, the former leader of the IWW, during his stay in Russia in 1922–23. McKay appreciated Haywood's sympathetic attitude concerning the Negro worker's importance to the working-class movement. News of McKay's association with the IWW eventually found its way back to Jamaica and deeply disturbed certain members of his family. U. Theo McKay wrote Claude that he was aware of McKay's association with the IWW but expressed confidence that Claude would do nothing to bar him from returning to the

United States. For as U. Theo put it, "it is not in our blood to be revolutionaries." See U. Theo McKay to Claude McKay, 1 March 1929; McKay Papers, James Weldon Johnson Collection.

23. "Socialism and the Negro," 2.

24. "The Capitalist Way: Lettow-Vorbeck," 6.

25. Ibid.

26. Also cited in James Weinstein, *The Decline of Socialism in America: 1912–1925*, 73.

27. Ross, J. E. *Spingarn and the Rise of the NAACP*, 18–19.

28. Weinstein, *Decline of Socialism in America*, 70.

29. W. E. B. Du Bois, "A Socialist of the Path," *Horizon*, February 1907, 7–8; reprinted in Francis L. Broderick, August Meier, and Elliot Rudwick, eds., *Black Protest in the Twentieth Century* (Indianapolis, Ind., Bobbs-Merrill, 1971), 63–64.

30. Wilson Record, *The Negro and the Communist Party*, 70.

31. *A Long Way from Home*, 86–88.

32. McKay to H. L. Mencken, 1 June 1922; McKay Papers, James Weldon Johnson Collection.

33. Joseph Freeman, *An American Testament: A Narrative of Rebels and Romantics*, 27.

34. *A Long Way from Home*, 96–97.

35. Ibid., 99–105, 116–33. Quotations are from 130.

36. Ibid., 108–9.

37. Philip S. Foner and James S. Allen, eds., *American Communism and Black Americans: A Documentary History, 1919–1929*, 16–18; Foner, *American Socialism and Black Americans*, 309–11; Robert Hill, ed., *The Marcus Garvey and Universal Improvement Association Papers*, 1:523–24.

38. Foner, *American Socialism and Black Americans*, 311.

39. The *Crusader*, September 1919 (vol. 2, no. 1); May 1920 (vol. 2, no. 9); and January 1921 (vol. 3, no. 6).

40. Robert Hill, ed., *The Crusader* xxx–xxxi.

41. Ibid., xxxii.

42. "How Black Sees Green and Red," 17–21.

43. Hill, *Crusader*, xxxix.

44. "Claude McKay with the Liberator," *Crusader*, April 1921 (vol. 4, no. 2), 21; reprinted in Hill, *Crusader*, 1085. The *Crusader* printed a number of his poems; McKay also reviewed books for the *Crusader*. See McKay, "English Journalists Investigate Bolshevism."

45. Quoted in Hill, *Crusader*, xxx.

46. Harry Haywood, *Black Bolshevik: Autobiography of an Afro-American Communist*, 124.

47. Hill, *Crusader*, xxv.

48. Haywood, *Black Bolshevik*, 125.

49. Mark I. Solomon, *Red and Black: Communism and Afro-Americans, 1929–1933*, 78.

50. Hill, *Crusader*, xxiv.

51. Foner and Allen, *American Communism and Black Americans*, 44–

49. Minor's article, "The Ten Black Millions," analyzing the oppressed character and potential of the black masses, received a great deal of attention in the black press. It was originally published in the February 1924 issue of the *Liberator* and later reprinted in the *Amsterdam News*.

52. Hill, *Crusader*, xl; Rose Pastor, a worker in a cigar factory, married J. G. Phelps Stokes, a millionaire philanthropist and social worker. She eventually left her husband and became a Communist speaker and editor of the radical journal, the *Toiler*.

53. *A Long Way from Home*, 109.

54. Ibid., 110–12.

55. McKay to Walter White, 3 February 1922; NAACP Files, Box C-90. McKay to Hubert Harrison, 7 January 1922 (enclosed in a letter to Walter White, n.d.); NAACP Files, Box C-90.

56. Max Eastman to Florence Deshon, 14 June 1921 and Max Eastman to Florence Deshon (n.d.) 1921, Deshon MSS, Indiana University.

57. *A Long Way from Home*, 148.

58. Cooper, *Passion of Claude McKay*, 17.

59. Lewis, *When Harlem Was in Vogue*, 51.

60. Benjamin Brawley, "The Negro Literary Renaissance," *Southern Workman*, April 1927, 28; Allison Davis, "Our Negro Intellectuals," *Crisis*, August 1928, 268; Walter White, quoted in Cooper, *Passion of Claude McKay*, 17; and James Weldon Johnson, in the *New York Age* quoted in R. G. Johnson, "The Poetry of Dunbar and McKay: A Study" (Master's thesis, University of Pittsburgh, 1950), 29.

61. Arna Bontemps, "The Negro Renaissance: Jean Toomer and the Harlem Writers of the 1920's," in Hill, *Anger and Beyond*, 22.

62. Reprinted in Eastman, *Selected Poems of Claude McKay*, 60.

63. Review of *He Who Gets Slapped*, by Leonid Andreyev, 24–25; *A Long Way from Home*, 130–50. To indicate how deeply he is affected by this incident, McKay devoted an entire chapter, "He Who Gets Slapped," to it in his 1937 autobiography.

64. Review of *He Who Gets Slapped*, 25.

65. Freeman, *American Testament*, 257–58.

66. Review of *Birthright*, by T. S. Stribling, 15–16.

67. See Jeffry Perry, "Hubert Henry Harrison: The Father of Harlem Radicalism" (Ph.D. diss., Columbia University, 1986).

68. Review of *Birthright*, 15–16.

69. McKay to Max Eastman, 3 April 1923; McKay MSS, Indiana University.

70. Freeman, *American Testament*, 27.

71. Eastman, *Road to Revolution*, 270; see Michael Gold, *Jews without Money*.

72. Eastman, *Road to Revolution*, 222.

73. McKay to Max Eastman, 3 April 1923; McKay MSS, Indiana University.

74. Max Eastman to McKay, 23 March 1923; McKay MSS, Indiana University. According to Eastman, he favored Gold because his editions had more "pep." In view of the financial problems the *Liberator* was experi-

encing at the time, this was extremely important; see John Hart, *Floyd Dell*, 108. After McKay resigned, Freeman shared the editorship with Gold until August, when Dell replaced Gold. This arrangement lasted until October 1922, when Dell was replaced by Robert Minor, who published the last issue in October 1924. *The Liberator* then merged with the *Labor Herald and the Soviet Russia Pictorial—The Worker's Monthly*.

75. McKay to Max Eastman, 3 April 1923, McKay MSS, Indiana University.

76. Max Eastman to McKay, March 1923; McKay MSS, Indiana University.

77. McKay to Max Eastman, 3 April 1923; McKay MSS, Indiana University.

78. *Negroes in America*, 4, 90, 83–87. The "explicit statement" was taken from an article McKay published in the *Bolshevik* (3 December 1922) under the title "The Negro Communist and His Race," and reprinted in the appendix of *The Negroes in America*. Although the author of the lynching article remained anonymous, the story is attributed to a Lucy Maverick. McKay justified the story in his book, declaring, "When such a story as this is written in the United States by a woman who belongs to a wealthy class and was brought up in the spirit of southern traditions and then is printed in a 'white magazine' such an event must be given the greatest significance."

79. McKay to H. L. Mencken, 31 March 1922; McKay Papers, James Weldon Johnson Collection.

80. Max Eastman to McKay, 12 April 1923; McKay MSS, Indiana University. Eastman reminded McKay that when he joined the *Liberator* staff, he wanted more than anything the free time to write poetry. He had not, in Eastman's words, "discovered this very solemnly consecrated political soul that now appears and looks down on the *Liberator*."

81. "How Black Sees Green and Red," 17, 20–21.

82. "Garvey as a Negro Moses," 8–9.

83. V. F. Calverton, "The Negro" (unpublished manuscript, n.d., V. F. Calverton Papers, New York Public Library).

84. James Weldon Johnson, *Along This Way*, 376.

85. Edward H. Carr, *Studies in Revolution*, 15–37.

86. Donald W. Treadgold, *Twentieth Century Russia*, 40–50.

87. Theodore Draper, *American Communism and Soviet Russia*, 67.

88. McKay to H. L. Mencken, 3 July 1922; McKay Papers, James Weldon Johnson Collection.

89. McKay to James Weldon Johnson, 8 May 1935; McKay Papers, James Weldon Johnson Collection. William A. Nolan suggests that McKay's trip was arranged and paid for by the Russian government; see his *Communism Versus the Negro*, 35.

90. Federal Bureau of Investigation, file no. 613497.

91. *A Long Way from Home*, 157. Actually, McKay was not attached to any Negro newspaper or magazine. However, he was hoping Mencken would be able to secure him a commission from the *Baltimore Sun* to do a series of articles.

92. Ibid., 159–66.
93. Ibid., 168.
94. Henry Lee Moon, *Balance of Power: The Negro Vote*, 118–131. Because of cruel, systematic, and sadistic inhumanity many Negroes felt that they had nothing to lose by supporting a fundamental change in the social order. See Cyril Briggs, "Bolshevism's Menace: To Whom and to What?," *Crusader*, February 1920, 5–6.
95. *A Long Way from Home*, 71–72. At one point McKay had almost arrived at the conclusion that Shaw was correct.
96. "Soviet Russia and the Negro," 61–65, 114–18; reprinted in Cooper, *Passion of Claude McKay*, 95–106.
97. Cooper, *Passion of Claude McKay*, 101, 102, 103.
98. McKay to Mencken, 5 September 1923; Mencken Papers, New York Public Library.
99. McKay to H. L. Mencken, 17 July 1923; Mencken Papers, New York Public Library.
100. Ibid.
101. Sterling D. Spero and Abram L. Harris, *The Black Worker*, 414–17.
102. Record, *The Negro and the Communist Party*, 22–23.
103. This speech was reprinted as "Report on the Negro Question," *International Press Correspondence* 3 (5 January 1923): 16–17.
104. Ibid.
105. "The Race Question in the United States," 817.
106. "Report on the Negro Question," 16–17.
107. Leon Trotsky to Claude McKay, 13 March 1923. This letter was reprinted in *International Press Correspondence*, 3, no. 25, 197. Within a year Zinoviev openly attacked Trotsky's theory of the "permanent revolution," with its emphasis on the Soviet world leadership of the proletariat and its implicit challenge to the Leninist position on the role of the poor peasantry in building socialism. In January 1925, the Central Committee, led by Stalin and Zinoviev, removed Trotsky from the War Commissariat. See Treadgold, *Twentieth Century Russia*, 216–28.
108. Gregory Zinoviev to McKay, 8 May 1923; "Zinoviev on National and Racial Problems," NAACP Administrative Files, Library of Congress.
109. Theodore Draper, *Roots of American Communism*, 387. Though McKay's comments before the Fourth Congress did not result in a change in the Communist party's tactics or attitudes, Draper's assessment of McKay's address as insignificant is not entirely accurate. The commission, headed by Safarov, reiterated the Third International's major theme: that the American Negro, because of his history, should play an important role in the liberation struggles of the African race.
110. *A Long Way from Home*, 173, 177, 178, 182, 208.
111. FBI files: memo 1/9/23; 2/3/23; 3/12/23; 3/26/23; 3/10/23; 4/1/23; memo to J. E. Hoover 1/23/23 (61-3497).
112. FBI files: 12/16/21; 1/23/23; 2/3/23 (61-3497).
113. "Enslaved" had first appeared in the *Liberator* for July 1921; "America" appeared in the December 1921 issue of the *Liberator*.

114. Instructions were sent to the Immigration Service, Customs, U.S. Shipping Commissioner, U.S. Shipping Board, Sea Service Bureau, and local police departments. See FBI files: memo 3/23/23 (61-3497).

115. FBI files: 12/13/22 (61-3497).

116. "The Communist International and the Negro," *Worker*, 10 March 1923; reprinted in Foner and Allen, *American Communism and Black Americans*, 30–32.

117. See Hill, *Crusader*, xxxvii.

118. FBI files: 2/3/23; 12/13/22 (61–3497).

119. "The Negro Communist and His Race," *Bolshevik*, 3 December 1922.

120. *A Long Way from Home*, 162–63.

121. FBI files: 27 October 1923 (61–3497).

122. McKay to James W. Johnson, 8 May 1935; McKay Papers, James Weldon Johnson Collection.

123. McKay to Walter White, 8 July 1923 (Berlin); NAACP Files, Box C-90.

124. Solomon, *Red and Black*, 73.

125. McKay to Josephine Herbst, 22 November 1923; Herbst Papers, Yale University. McKay met Herbst through Pierre Loving, a writer and critic. McKay described Herbst as "very kind and helpful in a practical and also artistic way." See *A Long Way from Home*, 241.

126. "Negroes in Russia," *Messenger*, April 1923, 653.

127. "Negroes Wrongs Aired at Moscow," *New York Amsterdam News*, 6 December 1923, 26.

128. Abram Harris, "The Negro Problem as Viewed by Negro Leaders," *Current History*, 18 (June 1923): 411–18.

129. "Claude McKay Before the International," *Opportunity*, September 1923, 259. The *Opportunity* had specifically pointed to an 18 November 1922 issue of *Izvyestia*.

130. Francis Broderick, *W. E. B. Du Bois: Negro Leader in a Time of Crisis*, 138.

131. W. E. B. Du Bois, "The Negro and Radical Thought," *Crisis*, July 1921, 102.

132. "Soviet Russia and the Negro," 61–65.

133. W. E. B. Du Bois, *The Autobiography of W. E. B. Du Bois: A Soliloquy on Viewing My Life from the Last Decade of Its First Century*, 421.

134. *A Long Way from Home*, 226.

135. McKay did not belong to that group of radicals who possessed the revolutionary temper and integrity to produce the instruments of collective revolutionary endeavor: theory, agitation, and revolver; see Al Richmond, *A Long View from the Left*, 49.

4. *"How Shall the Negro Be Portrayed?"*

1. McKay had alluded to this in his speech to the Fourth Congress of the Third International; see "Report on the Negro Question," *International Press Correspondence* 3 (5 January 1923): 16.

2. Johnson, *Along This Way*, 375. Johnson took this view and cited McKay's long absence from the United States as a reason for his eclipsed reputation as a poet.

3. Robert Bone, *The Negro Novel in America*, 95.

4. McKay to Josephine Herbst, 22 November 1923; Herbst Papers, Yale University. In McKay's autobiography he stated he had suffered from the "grippe"; see *A Long Way from Home* 230–33.

5. Unpublished poems contained in the Herbst Papers, Yale University.

6. McKay to Josephine Herbst, December 1923; Herbst Papers, Yale University. Herbst had first corresponded with McKay at the request of Max Eastman in 1922. McKay was feeling abandoned and needed someone to confide in. As a result of this correspondence, he disclosed to Herbst that he had contracted syphilis (Herbst to Harold Cruse, 10 September 1968; Herbst Papers, Yale University).

7. While McKay overcame the initial effects of his illness, he continued to suffer headaches until his death.

8. Norman Hapgood, 1923; Mencken Papers, New York Public Library.

9. Walter White to Joel Spingarn, 24 January 1924; NAACP Papers, Box C-90. White wrote asking Spingarn for his help and mentioned that the Socialists under Grace Campbell's direction were also attempting to help McKay. White wrote McKay that Spingarn had contributed $50 to his fund.

10. Louise Bryant Bullitt to McKay, 26 September 1926; McKay Papers, James Weldon Johnson Collection.

11. McKay to Grace Campbell, 7 January 1924; NAACP Papers, Box C-90.

12. McKay to Louise Bryant Bullitt, 24 June 1926; McKay Papers, James Weldon Johnson Collection.

13. McKay to Nancy Cunard, 25 January 1933; McKay Papers, James Weldon Johnson Collection. Cunard was among a handful of whites who took a serious interest in the study of African-American and African culture. It is purported that once Salvador Dali was asked if he knew anything about Negroes. He replied, "Everything, I've met Nancy Cunard." See Robert E. Hemenway, *Zora Neale Hurston: A Literary Biography*, 25.

14. McKay to Josephine Herbst, 7 August 1924; Herbst Papers, Yale University. According to McKay, by 1911 he had stopped reading or writing prose.

15. McKay to Walter White, 27 February 1925; NAACP Papers, Box C-92.

16. McKay to Walter White, 25 September 1925, and McKay to Walter White, 15 October 1925; NAACP Papers, Box C-93.

17. Louise Bryant Bullitt to McKay, 26 September 1926; McKay Papers, James Weldon Johnson Collection. She informed McKay that she had sent his short stories to Harcourt and they had turned them down. But she also noted that they had indicated a strong interest in Negro stories.

18. Langston Hughes to Walter White, 17 December 1925; and Walter White to Langston Hughes, 18 December 1925; NAACP Papers, Box C-93.

19. Though White was not McKay's official agent, McKay repeatedly criticized him for not trying hard enough. For a discussion of White's aid to several writers of the Renaissance period, see Charles Cooney, "Walter White and the Harlem Renaissance," *Journal of Negro History* 7 (July 1972): 231–40.

20. McKay to H. L. Mencken, 1 May 1924; Mencken Papers, New York Public Library. White to McKay, 6 November 1924; NAACP Papers, Box C-93. It had been White who suggested McKay seek Sinclair Lewis's assistance. Lewis had been extremely helpful to White; see Sinclair Lewis to White, 12 November 1924; NAACP Papers, Box C-92.

21. McKay to Walter White, 4 August 1924; NAACP Papers, Box C-93.

22. McKay to Walter White, 20 May 1925; NAACP Papers, Box C-92.

23. White to McKay, 20 May 1925; NAACP Papers, Box C-92.

24. McKay to White, 15 June 1925; NAACP Papers, Box C-92.

25. Ibid.

26. White to James Oppenheimer and Guinberg, 22 May 1925; NAACP Papers, Box C-92.

27. Walter White to McKay, 8 July 1925; NAACP Papers, Box C-92. White felt that the advantage of having a book published by a firm just starting out was that out of necessity they would have to push every book on their list. White pointed to the excellent job the Viking Press had done for James Weldon Johnson's book which was coming out in the fall. White to Arthur Schomburg, 23 July 1925; NAACP Papers, Box C-92.

28. McKay to H. L. Mencken, 2 August 1925; Mencken Papers, New York Public Library.

29. Arthur Schomburg to Walter White, 25 July 1925; NAACP Papers, Box C-93.

30. McKay to H. L. Mencken, 2 August 1925; Mencken Papers, New York Public Library.

31. Virginia Gardner, *Friend and Lover: The Life of Louise Bryant*, 258–59.

32. Ibid.

33. Ibid., 266–70, 298.

34. Walter White to Arthur Schomburg, 27 August 1925; NAACP Papers, Box C-93.

35. Nathan Huggins, *Harlem Renaissance*, 99–118; Addison Gayle, Jr., *The Way of the New World: The Black Novel in America*, 104–11.

36. Louise Bryant Bullitt to McKay, 18 December 1926; McKay Papers, James Weldon Johnson Collection. Bullitt to McKay, 4 January 1927; McKay Papers, James Weldon Johnson Collection.

37. William Aspenwell Bradley to McKay, 25 February 1927; McKay Papers, James Weldon Johnson Collection. Bradley, whom McKay had scolded for accepting such an ambiguous contract, argued that his function as a literary agent had not been primarily to sell a book, but to establish contact with a reliable publishing house and secure a contract covering a certain period of literary output.

38. William Aspenwell Bradley to McKay, 13 April 1927; McKay Papers, James Weldon Johnson Collection.

39. McKay to Josephine Herbst, 1 September 1924; Herbst Papers, Yale University.

40. McKay to H. L. Mencken, 18 December 1923; Mencken Papers, New York Public Library. Apparently, McKay used the term "semi-underworld" to refer to the lower class of Harlem.

41. Bone, *Negro Novel in America*, 68–69; Huggins, *Harlem Renaissance*, 121–27; Bernard W. Bell, *The Afro-American Novel and Its Tradition*, 116–19.

42. *Home to Harlem*, 15, 273.

43. Ibid., 243.

44. Ibid., 242, 153.

45. Before World War I many white writers and artists believed that their work served society. After the war many rejected service as mere propaganda and turned to personal issues.

46. W. E. B. Du Bois, "Review of *Home to Harlem*," *Crisis*, September 1928, 202.

47. Bone, *Negro Novel in America*, 96.

48. Marcus Garvey, "*Home to Harlem*, Claude McKay's Damaging Book Should Earn Wholesale Condemnation of Negroes," *Negro World*, 29 September 1928, 1.

49. Harvey Wickersham, *The Impuritans* (New York: Dial Press, 1929), 280–89.

50. "Review of *Home to Harlem*," *New York World*, 16 March 1928.

51. Herschell Brickell, "Review of *Home to Harlem*," *Opportunity*, May 1928, 151–52.

52. Langston Hughes to Alain Locke, 1 March 1928; Hughes Letters, Locke Papers, Howard University.

53. Burton Rascoe, "The Seamy Side," review of *Home to Harlem*, *Bookman*, 25 May 1928, 183–84.

54. T. S. Matthews, "What Gods! What Gongs!," review of *Home to Harlem*, *New Republic*, 30 May 1928, 50–51.

55. William Pickens, *The New Negro: His Political, Civil, and Mental Status and Related Essays*, 4.

56. A. Philip Randolph, "The Negro and the New Social Order," *Messenger*, March 1919, 26; "The New Philosophy of the Negro," *Messenger*, December 1919, 5; editorial, "New Leadership for the Negro," *Messenger*, May–June 1919, 29.

57. Alain Locke, ed., *The New Negro*, 3.

58. Pickens, *The New Negro*, 224.

59. Countee Cullen, "The League of Youth," *Crisis*, August 1923, 167.

60. Harold Cruse, *The Crisis of the Negro Intellectual*, 96.

61. Alain Locke, *A Decade of Negro Self-Expression*, 8.

62. James Weldon Johnson to Walter White, 13 April 1923; NAACP Files, Box C, no. 90.

63. Editorial, "The Debut of Younger School of Negro Writers," *Opportunity*, May 1924, 143.

64. Editorial, "On Writing About Negroes," *Opportunity*, August 1925, 227–28. From the beginning Charles S. Johnson, editor of *Opportunity*, argued that the purpose for establishing the magazine had been partly sociological and partly literary; see Augustus J. Jackson, "The Renaissance of Negro Literature, 1922–1929" (Master's thesis, Atlanta University, 1936).

65. W. E. B. Du Bois, *The Gift of Black Folks: The Negro in the Making of America*, 204.

66. Alain Locke, "The New Negro," in Locke, *The New Negro*, 3–16; reprinted in John Bracey, Jr., August Meier, and Elliott Rudwick, eds., *Black Nationalism in America*, 334–47.

67. Contrary to what some historians have argued, this seemed to be the dominant feeling of most blacks. They wanted to attain first-class citizenship, to obtain the rights and privileges that white people had enjoyed for years. Even the Garvey movement, which was the only significant indicator of what the masses of blacks felt, reflected this desire. Utilizing the symbols of black nationalism, Garvey tapped the rejection, disillusionment, and despair of blacks who felt they had been on the threshold of attaining the rewards of first-class citizenship. It was this frustration—not a rejection of American middle-class values—that accounted for this reaction. Aside from his "Back to Africa" plan, Garvey's movement was very bourgeois.

68. V. F. Calverton, "The New Negro," *Current History* 33 (February 1926), 694–98. Calverton argued that the new Negro was no longer a promise but an actuality. His passivity had been transformed into an intellectual resistance. Individual isolation was replaced by racial cooperation.

69. Anderson, *This Was Harlem*, 221–22.

70. *A Long Way from Home*, 321–23.

71. McKay to Locke, 18 April 1927; McKay Letters, Locke Papers, Howard University. McKay was convinced that the American Negro intelligentsia had no real interest in art, except as a decoration for their social affairs and he had no intention of being used by them.

72. *Negroes in America*, 62.

73. McKay to Locke, 27 July 1926; McKay Letters, Locke Papers, Howard University.

74. "Negro Life and Negro Art" (unpublished manuscript dated 1927, NAACP Files, Library of Congress, 1–2).

75. W. E. B. Du Bois, "Criteria of Negro Art," *Crisis*, October 1926, 295–96.

76. William Pickens, "Art and Propaganda," *Messenger*, April 1924, 111.

77. Walter White to Eugene Saxon, 23 May 1924; NAACP Files, Box C–90.

78. James W. Johnson, "The Dilemma of the Negro Artist," *American Mercury*, December 1928; "Negro Authors and White Publishers," *Crisis*, July 1929, 228–229.

79. Louise Bryant Bullitt to McKay, 14 February (year unknown); Schomburg Special Collection, New York Public Library.

80. McKay to White, 7 September 1925; NAACP Files, Box C–93.

81. Ibid.

82. *Banjo: A Story without a Plot*, 200.

83. Ibid., 200, 201.

84. The *Crisis* symposium had been conducted almost two years before the famous discussion over the same topic between Langston Hughes and George Schuyler appeared in *Nation;* "The Negro in Art: How Shall He Be Portrayed?" *Crisis*, August 1926, 193–94.

85. "The Negro in Art: How Shall He Be Portrayed?" *Crisis*, March 1926, 219. There may have been some truth to accusations that Van Vechten was predisposed toward the unhealthy, exotic aspects of life. Mabel Luhan Dodge once remarked, "How Carl loved the grotesque. He loved to twist and squirm with laughter at the oddity of strong contrasts"; see Dodge, *Movers and Shakers*, 29.

86. "How Shall the Negro Be Portrayed?" *Crisis*, April 1926, 278–79.

87. "How Shall the Negro Be Portrayed?" *Crisis*, June 1926, 72.

88. "How Shall the Negro Be Portrayed?" *Crisis*, August 1926, 264.

89. Ellen Glasgow to Carl Van Vechten, 28 July 1926, and Henry Hanson to Carl Van Vechten (n.d); Van Vechten Papers, New York Public Library.

90. W. E. B. Du Bois, "Postscript: Mencken," *Crisis*, October 1927, 276.

91. "The Negro in Art: How Shall He Be Portrayed?" *Crisis*, August 1926, 279.

92. McKay to James W. Johnson, 9 May 1928; McKay Papers, James Weldon Johnson Collection.

93. McKay to James Ivy, 20 May 1928; McKay Papers, James Weldon Johnson Collection.

94. McKay to Arthur Schomburg, 17 July 1925; McKay Papers, James Weldon Johnson Collection.

95. "Negro Life and Negro Art," 6.

96. "A Negro Writer to His Critics," *New York Herald-Tribune Books,* 6 March 1932; reprinted in Cooper, *Passion of Claude McKay*, 278–79.

97. "How Shall the Negro Be Portrayed?" *Crisis*, April 1926, 278–79.

98. Langston Hughes, "The Negro Artist and the Racial Mountain," *Nation,* June 1926, 692–94. Schuyler denied that he had intentionally sought the debate between himself and Hughes; the *Nation* had; see Schuyler Interview, Columbia Oral History Project, Columbia University, 76.

99. Hughes, "The Negro Artist and the Racial Mountain," 694.

100. Editorial, "American Negro Art," *Opportunity*, August 1926, 238–39. *Opportunity* had concluded that it was more important that blacks develop artists first, and then let the question of a distinctive art settle. This was in reference to the Hughes-Schuyler debate.

101. Hughes, "The Negro Artist and the Racial Mountain," 693.

102. Langston Hughes, *Not without Laughter.*

103. Langston Hughes, *The Best of Simple*, viii.

104. McKay to Josephine Herbst, 22 November 1923; Herbst Papers, Yale University. He referred to Fauset's prose as "pretty primroses."

105. McKay to Harold Jackman, 1927; McKay Papers, James Weldon Johnson Collection.

106. "Negro Writer to His Critics," 134.

107. Many black writers and critics shared McKay's opinion, but there was no consensus on the best way to combat it. See A. J. Rogers, "Nigger Heaven," *Messenger*, December 1926, 365.

108. Huggins, *Harlem Renaissance*, 116.

109. "Negro Life and Negro Art," 7. He also believed that by virtue of the greater numbers of white writers, blacks would lose out in the competition.

110. Edward Margolies, *Native Sons: A Critical Study of Twentieth-Century American Authors*, 1–40.

111. McKay to Joel Spingarn, 9 January 1917; Spingarn Papers, New York Public Library.

112. Charlotte R. Osgood Mason to McKay, 12 March 1928; McKay Papers, James W. Johnson Collection. Mason had indicated to McKay that she preferred his novel to *Nigger Heaven* because of the absence of apologetics.

113. Nancy Cunard to McKay, 23 March 1932 (postcard); McKay Papers, James Weldon Johnson Collection.

114. "Negro Writer to His Critics," 134.

115. McKay to James Weldon Johnson, 9 May 1928; McKay Papers, James Weldon Johnson Collection.

116. McKay to Charlotte Osgood Mason, 13 February 1930; McKay Letters, Locke Papers, Howard University.

117. Johnson, "The Dilemma of the Negro Author," *American Mercury*, December 1928, 477–81.

118. Leon Whipple, "Letters and Life—The Negro Artistic Awakening," *Survey*, April 1926, 517–19.

5. Banjo

1. Huggins, *Harlem Renaissance*, 173.

2. Louise Bryant Bullitt to McKay, 2 March 1927; McKay Papers, James Weldon Johnson Collection. She also advised McKay that her late husband, John Reed, had sometimes written an entire story seventeen times. Louise Bryant Bullitt to McKay, 18 January 1928; McKay Papers, James Weldon Johnson Collection. Bullitt displayed a deep interest in McKay throughout her life. Even as she lay dying from cancer in a Baden, Germany, sanitorium, she continued to try to help him.

3. William Aspenwell Bradley to McKay, 30 October 1927; McKay Papers, James Weldon Johnson Collection.

4. W. E. B. Du Bois, review of *Banjo*, *Crisis*, July 1929, 234.

5. W. E. B. Du Bois, "Back to Africa," *Century*, February 1927, 539–48.

6. Walter White to Harry Hausen, 4 June 1929; NAACP Files, Box C-93. White did not find much fault with McKay's lack of form. He felt McKay

had achieved a kind of triumph, for life in the ditch had no form. He did indicate that the story was not for Sunday school classes or Boston bookstores.

7. Lewis, *When Harlem Was in Vogue*, 239.

8. McKay to Harold Jackson, 1 August 1927; McKay Papers, James Weldon Johnson Collection.

9. *Banjo: A Story without A Plot*, 115–16.

10. Ibid., 116–17.

11. McKay to James Weldon Johnson, 5 September 1929; McKay Papers, James Weldon Johnson Collection.

12. Eugene Saxton to McKay, 12 November 1929; McKay Papers, James Weldon Johnson Collection. Saxton also offered another reason for the lack of sales. According to the sales department, the book's poor showing had been the result of competition with two or three other books on the market about Negroes—indicating the restricted market black artists had to contend with.

13. This may account for the lack of different types of blacks in McKay's *Home to Harlem*, and in Van Vechten's *Nigger Heaven*.

14. McKay to Max Eastman, 27 June 1930 and McKay to Eastman, 7 December 1929; McKay *MSS*, Indiana University.

15. Stephen Bronz, *Roots of Negro Racial Consciousness*, 80.

16. George Kent, *Blackness and the Adventure of Western Culture*, 25.

17. Brawley, "The Negro Literary Renaissance," *Southern Workman*, April 1927, 177–83. Brawley was generally very critical of the Negro Renaissance and of new art forms.

18. Benjamin Brawley to McKay, 23 June 1927; McKay Papers, James Weldon Johnson Collection; Benjamin Brawley, *The Negro Genius*, 194.

19. Wallace Thurman to McKay, 1928; McKay Papers, James Weldon Johnson Collection. Thurman described his role in the Renaissance as one of bringing order to a literary stampede.

20. William Stanley Braithwaite to George Haynes, 26 December 1928; Harmon Papers, Library of Congress. Some on the award committee agreed with Braithwaite's opinion of *Home to Harlem*, but still praised McKay's literary talents in justifying the award. Dr. J. Melvin Lee mentioned in his recommendation to the committee that in "some respects and these the most essential—I regarded *Quicksand*, by Nella Larsen, as the most important novel of the year to be written by a Negro." However, he decided to give McKay the gold medal on the strength of his portrayal of Pullman porter life.

21. Walter White to George Haynes, 20 September 1928; Harmon Papers, Library of Congress.

22. McKay to Walter White, 4 December 1924; NAACP Files, Box C-92. McKay suggested that Toomer could really do wonderful things if he would be simple and clear and not confuse the reality of Negro life with purple patches of mysticism.

23. McKay to Alain Locke, 7 October 1924; McKay Letters, Locke Papers, Howard University.

24. McKay to Alain Locke, 1 August 1926; printed in Cooper, *The Passion of Claude McKay*, 143–44.

25. McKay to Alain Locke, 18 April 1927; McKay Letters, Locke Papers, Howard University.

26. McKay to Simon and Schuster, 1 July 1927; McKay Letters, Locke Papers, Howard University.

27. McKay to Alain Locke, 18 April 1927; McKay Letters, Locke Papers, Howard University.

28. McKay to Alain Locke, 7 October 1924; McKay Letters, Locke Papers, Howard University.

29. Jessie Fauset to Alain Locke, 9 January 1933; Fauset Letters, Locke Papers, Howard University.

30. McKay to Harold Jackman, 1 August 1927; McKay Papers, James Weldon Johnson Collection. This letter also makes clear that McKay took compliments too seriously. He mentioned to Jackman that Charles S. Johnson had sent him $10 and commented that it was vital for him to be kept alive and his voice heard.

31. McKay to Walter White, 4 December 1924; NAACP Files, Box C-90.

32. McKay to Harold Jackman, 1927; McKay Papers, James W. Johnson Collection.

33. McKay to W. E. B. Du Bois, June 1928; letter reprinted in Herbert Aptheker, ed., *The Correspondence of W. E. B. Du Bois*, 1: 374.

34. Ibid. Also see W. E. B. Du Bois to McKay, 16 March 1927; McKay Papers, James Weldon Johnson Collection. He had enclosed $10 to pay for the two poems used in the *Crisis*.

35. McKay to W. E. B. Du Bois, 18 June 1928; letter reprinted in Aptheker, *Correspondence*, 1:374.

36. Ibid. Earlier McKay had expressed a different opinion of Du Bois and the *Crisis*. Writing to Du Bois, McKay commented that the October 1925 issue of the *Crisis* was a fine piece of literary criticism. McKay included the sheaf of poems that later caused heated controversy between Du Bois and McKay.

37. W. E. B. Du Bois to McKay, 2 August 1928; letter reprinted in Aptheker, *Correspondence*, 1:376.

38. Eugene Saxton of Harper had deleted phrases from McKay's original draft of *Home to Harlem* because of their "racy" connotations without first getting McKay's consent. Other white publishers had not returned any of the manuscripts he had sent them.

39. W. E. B. Du Bois, "Opinion," *Crisis*, April 1920, 298. Du Bois considered McKay's insinuations nonsense, but felt that McKay had awakened *Crisis* to an even greater need for procuring more Negro writers. Still, he defended *Crisis*'s influence in the Renaissance.

40. McKay to Alain Locke, 2 January 1928; McKay Letters, Locke Papers, Howard University.

41. McKay to Alain Locke, 4 June 1927; McKay Letters, Locke Papers, Howard University.

42. McKay to Harold Jackman, 1927; McKay Papers, James W. Johnson Collection.

43. McKay to Walter White, 15 December 1924; NAACP Files, Box C-92.

44. *A Long Way from Home*, 307–14; quotation from 307.
45. Ibid., 315–23; quotation from 322–23.
46. McKay to Max Eastman, 7 December 1929; McKay MSS, Indiana University.
47. *Banjo*, 3–17.
48. Ibid., 64.
49. Ibid., 65.
50. Ibid., 133–37.
51. Ibid., 182–83.
52. Ibid., 183–84.
53. Bone, *Negro Novel in America*, 71.
54. *Banjo*, 272–73.
55. Ibid., 292–93.
56. Ibid., 293.
57. Ibid., 314, 320–21.
58. Ibid., 316.
59. Ibid., 322, 323.
60. Ibid., 312.

6. Back to Harlem

1. S. P. Fullinwider, *The Mind and Mood of Black America*, 153. Fullinwider offers a provocative chapter on the impact of the Renaissance debates on some black writers.
2. McKay to Walter White, 4 December 1924; NAACP Files, Box C-92. McKay to Josephine Herbst, 22 February 1924; Herbst Papers, Yale University.
3. McKay to Walter White, 4 December 1924; NAACP Files, Box C-92.
4. William Aspenwall Bradley to McKay, 22 April 1929; McKay Papers, James Weldon Johnson Collection. Apparently McKay had made reference to his nervous condition in an earlier letter. McKay to Max Eastman, 7 December 1929; McKay MSS, Indiana University.
5. McKay to Max Eastman, 27 June 1930; McKay MSS, Indiana University.
6. McKay to Max Eastman, 1 December 1930; McKay MSS, Indiana University.
7. Ibid. This was obviously not true; McKay's distance may have accounted for the erroneous assumption.
8. In contrast, Eastman lived in a fashionable part of Greenwich Village, where he employed a "gentle elderly black woman," who was "slow footed but not shuffling"; see Eastman, *Road to Revolution*, 172.
9. McKay to Max Eastman, 31 March 1931; McKay MSS, Indiana University.
10. McKay to Max Eastman, 1 December 1931; McKay MSS, Indiana University. The house had cost him 600 francs for the year, but he received the second year's rent free for repairing the house.

11. McKay to Max Eastman, 1 September 1931; McKay MSS, Indiana University.
12. Ibid.
13. McKay to Max Eastman, 19 July 1931; McKay MSS, Indiana University.
14. Warren French, ed., *The Twenties: Fiction, Poetry, Drama*, 308.
15. To an extent, McKay's choice of Bita as his protagonist to lead a cultural rebellion is implausible. Given the male-dominated character of Jamaican society at the time, it is unlikely a woman, especially a dark-skinned one, would have had the freedom and independence of a Bita.
16. *Banana Bottom*, 17.
17. Ibid., p. 40. Jubilee is a small village just outside of Banana Bottom, where the mission was located and where the Craigs and Bita lived.
18. Ibid., 71–74.
19. Ibid., 169.
20. Ibid., 190–96.
21. Ibid., 247–50.
22. Bone, *Negro Novel in America*, 72. Bone is correct that McKay attained the proper distance; however, it is not as far as he suggests.
23. *Banana Bottom*, 81–82.
24. Ibid., 2. McKay's description of Jekyll's sexuality is interesting in light of Wayne Cooper's suggestion of a homosexual relationship between McKay and Jekyll.
25. Sterling Brown, "Banana Bottom," 217.
26. *Banana Bottom*, 100–101.
27. Ibid., 259–69.
28. Ibid., 9.
29. Ibid., 16.
30. Ibid., 221.
31. Ibid., 140–51.
32. Ibid., 172–76.
33. McKay to Max Eastman, 21 April 1931; McKay MSS, Indiana University.
34. McKay to Max Eastman, 24 May 1933; McKay MSS, Indiana University.
35. McKay to Max Eastman, 6 June 1933; McKay MSS, Indiana University.
36. Clifton Fadiman to Max Eastman, 12 September 1933; McKay Papers, James Weldon Johnson Collection.
37. McKay to Carl Van Vechten, 28 June 1933; McKay MSS, Indiana University.
38. McKay to Max Eastman, 5 July 1933; McKay MSS, Indiana University.
39. McKay to Max Eastman, 28 June 1933; McKay MSS, Indiana University.
40. McKay to Max Eastman, 21 June 1933; McKay MSS, Indiana University.
41. James Weldon Johnson on several occasions had assisted McKay in

getting prepared to come back to America. See Johnson to McKay, 27 February 1928; McKay Papers, James Weldon Johnson Collection. He mentioned to McKay that he and other African Americans wanted him to return and work with them on the "New Movement."

42. McKay to James Weldon Johnson, 27 August 1928; McKay Papers, James Weldon Johnson Collection.

43. McKay to James Weldon Johnson, 23 July 1933; James Weldon Johnson Collection.

44. McKay to Max Eastman, 30 October 1933; McKay MSS, Indiana University. He also mentions to him that he had been shadowed in Berlin in 1930. Letters sent to friends in Paris were missent to London, and a silly forged letter appeared over his signature in the *London Times* headed "A Subtle Propagandist."

45. McKay to American consul general, 18 January 1929; McKay Papers, James Weldon Johnson Collection.

46. McKay to Max Eastman, 18 June 1931; McKay MSS, Indiana University.

47. McKay to Max Eastman, April 1933; McKay MSS, Indiana University.

48. Walter White to Max Eastman, 7 September 1933; McKay Papers, James Weldon Johnson Collection. Both Arthur Schomburg and James W. Johnson had also spoken in his behalf. See James Weldon Johnson to McKay, 30 September 1933; McKay Papers, James Weldon Johnson Collection.

49. McKay to Joel Spingarn, 30 July 1933; Spingarn Papers, New York Public Library.

50. Walter White to Max Eastman, 19 September 1933; McKay Papers, James Weldon Johnson Collection.

51. Charlotte (no last name indicated) to Max Eastman, 26 September 1933; McKay Papers, James Weldon Johnson Collection.

52. McKay to Max Eastman, 5 October 1933; McKay MSS, Indiana University.

53. McKay to Max Eastman, 7 September 1933; McKay MSS, Indiana University.

54. McKay to Max Eastman, 25 October 1933; McKay MSS, Indiana University.

55. McKay to Max Eastman, 20 October, 1933; McKay MSS, Indiana University.

56. Gladys Wilson to McKay, 25 September 1928; McKay Papers, James Weldon Johnson Collection.

57. "Note on Harlem" (unpublished manuscript, V. F. Calverton Papers, box 4, folder 16, New York Public Library). The poem appeared later in *Modern Monthly*, July 1934, 368.

58. Bella Gross, "Home to Harlem: Claude McKay!," *Harlem Liberator*, 24 April 1934, 6.

59. Arthur Schomburg to Open, "Prospectus for the Establishment of a Negro Magazine" (unpublished manuscript, date 21 August 1934; McKay Papers, Schomburg Collection, New York Public Library).

60. Ibid.

61. McKay to Max Eastman, 11 July 1934; McKay MSS, Indiana University. Eastman had done the same thing in establishing the *Liberator*. He organized it to have controlling interest, to avoid the problems its predecessor, the *Masses*, suffered.

62. McKay to Carl Van Vechten, 26 July 1934; Van Vechten Papers, Yale University. McKay prevailed upon Van Vechten to be one of its sponsors, but Van Vechten never responded.

63. McKay to Max Eastman, 11 September 1934, and McKay to Eastman, 12 August 1934; McKay MSS, Indiana University.

64. McKay to Max Eastman, 11 September 1934, and McKay to Eastman, 1 September 1934; Van Vechten Papers, Yale University.

65. McKay to Max Eastman, 25 October 1934, and 10 November 1934; McKay MSS, Indiana University.

66. Ibid.

67. The camp reminded McKay of what took place in Russia after the revolution; see McKay to Max Eastman, 3 November 1934, McKay MSS, Indiana University.

68. McKay to Max Eastman, 19 December 1934; 3 December 1934; 25 November 1934; McKay MSS, Indiana University.

69. McKay to Max Eastman, 3 December 1934; McKay MSS, Indiana University.

70. McKay to Max Eastman, 3 November 1934; McKay MSS, Indiana University.

71. McKay to Max Eastman, 25 November 1934; McKay MSS, Indiana University.

72. McKay to Max Eastman, 16 December 1934; McKay MSS, Indiana University.

73. McKay to Max Eastman, 7 December 1934; McKay MSS, Indiana University.

74. McKay to Max Eastman, 19 December 1934, and McKay to Eastman, 30 April 1934; McKay MSS, Indiana University.

75. Cooper, *Passion of Claude McKay*, 36, 215. McKay left Greycourt and returned to New York City, where he shared an apartment on West 63rd Street with the black sculptor Selma Burke, who was then an art student and a model. The exact nature of McKay's relationship with Burke is unclear. However, McKay was furious when she left to spend an evening with an acquaintance of Max Eastman's. See McKay to Max Eastman (undated); McKay MSS, Indiana University.

76. James Weldon Johnson to McKay, 20 April 1935; Rosenwald Fund Archives, Fisk University.

77. Edward R. Embree to McKay, 7 May 1935; Rosenwald Fund Archives.

78. James Weldon Johnson to Edwin R. Embree, 11 May 1935; Rosenwald Fund Archives.

79. Edwin R. Embree to James Weldon Johnson, 20 June 1935, and McKay to Edwin R. Embree, 31 March 1936; Rosenwald Fund Archives. McKay did not communicate to Embree the name of the publisher.

However, according to McKay, the $300 was to be paid in installments. It is likely that the publisher was the firm of Lee Furman, which published the autobiography two years later.

7. I Have Come to Lead the Renaissance

1. McKay to James Weldon Johnson, 8 August 1935; McKay Papers, James Weldon Johnson Collection.

2. McKay to James Weldon Johnson, 9 January 1937; James Weldon Johnson Collection.

3. Tarry, *The Third Door*, 127.

4. "Writers Fail to Agree on Membership," *New York Amsterdam News*, 24 July 1937.

5. *Harlem: Negro Metropolis*, 246–47.

6. McKay to James Weldon Johnson, 9 May 1935; McKay Papers, James Weldon Johnson Collection.

7. McKay to Edwin R. Embree, 30 April 1935; McKay Papers, Rosenwald Fund Archives, Fisk University. McKay had outlined these observations in his application for a Rosenwald grant.

8. McKay to Helen Boardman, 18 July 1935 and Helen Boardman to McKay, 19 July 1937; McKay Papers, James W. Johnson Collection. McKay had been so vociferous in his opposition to her that on one occasion she fled a meeting yelling, "I resign, I resign."

9. McKay to James Weldon Johnson, 22 August 1937; McKay Papers, James Weldon Johnson Collection. McKay made this comment to Johnson in defending his opposition to Boardman.

10. *A Long Way from Home*, 350–51.

11. Harvard Sitkoff, *A New Deal For Blacks: The Emergence of Civil Rights as a National Issue: The Depression Decade*, 252.

12. *A Long Way from Home*, 351.

13. "For Group Survival," 19–26.

14. "Segregation in Harlem?", 5.

15. Roy Wilkins, *The Autobiography of Roy Wilkins: Standing Fast*, 152; Sitkoff, *A New Deal*, 251–53.

16. McKay to James Weldon Johnson, 16 May 1935; McKay Papers, James Weldon Johnson Collection.

17. "For Group Survival," 26.

18. McKay to James Weldon Johnson, 8 August 1937; McKay Papers, James Weldon Johnson Collection.

19. McKay to Friends (form letter), 10 August 1937; McKay Papers, James Weldon Johnson Collection.

20. McKay to Friends (form letter), 23 October 1937; McKay Papers, James Weldon Johnson Collection.

21. McKay to Countee Cullen, 12 May (no year); Countee Cullen Papers, Amistad Collection, Tulane University.

22. McKay to James Weldon Johnson, 22 August 1937; McKay Papers, James Weldon Johnson Collection.

23. Tarry, *The Third Door*, 133; McKay to James Weldon Johnson, 28 September 1937; James Weldon Johnson Collection.

24. McKay to James Weldon Johnson, October 1937; McKay Papers, James Weldon Johnson Collection.

25. Tarry, *The Third Door*, 133.

26. McKay to James Weldon Johnson, October 1937; McKay Papers, James Weldon Johnson Collection.

27. Alain Locke, "Spiritual Truancy," in *The New Challenge*, vol. 2 (1937); reprinted in Nathan Irvin Huggins, *Voices from the Harlem Renaissance*, 404–6.

28. Ibid.

29. Ibid.

30. Ibid.

31. James Weldon Johnson to McKay, 12 April 1937; McKay Papers, James Weldon Johnson Collection.

32. McKay to James Weldon Johnson, 12 April 1938; McKay to Johnson, 9 May 1938, and McKay to Johnson, 14 May 1938; McKay Papers, James Weldon Johnson Collection.

33. Anderson, *This Was Harlem*, 280–81.

34. See Joyce B. Ross, "The Twilight of White Liberalism," in *J. E. Spingarn and the Rise of the NAACP*, 217–45.

35. Sitkoff, *A New Deal*, 210.

36. Mark Naison, *Communists in Harlem during the Depression*, 202.

37. Sitkoff, *A New Deal*, 210.

38. McKay to James Weldon Johnson, 8 April 1937; McKay Papers, James Weldon Johnson Collection.

39. McKay to James Weldon Johnson, 16 May 1935; McKay Papers, James Weldon Johnson Collection. McKay had been right in his prediction, for the Congress was eventually taken over by the Communists.

40. Naison, *Communists in Harlem*, 169–92, 193.

41. Harvey Klehr, *The Heyday of American Communism: The Depression Decade*, 373.

42. See Record, *The Negro and the Communist Party*, for a treatment of Communist influence on blacks in the thirties. "Countee Cullen Accepts Bid to 'Lib' Banquet," *Harlem Liberator*, 9 June 1934, 6. Cullen supported the League of Struggle for Negro Rights. The *Liberator* was a Communist paper.

43. Sitkoff, *A New Deal*, 210–11; Record, *The Negro and the Communist Party*, 111; "Langston Hughes Greets F.S.U. Convention," *Harlem Liberator*, 27 April 1934, 2; Langston Hughes, "To Negro Writers," in Henry Hart, ed., *American Writers' Congress*, 140.

44. McKay to Carl Cowl, 14 January 1948; McKay Papers, James Weldon Johnson Collection. McKay's remark had been prompted by Arna Bontemps's desire to include some of McKay's poems in an anthology he was compiling. McKay did not want to appear in the same anthology with Hughes.

45. "I Believe in the Social Revolution and the Triumph of Worker's Democracy," *Socialist Call*, 17 July 1937, 8.

46. "Where the News Ends," 8; reprinted in Cooper, *Passion of Claude McKay*, 229–32. McKay claimed that a New York section of the Federal Writers' Project was underhandedly abolished by Communist "stooges"; see McKay to Orick Johns, director of the Federal Writers' Project, New York (n. d.); McKay Papers, Schomburg Collection, New York Public Library. The Federal Writers' Project had provided other writers, like Richard Wright (a member of the American Writers' Congress), Ralph Ellison, Willard Motley, Era Bell Thompson, Margaret Walker, and Robert Hayden with an opportunity to use their talents without the handicap of a hostile market; see Richard Bardolph, *The Negro Vanguard*, 377.

47. Alan M. Wald, *The New York Intellectuals: The Rise and Decline of the Anti-Stalinist Left from the 1930s to the 1980s*, 75–82; and Klehr, *Heyday of American Communism*, 349–355.

48. McKay to Gilmore, 5 March 1941; McKay Papers, James Weldon Johnson Collection.

49. "Author Decries Inroads Made by Communists," *New York Amsterdam News*, 17 September 1938.

50. Naison, *Communists in Harlem*, 171.

51. McKay to Max Eastman, 17 July 1944; McKay MSS, Indiana University.

52. "Negro Author Sees Disaster if the Communist Party Gains Control of Negro Workers," *New Leader*, 10 September 1938, 5.

53. "Claude McKay Replies to Poston on Solution to Negro Problems," *New Leader*, 7 December 1940, 5.

54. Richmond, *A Long View from the Left*, 90–91. Richmond describes how uncomfortable and difficult it was initially for even white comrades to "close ranks" to defend the nine Scottsboro boys, until one of the white women confessed that neither she nor her companion was raped—attesting to the deep-seated prejudice in America. Haywood, *Black Bolshevik*, 358–63. Haywood's recollection was that the Communists never failed to view the case except in broader "class terms."

55. Wald, *New York Intellectuals*, 49, 57, 60, 61; also see Klehr's chapter "The Negroes," in *Heyday of American Communism*, 324–48; Solomon, *Red and Black*, 451–521.

56. Herbert Garfinkel, *When Negroes March*, 42–47.

57. McKay to Gilmore, 5 March 1941; McKay Papers, James Weldon Johnson Collection.

58. Record, *The Negro and the Communist Party*, 209–26.

59. Naison, *Communists in Harlem*, 289.

60. Ibid., 291–92.

61. Richmond, *A Long View from the Left*, 283–86, 289.

62. Haywood, *Black Bolshevik*, 495.

63. McKay to Max Eastman, 30 June 1944; McKay MSS, Indiana University.

64. *Harlem: Negro Metropolis*, 181–262. See also Roi Ottley, "Review of *Harlem: Negro Metropolis*," *New York Times*, 24 November 1940, 5.

65. McKay to Max Eastman, 17 July 1944; McKay MSS, Indiana University.

66. McKay to Max Eastman, 1939; McKay MSS, Indiana University. Martin Dies of Texas, chairman of the House Committee on Un-American Activities, pursued a policy of harrying radicals.

67. McKay to Carl Cowl, 17 October 1947; McKay Papers, James Weldon Johnson Collection.

68. McKay to Carl Cowl, November 1947; McKay Papers, James Weldon Johnson Collection.

69. Charles Paterno to McKay, 3 March 1939 (from WPA); McKay to Max Eastman, 2 March 1939; McKay to Max Eastman, 23 March 1939; McKay MSS, Indiana University.

70. McKay to Max Eastman, 2 March 1939; McKay MSS, Indiana University.

71. "Native Liberation Might Have Been Stopped: The Franco Revolt," *New Leader*, 18 February 1939, 2, 5; reprinted in Cooper, *Passion of Claude McKay*, 285–89.

72. Tarry, *The Third Door*, 132.

73. McKay to Carl Cowl, 13 February 1947; McKay Papers, James Weldon Johnson Collection; McKay to Max Eastman, 30 June 1944; McKay to Eastman, 2 March 1939; McKay MSS, Indiana University.

74. McKay to Max Eastman, 2 March 1944; McKay to Eastman, 9 March 1939; McKay MSS, Indiana University.

75. McKay to Max Eastman, 30 June 1944; McKay MSS, Indiana University.

8. A Long Way from Home

1. Bracey, Meier, and Rudwick, *Black Nationalism in America*, xlvi.

2. Horace R. Clayton and St. Clair Drake, *Black Metropolis: A Study of Negro Life in a Northern City* (New York: Harcourt, Brace and World, 1945), 430–32; Thomas Blair, *Retreat to the Ghetto: The End of a Dream?* 13.

3. Sitkoff, *A New Deal for Blacks*, 262–63.

4. Bracey, Meier, and Rudwick, *Black Nationalism in America*, xlvi.

5. *Harlem: Negro Metropolis*, 185–86.

6. Naison, *Communists in Harlem*, 117.

7. Wilbur Young, "Activities of Bishop Amiru, Al-Mumin Sufi A. Hamid," Federal Writers' Project Papers, Reel 1; *Harlem: Negro Metropolis*, 191–92; *New York Age*, 1 October 1932; Melville Weiss, "Don't Buy Where You Can't Work," (Master's thesis, Columbia University, 1941), 56–57; *New York Amsterdam News*, 26 May 1934.

8. "Harlem Runs Wild," 382–83.

9. Ibid., 383.

10. *Harlem: Negro Metropolis*, 181–262.

11. McKay to S. Katz, 28 August 1938; McKay Papers, James Weldon Johnson Collection.

12. "Everybody's Doing It: Anti-Semitic Propaganda Fails to Attract Negroes; Harlemites Face Problems of All Other Slum Dwellers," 5–6.

NOTES TO PAGES 167-73

13. "Claude McKay Replies to Poston on Solution of Negro Problems," 5.

14. Ibid. Walter White, however, was less willing to excuse Jews for their exploitation of blacks in Harlem and other communities. He wrote to McKay about Jewish merchants who get their start in black neighborhoods—often by charging high prices for inferior goods—and who get to the top. He cited Baltimore, Maryland, as proof. Jews owned seven of the nine stores and wouldn't let a Negro work in their stores; see Walter White to McKay, 23 December 1938; McKay Papers, James Weldon Johnson Collection.

15. Cruse, *Crisis of the Negro Intellectual*, 481.

16. McKay to Max Eastman, 4 May 1944; McKay MSS, Indiana University. McKay indicated to Eastman that he believed the *New Leader* purposely got Poston, a Negro, to attack his book as anti-Semitic and antilabor and then forced him to respond.

17. McKay to Max Eastman, 30 June 1944; McKay MSS, Indiana University.

18. McKay to Max Eastman, 21 March 1945; McKay MSS, Indiana University.

19. McKay to James Weldon Johnson, 16 May 1935; McKay Papers, James Weldon Johnson Collection; Levy, *James Weldon Johnson*, 344–45.

20. McKay to James Weldon Johnson, 31 May 1935; McKay Papers, James Weldon Johnson Collection.

21. William Harris, *The Harder We Run: Black Workers since the Civil War*, 108.

22. "Labor Steps Out in Harlem," 399–402.

23. Naison, *Communists in Harlem*, 262–63.

24. "Labor Steps Out in Harlem," 400.

25. *Harlem: Negro Metropolis*, 211–16; Naison, *Communists in Harlem*, 262–63; "Labor Steps Out in Harlem," 400–402.

26. "Labor Steps Out in Harlem," 402; Harris, *The Harder We Run*, 108–9.

27. Adam Clayton Powell, Jr., "Soap Box," *New York Amsterdam News*, 30 October 1937, 13.

28. "Claude McKay Versus Powell," 4; see also Adam Clayton Powell, Jr., "Soap Box," *New York Amsterdam News*, 11 December 1937, 13. Powell wrote glowingly of Kemp's contribution to the economic uplift of blacks. Kemp had just died.

29. Powell, "Soap Box," *New York Amsterdam News*, 30 October 1937.

30. For an in-depth discussion of black nationalism, see Bracey, Meier, and Rudwick, *Black Nationalism in America*, xxx–lx.

31. "McKay Says Schuyler Is Writing Nonsense," 20 November 1937, 12.

32. McKay to Joel Spingarn, 12 March 1937; McKay Papers, James Weldon Johnson Collection.

33. Asa Philip Randolph to McKay, 14 April 1941; McKay Papers, James Weldon Johnson Collection. Randolph felt McKay was right in his belief that part of the Negro intelligentsia believed that to stress race

vigorously smacked of chauvinism. But Randolph urged McKay not to abandon the idea of the need for "race leadership" in the black man's struggle for liberation.

34. *Harlem: Negro Metropolis*, 183–84.

35. "McKay Says Schuyler Is Writing Nonsense," 12.

36. Levy, *James Weldon Johnson*, 316, 346.

37. McKay to Walter White, 4 December 1924; NAACP Papers, Box C-92.

38. McKay to Carl Cowl, 17 October 1947; McKay Papers, James Weldon Johnson Collection.

39. McKay to Carl Cowl, 13 January 1948; McKay Papers, James Weldon Johnson Collection. The article appeared in the January issue of the *Saturday Review of Literature*.

40. McKay to Carl Cowl, 12 February 1947; McKay Papers, James Weldon Johnson Collection.

41. *A Long Way from Home*, 347.

42. McKay to Joel Spingarn, 18 December 1934; Spingarn Papers, New York Public Library. It was in this letter that McKay included the excerpt from the Eastman letter.

43. McKay to Joel Spingarn, 24 December 1934; Spingarn Papers, New York Public Library.

44. McKay to Joel Spingarn, 7 March 1937, and McKay to Spingarn, 12 March 1937; Spingarn Papers, New York Public Library.

45. Ross, J. E. *Spingarn and the Rise of the NAACP*, 242–43; Levy, *James Weldon Johnson*, 338–39.

46. McKay to Joel Spingarn, 12 March 1937; Spingarn Papers, New York Public Library. McKay replied to Spingarn that he agreed it was possible, for "such things belong to the experience of all humanity. Jesus and Judas are the classical examples of Christendom. And many great souls have been broken or murdered by peoples whom they were trying to raise up." Spingarn had made this comment in an earlier statement to McKay.

47. McKay to Edwin R. Embree, 30 April 1935; Rosenwald Fund Archives, Fisk University. The book had been finished while McKay was a member of the Federal Writers' Project in New York.

48. McKay to Lewis Gannett, 27 October 1937; Braithwaite Papers, Harvard University. Gannett was a staff member of the *New York Herald Tribune*.

49. Random House, Farrar, Straus, Viking Press, and Macmillan turned McKay down; see correspondence between McKay and publishers contained in McKay Papers, James Weldon Johnson Collection.

50. Herbert Weinstock of Knopf to Carl Cowl, 30 October 1947; McKay Papers, James Weldon Johnson Collection.

51. Elmer Carter of the Unemployment Insurance Appeal Board, New York Department of Labor, to McKay, 6 September 1939; McKay Papers, James Weldon Johnson Collection.

52. McKay to Max Eastman, 30 July 1942; McKay MSS, Indiana University. He asked Max to contact Elmer Davis to get him a job with the Office of War Information.

53. McKay to Countee Cullen, 11 May 1943; Cullen Papers, Amistad Collection, Tulane University.

54. McKay to Countee Cullen, 1943; Cullen Papers, Amistad Collection, Tulane University.

55. Cooper, *Passion of Claude McKay*, 40.

56. Ibid.; Freda Kirchway to Edwin R. Embree (of Postal Telegraph), November 1943; McKay Papers, Rosenwald Fund Archives.

57. Freda Kirchway to Edwin K. Embree, 16 November 1947; McKay Papers, Rosenwald Fund Archives.

58. McKay to Countee Cullen, 11 October 1943; Cullen Papers, Amistad Collection, Tulane University.

59. Ibid.

60. McKay to Countee Cullen, 10 August 1943, and McKay to Cullen, 28 August 1943; Cullen Papers, Amistad Collection, Tulane University.

61. Ibid.

62. Cooper, *Passion of Claude McKay*, 40.

63. McKay to Max Eastman, 4 May 1944; McKay MSS, Indiana University.

64. Editorial, "Fearless Bishop Sheil," *Chicago Defender*, 24 February 1945.

65. McKay to Max Eastman, 1 June 1944; McKay MSS, Indiana University. Sheil had also been founder of the Chicago Catholic Youth Organization, which the *Chicago Defender* pointed out was a good example of democracy applied to sports.

66. McKay to Max Eastman, 30 June 1944; McKay MSS, Indiana University.

67. McKay to Max Eastman, 16 August 1944; McKay MSS, Indiana University.

68. "Why I Became a Catholic," 32.

69. Max Eastman to McKay, 7 June 1944; McKay MSS, Indiana University.

70. McKay to Max Eastman, 28 November 1944, and McKay to Eastman, 16 September 1946; McKay MSS, Indiana University.

71. Betty Britton to McKay, 12 July 1944; Britton to McKay, 20 September 1944; McKay Papers, James Weldon Johnson Collection.

72. See Eddie Doherty, "Poet's Progress," *Extension*, September 1946, 5, 46.

73. Betty Britton to McKay, 24 August 1944; McKay Papers, James Weldon Johnson Collection.

74. McKay to Carl Cowl, 9 April 1947; McKay Papers, James Weldon Johnson Collection.

75. McKay to Bishop J. Sheil, 30 January 1947; McKay Papers, Schomburg Collection, New York Public Library.

76. Betty Britton to McKay, 20 January 1947; McKay Papers, James Weldon Johnson Collection.

77. "Right Turn to Catholicism" (unpublished manuscript), 21–22; McKay Papers, James Weldon Johnson Collection.

78. Ibid., 21–22, 23.

79. Tarry, *The Third Door*, 269; Cooper, *Passion of Claude McKay*, 41.
80. Tarry, *The Third Door*, 270.
81. Max Eastman to Eliena Eastman, 25 May 1948; Eastman MSS, Indiana University.
82. Bishop Sheil, in his introduction to "My Green Hills of Jamaica" (unpublished manuscript, McKay Papers, Schomburg Collection). McKay seemed to understand his own dilemma when he wrote, "I can't get my mind and my emotions in harmony together, that's my whole tragedy" (McKay to Max Eastman, 28 June 1938, McKay MSS, Indiana University).
83. "When I Have Passed Away" (unpublished poem), Braithwaite Papers, Harvard University.

Bibliography

The Writings of Claude McKay

ARTICLES, REVIEWS, AND OTHER SHORT PIECES

"The American Type." Review of *Three Soldiers*, by John Dos Passos. *Liberator*, January 1922, 8–9.

"Anti-Semite Propaganda Fails to Attract Negroes." *New Leader*, 20 May 1939, 5–6.

"Author Assails Negro Congress for Message Sent to Washington on Jews: Calls Body Organization of Leaders; No Followers." *New York Amsterdam News*, 26 November 1939, 11.

"Author Decries Inroads Made by Communists." *New York Amsterdam News*, 17 September 1938.

"Birthright." Review of *Birthright*, by T. S. Stribling. *Liberator*, August 1922, 15–16.

"A Black Man Replies." *Workers' Dreadnought*. 24 April 1920.

"A Black Star." Review of 1921, *Emperor Jones*, by Eugene O'Neill. *Liberator*, August 25.

"Boyhood in Jamaica." *Phylon* 13 (Spring 1953): 134–45.

"The Capitalist Way: Lettow-Vorbeck." *Workers' Dreadnought*, 7 February 1920, 6.

"Claude McKay Replies to Poston on Solution of Negro Problems." *New Leader*, 7 December 1940, 6.

"Claude McKay Versus Powell." *New York Amsterdam News*, 6 November 1937, 4.

"Dynamite in Africa: Are the Popular Fronts Suppressing Colonial Independence?" *Common Sense*, March 1938, 8–11.

"English Journalists Investigate Bolshevism." *Crusader*, April 1921, 18–19.

"Everybody's Doing It: Anti-Semitic Propaganda Fails to Attract Negroes; Harlemites Face Problems of All Other Slum Dwellers." *New Leader*, 20 May 1939, 5–6.

"Father Divine's Rebel Angel." *American Mercury*, September 1940, 73–80.

"Fear of Segregation Furthers Negro Disunity." *New Leader*, 15 November 1941, 4.

"For Group Survival." *Jewish Frontier*, October 1937, 43–45.

"Garvey as a Negro Moses." *Liberator*, April 1922, 8–9.

"Harlem Runs Wild." *Nation*, 3 April 1935, 382–83.

BIBLIOGRAPHY

"He Who Gets Slapped." Review of He Who Gets Slapped, by Leonid Andreyev. *Liberator*, May 1922, 24–25.
"How Black Sees Green and Red." *Liberator*, June 1921, 17, 20–21.
"I Believe in the Social Revolution and the Triumph of Worker's Democracy." *Socialist Call*, 17 July 1937, 8.
"A Job in London." *Opportunity*, March 1937, 72–75.
"Labor Steps Out in Harlem." *Nation*, 16 October 1937, 399–402.
"Lest We Forget." *Jewish Frontier*, January 1940, 9–11.
"Letter to the Editor." *Crisis*, July 1921, 102.
"Letter to the Editor." *Messenger*, October 1920, 7.
"A Little Lamb to Lead Them: A True Narrative." *African*, March–April 1938, 107–8, 112.
"The Little Lincoln." *Liberator*, February 1922, 22–25.
"Looking Forward." *New York Amsterdam News*, 20 May 1939, 13.
"The Looking Glass." *Crisis*, November 1918, 23.
"McKay Says Schuyler Is Writing Nonsense." *New York Amsterdam News*, 20 November 1937, 12.
"A Moscow Lady." *Crisis*, September 1924, 225–28.
"Mystic Happiness in Harlem." *American Mercury*, August 1939, 444–50.
"Native Liberation Might Have Been Stopped: The Franco Revolt." *New Leader*, 18 February 1939, 2, 5.
"Negro Author Sees Disaster if the Communist Party Gains Control of Negro Workers." *New Leader*, 10 September 1938, 5.
"A Negro Extravaganza." Review of *Shuffle Along*, by Eubie Blake and Noble Sissle. *Liberator*, December 1921, 24–26.
"A Negro Poet." *Pearson's Magazine*, September 1918, 275–76.
"New Crime Wave Old Story to Harlemites: Poverty Brings Prostitution, 'Muggings,' Robberies." *New Leader*, 29 November 1941, 5.
"North African Triangle." *Nation*, 8 May 1943, 663–65.
"On Becoming a Roman Catholic." *Epistle*, Spring 1945, 43–45.
"The Race Question in the United States." *International Press Correspondence*, 21 November 1922, 817.
"Report on the Negro Question." *International Press Correspondence*, 5 January 1923, 16.
"Segregation in Harlem?" *Column Review*, December 1941, 5.
"Socialism and the Negro." *Workers' Dreadnought*, 31 January 1920, 1–2.
"Soviet Russia and the Negro." *Crisis*, December 1923, 61–65.
"There Goes God! The Story of Father Divine and His Angels." *Nation*, 6 February 1935, 155–63.
"This Race Problem." *March of Progress*, Spring 1945, 264–67.
"An Unpublished Letter from Claude McKay, Poet and Literateur." *Negro History Bulletin*, no. 13 (April 1968): 10–11.
"What Is and What Isn't." *Crisis*, April 1924, 261.
"What Is Lacking in the Theatre." *Liberator*, March 1922, 20–21.
"Where the News Ends." *New Leader*, 10 June 1939, 8.
"Why I Became a Catholic." *Ebony*, March 1946, 32.

Bibliography

BOOKS

Banana Bottom. New York: Harper, 1929. Reprinted. Chatham, N.J.: Chatham Bookseller, 1970.
Banjo: A Story without A Plot. New York: Harper, 1929.
Constab Ballads. London: Watts, 1912.
The Dialect Poetry of Claude McKay. 2 vols. in 1. Vol. 1, *Songs of Jamaica.* Vol. 2, *Constab Ballads.* Freeport, N.Y.: Books for Libraries, 1972.
Gingertown. New York: Harper, 1932.
Harlem: Negro Metropolis. New York: E. P. Dutton and Co., 1940.
Harlem Shadows. New York: Harcourt, Brace, 1922.
Home to Harlem. New York: Harper, 1928.
A Long Way from Home. New York: Lee Furman, 1937.
The Negroes in America. Translated by Robert J. Winter. Edited by Alan J. McLeod. New York: Kennikat Press, 1979. [Originally published as *Negry v Amerike*, USSR, 1923.]
Songs of Jamaica. Kingston, Jamaica: Aston W. Gardner, 1912.
Spring in New Hampshire and Other Poems. London: Grant Richards, 1920.

UNPUBLISHED WRITINGS

Braithwaite, William Stanley. Papers. Houghton Library, Harvard University, Cambridge, Massachusetts.
Cullen, Countee. Papers. Amistad Collection. Amistad Research Center, Tulane University, New Orleans, Louisiana.
Deshon, Florence. MSS. Lilly Library, Indiana University, Bloomington, Indiana.
Eastman, Eliena. MSS. Lilly Library, Indiana University, Bloomington, Indiana.
Fauset, Jessie. Letters. Alain Locke Papers. Moorland-Spingarn Research Center, Howard University, Washington, D.C.
Harmon Foundation Papers. Manuscript Division, Library of Congress, Washington, D.C.
Herbst, Josephine. Papers. Beinecke Rare Book and Manuscript Library, Yale University, New Haven, Connecticut.
Hughes, Langston. Letters. Alain Locke Papers. Moorland-Spingarn Research Center, Howard University, Washington, D.C.
McKay, Claude. Introductory Remarks to Reading of "If We Must Die." Included in "Anthology of Negro Poets." Folkways Records, FP91.
McKay, Claude. Letters. Alain Locke Papers. Moorland-Spingarn Research Center, Howard University, Washington, D.C.
McKay, Claude. MSS. Lilly Library, Indiana University, Bloomington, Indiana.
McKay, Claude. "My Green Hills of Jamaica." Manuscript. Claude Mc-

Kay Papers, Special Collection, Schomburg Branch, New York Public Library, New York, New York.

McKay, Claude. "Negro Life and Negro Art." Manuscript. NAACP Letter File. Manuscript Division, Library of Congress, Washington, D.C.

McKay, Claude. "Notebook." Manuscript. Claude McKay Papers, Special Collection, Schomburg Branch, New York Public Library, New York, New York.

McKay, Claude. Papers. James Weldon Johnson Collection of Negro Literature and Art, American Literature Collection, Beinecke Rare Book and Manuscript Library, Yale University, New Haven, Connecticut.

McKay, Claude. Papers. Special Collection, Schomburg Branch, New York Public Library, New York, New York.

McKay, Claude. "Right Turn to Catholicism." Manuscript. Claude McKay Papers, Schomburg Collection, New York Public Library, New York, New York.

Mencken, H. L. Papers. New York Public Library, New York, New York.

National Association for the Advancement of Colored People Letter File. Manuscript Division, Library of Congress, Washington, D.C.

Spingarn, Joel E. Papers. New York Public Library, New York, New York.

Van Vechten, Carl. Papers. Beinecke Rare Book and Manuscript Library, Yale University, New Haven Connecticut.

Washington, Booker T. Papers, Manuscript Division, Library of Congress, Washington, D.C.

Newspapers and Periodicals Consulted

American Mercury. Scattered issues, Vols. 3–51. New York, 1924–1940.

Crisis: A Record of the Darker Races. Vols. 17–44. New York, 1917–40.

Crusader. Scattered issues. Vols. 3–4. New York, 1920–21.

Current History. Vols. 17–30. New York, 1923–1929.

Daily Gleaner. Scattered issues. Kingston, Jamaica, 1900–1920.

Harlem Liberator. Scattered issues. New York, 1930–1934.

Liberator. Vols. 1–10. New York, 1918–1924.

Messenger. Vols. 1–8. New York, 1918–1927.

Nation. Scattered issues. Vols. 122–50. New York, 1926–1935.

New York Amsterdam News. Scattered issues. 1920–1940.

Opportunity. Vols. 1–27. New York, 1918–49.

Pearson's Magazine. Vols. 39–151. New York, 1918–1920.

Phylon. Scattered issues. Vols. 1–13.

Workers' Dreadnought. London, England, 1919–1921.

Secondary Works

ARTICLES, REVIEWS, AND OTHER SHORT PIECES

Braithwaite, Stanley William. "Some Contemporary Poets of the Negro Race." *Crisis*, April 1919, 277.

Brawley, Benjamin. "The Negro Literary Renaissance." *Southern Workman.* April 1927, 28.

Brickell, Herschell. "Home to Harlem." Review of *Home to Harlem,* by Claude McKay. *Opportunity,* May 1928.

Briggs, Cyril. "Bolshevism's Menace: To Whom and to What?" *Crusader,* February 1920, 5–6.

———. "We Must Unite for the Struggle." *Negro Champion,* 27 October 1928.

Brown, Sterling. "The Negro Character as Seen Through White Authors." *Journal of Negro Education,* April 1933, 42–49.

Calverton, V. F. "The New Negro." *Current History,* February 1926, 694–98.

Chapman, Abraham. "The Harlem Renaissance in Literary History." *College Language Association* 2 (September 1967): 38–58.

Cooper, Wayne, and C. Robert Reinders. "A Black Briton Comes Home: Claude McKay in England." *Race,* January 1967, 67–83.

Cooney, Charles. "Walter White and the Harlem Renaissance." *Journal of Negro History* 17 (July 1972): 231–40.

Cullen, Countee. "The League of Youth." *Crisis,* August 1923, 167.

Davis, Allison. "Our Negro Intellectuals." *Crisis,* August 1928, 268–69.

Du Bois, W. E. B. "Back to Africa." *Century,* July 1929, 539–48.

———. "Criteria of Negro Art." *Crisis,* October 1926, 295–96.

———. "The Negro and Radical Thought." *Crisis* July 1921, 102.

———. "Postscript: Mencken." *Crisis,* October 1927, 279.

———. Review of *Banjo,* by Claude McKay. *Crisis,* July 1929, 234.

———. Review of *Home to Harlem,* by Claude McKay. *Crisis,* September 1928, 202.

Garvey, Marcus. "*Home to Harlem:* Claude McKay's Damaging Book Should Earn Wholesale Condemnation of Negroes." *Negro World,* 29 September 1928.

Harris, Abram L. "The Negro Problem as Viewed by Negro Leaders." *Current History,* June 1923, 411–418.

Hughes, Langston. "The Negro Artist and the Racial Mountain." *Nation* 122 (June 1926): 692–694.

———. "The Twenties: Harlem and Its Negritude." *African Forum* 1 (1966): 11–20.

Keller, Francis Richardson. "The Harlem Literary Renaissance." *North American Review* 5 (May 1968): 29–34.

Matthews, T. S. "What Gods! What Gongs!" Review of *Home to Harlem,* by Claude McKay. *New Republic,* 30 May 1928, 50–51.

New York World. "Home to Harlem." 16 March 1928.

Ottley, Roi. "Review of *Negro Metropolis.*" *New York Times Book Review,* 24 November 1940.

Pickens, William. "Art and Propaganda." *Messenger,* April 1924, 111.

Powell, Adam Clayton, Jr. "Soap Box." *New York Amsterdam News,* 30 October 1937; 11 December 1937.

Randolph, A. Philip. "The Negro and the New Social Order." *Messenger,* March 1919, 26.

————. "New Leadership for the Negro." *Messenger,* May–June 1919, 29.

————. "The New Philosophy of the Negro." *Messenger,* December 1919, 5.

Rascoe, Burton. "The Seamy Side." Review of *Home to Harlem,* by Claude McKay. *Bookman,* 23 March 1928, 183–84.

Rogers, J. A. "Rogers Finds Claude McKay, Abroad and in Want." *Afro-Baltimore,* 18 June 1927.

————. "Nigger Heaven." *Messenger,* December 1926, 365.

Smith, Robert. "Claude McKay: An Essay in Criticism." *Phylon* 9 (1948): 270–73.

Whipple, Leon. "Letters and Life: The Negro Artistic Awakening." *Survey,* April 1926, 517–19.

BOOKS

Aaron, Daniel. *Writers on the Left: Episodes in American Literary Communism.* New York: Harcourt, Brace and World, 1961.

Abrahams, Peter. *Jamaica: An Island Mosaic.* London: Her Majesty's Stationery Office, 1957.

American Society for African Culture. *The American Negro Writer and His Roots: Selected Papers from the First Conference of Negro Writers, 1959.* New York: American Society of African Culture, 1960.

Anderson, Jervis. *A. Philip Randolph: A Biographical Portrait.* New York: Harcourt Brace Jovanovich, 1973.

————. *This Was Harlem: A Cultural Portrait, 1900–1950.* New York: Farrar, Straus, Giroux, 1982.

Aptheker, Herbert, ed. *The Correspondence of W. E. B. Du Bois.* Vol. 1. *Selections, 1877–1934.* Amherst: University of Massachusetts Press, 1973.

Bardolph, Richard. *The Negro Vanguard.* New York: Random House, 1961.

Barton, Rebecca Chalmers. *Black Voices in American Fiction, 1900–1930.* New York: Dowling College Press, 1976.

Bell, Bernard W. *The Afro-American Novel and Its Tradition.* Amherst: University of Massachusetts Press, 1987.

Blair, Thomas. *Retreat to the Ghetto: The End of a Dream?* New York: Hill and Wang, 1977.

Bone, Robert. *Down Home: A History of Afro-American Short Fiction from Its Beginning to the End of the Renaissance.* New York: G. P. Putnam's Sons, 1975.

————. *The Negro Novel in America.* New Haven: Yale University Press, 1968.

Bontemps, Arna. *One Hundred Years of Negro Freedom.* New York: Dodd, Mead and Co., 1966.

Bracey, John H., Jr., August Meier, and Elliott Rudwick, eds. *Black*

Nationalism in America. Indianapolis: Bobbs-Merrill Company, 1970.

Brawley, Benjamin. *The Negro Genius.* New York: Dodd, Mead, 1937.

Broderick, Francis L. *W. E. B. Du Bois: Negro Leader in Time of Crisis.* Stanford: Stanford University Press, 1959.

Bronz, Stephen. *Roots of Negro Racial Consciousness.* New York: Libra Publishers, 1964.

Brown, Sterling A., Arthur Davis, and Ulysses Lee, eds. *The Negro Caravan.* New York: Citadel Press, 1941.

Butcher, Margaret J. *The Negro in American Culture.* New York: Knopf, 1956.

Carr, Edward H. *Studies in Revolution.* New York: Grosset and Dunlap, 1964.

Churchill, Allen. *The Improper Bohemians.* New York: E. O. Dutton and Company, 1959.

Clayton, Horace, and St. Clair Drake. *Black Metropolis: A Study of Negro Life in a Northern City.* New York: Harcourt, Brace and World, 1945.

Cooke, M. G., ed. *Modern Black Novelists: A Collection of Critical Essays.* Englewood Cliffs, N.J.: Prentice-Hall, 1971.

Cooper, Wayne F. *Claude McKay: Rebel Sojourner in the Harlem Renaissance.* Baton Rouge: Louisiana State University Press, 1987.

————, ed. *The Passion of Claude McKay: Selected Poetry and Prose, 1912–1948.* New York: Schocken Books, 1973.

Cowley, Malcolm. *Exile's Return: A Literary Odyssey of the 1920's.* New York: Viking Press, 1951.

Cronon, David E. *Black Moses: The Story of Marcus Garvey and the Universal Negro Improvement Association.* Madison: University of Wisconsin Press, 1955.

Cruse, Harold. *The Crisis of the Negro Intellectual.* New York: William Morrow and Co., 1967.

Curtin, Philip D. *Two Jamaicas: The Role of Ideas in a Tropical Colony, 1830–1865.* Cambridge: Harvard University Press, 1955.

Davis, Arthur. *From the Dark Tower: Afro-American Writers 1900 to 1960.* Washington, D.C.: Howard University Press, 1974.

Draper, Theodore. *American Communism and Soviet Russia.* New York: Viking Press, 1960.

————. *The Roots of American Communism.* New York: Viking Press, 1960.

Du Bois, W. E. B. *The Autobiography of W. E. B. Du Bois: A Soliloquy on Viewing My Life from the Last Decade of Its First Century.* New York: International Publishers, 1968.

————. *Dusk of Dawn: An Essay toward an Autobiography of a Race Concept.* New York: Harcourt and Brace, 1940.

————. *The Gift of Black Folk: The Negro in the Making of America.* Boston: Straford Co., 1924.

————. *Shall the Negro Seek Cultural Equality?* (Debate with Lothrop Stoddard of Harvard University, Chicago, 17 March 1929.) Chicago: University Forum, 1929.

———. *The Souls of Black Folks*. Greenwich, Conn.: Fawcett Publication, 1903.

Eastman, Max. *Road to Revolution*. New York: Random House, 1964.

———, ed. *Selected Poems of Claude McKay*. New York: Harcourt, Brace and World, 1953.

Egbert, Donald D., and S. Persons. *Socialism and American Life*. Princeton: Princeton University Press, 1952.

Ferguson, Blacke E. *Countee Cullen and the Negro Renaissance*. New York: Dodd and Mead, 1966.

Foner, Philip S. *American Socialism and Black Americans: From the Age of Jackson to World War II*. Westport, Conn.: Greenwood Press, 1977.

Foner, Philip S., and James Allen, eds. *American Communism and Black Americans: A Documentary History, 1919–1929*. Philadelphia: Temple University Press, 1987.

Franklin, John Hope. *From Slavery to Freedom: A History of Negro Americans*. Rev. 4th ed. New York: Knopf, 1961.

Freeman, Joseph. *An American Testament: A Narrative of Rebel and Romantics*. New York: Farrar and Rinehart, 1936.

French, Warren, ed. *The Twenties: Fiction, Poetry, Drama*. Deland, Fla.: Everett/Edwards, 1975.

Fullinwider, S. P. *The Mind and Mood of Black America*. Homewood, Ill.: Dorsey Press, 1969.

Gardner, Virginia. *Friend and Lover: The Life of Louise Bryant*. New York: Horizon Press, 1982.

Gayle, Addison, Jr. *Black Expression: Essays by and about Black Americans in the Creative Arts*. New York: Weybright and Talley, 1969.

———. *Bondage, Freedom, and Beyond*. New York: Zenith Books/Doubleday, 1971.

———. *The Way of the New World: The Black Novel in America*. Garden City, N.Y.: Anchor Press/Doubleday, 1976.

Gilbert, James Burkhart. *Writers and Partisans: A History of Literary Radicalism in America*. New York: John Wiley and Sons, 1968.

Giles, James R. *Claude McKay*. Boston: Twayne Publishers, 1976.

Gold, Michael. *Jews without Money*. New York: Horace Liveright, 1930.

The Handbook of Jamaica. Kingston, Jamaica: Government Printing Establishment, 1888–1890.

Harris, William. *The Harder We Run: Black Workers since the Civil War*. New York: Oxford University Press, 1982.

Harrison, Hubert. *When Africa Awakes*. New York: Porro Press, 1920.

Hart, Henry, ed. *American Writers Congress*. New York: International Publishers, 1935.

Hart, John. *Floyd Dell*. New York: Twayne Publishers, 1971.

Hemenway, Robert E. *Zora Neale Hurston: A Literary Biography*. Urbana: University of Illinois Press, 1977.

Henriques, Fernando. *Family and Colour in Jamaica*. London: Eyre and Spottiswoods, 1953.

Hicks, Granville, Michael Gold, Isadore Schneider, and Joseph North.

Proletarian Literature in the United States. New York: International Publishers, 1935.

Hill, Herbert, ed. *Anger and Beyond: The Negro Writer in the United States.* New York: Harper and Row, 1966.

Hill, Robert A., ed. *The Crusader.* New York: Garland Press, 1988.

———. *The Marcus Garvey and U.N.I.A. Papers.* Vol. 1, *1826–1919.* Berkeley: University of California Press, 1983.

Hoffman, Frederick J. *The Twenties: American Writing in the Post-war Decade.* New York: Viking Press, 1955.

Hooker, James R. *Black Revolutionary: George Padmore's Path from Communism to Pan-Africanism.* New York: Praeger Publications, 1967.

Huggins, Nathan Irvin. *Harlem Renaissance.* New York: Oxford University Press, 1971.

———, ed. *Voices from the Harlem Renaissance.* New York: Oxford University Press, 1976.

Hughes, Langston. *The Best of Simple.* New York: Knopf, 1930.

———. *The Big Sea: An Autobiography.* New York: Knopf, 1945.

———. *Not without Laughter.* New York: Hill and Wang, 1930.

Hurston, Zora Neale. *Dust Tracks on a Road.* Philadelphia: Lippincott, 1971.

———. *Tell My Horse.* New York: J. B. Lippincott, 1938.

Ikonné, Chidi. *From Du Bois to Van Vechten: The Early New Negro Literature, 1903–1926.* Westport, Conn.: Greenwood Press, 1981.

Jacobson, Julius, ed. *The Negro and the American Labor Movement.* Garden City, N.Y.: Anchor Books/Doubleday, 1968.

Jekyll, Walter. *Jamaican Song and Story: Annancy Stories, Digging Songs, Ring Tunes, and Dancing Tunes.* London: David Nutt, 1907. Reprint. New York: Dover Publications, 1966.

Johnson, James Weldon. *Along This Way: The Autobiography of James Weldon Johnson.* New York: Viking Press, 1933.

———. *Black Manhattan.* 1930. Reprint. New York: Atheneum, 1972.

Jones, LeRoi. *Blues People.* New York: William Morrow, 1963.

Kent, George. *Blackness and the Adventure of Western Culture.* Chicago: Third World Press, 1972.

Klehr, Harvey. *The Heyday of American Communism: The Depression Decade.* New York: Basic Books, 1984.

Levy, Eugene. *James Weldon Johnson: Black Leader, Black Voice.* Chicago: University of Chicago Press, 1973.

Lewis, David Levering. *When Harlem Was in Vogue.* New York: Knopf, 1981.

Locke, Alain. *A Decade of Negro Self-Expression.* Charlottesville, Va.: Michie Co., 1928.

———, ed. *The New Negro: An Interpretation.* 1925. Reprint. New York: Atheneum, 1977.

Lueders, Edward. *Carl Van Vechten and the Twenties.* New York: University of New Mexico Press, 1955.

Luhan, Mable Dodge. *Movers and Shakers.* New York: Harcourt and Brace, 1936.

Margolies, Edward. *Native Sons: A Critical Study of Twentieth-Century American Authors*. New York: J. B. Lippincott, 1968.

May, Henry F. *The End of Innocence*. New York: Knopf, 1959.

Meier, August. *Negro Thought in America, 1880–1915: Racial Ideologies in the Age of Booker T. Washington*. Ann Arbor: University of Michigan, 1963.

Meier, August, and Elliott Rudwick. *From Plantation to Ghetto*. New York: Hill and Wang, 1970.

————, eds. *Black Protest in the Twentieth Century*. Indianapolis: Bobbs-Merrill, 1971.

Moon, Henry Lee. *Balance of Power: The Negro Vote*. New York: Doubleday and Co., 1948.

Naison, Mark. *Communists in Harlem during the Depression*. New York: Grove Press, 1984.

Nettleford, Rex M. *Mirror Mirror: Identity, Race, and Protest in Jamaica*. Jamaica: Collins and Sangster, 1970.

New York Legislature. Joint Committee Investigating Seditious Activities. *Revolutionary Radicalism: Its History, Purpose, and Tactics with an Exposition and Discussion of the Steps Being Taken and Required to Curb It, Being the Report of the Legislative Committee Investigating Seditious Activities*. Filed April 24, 1920, in the Senate of the State of New York. 4 vols. Albany, N.Y.: J. B. Lyon, 1920.

Nolan, William A. *Communism Versus the Negro*. Chicago: Regnery, 1935.

Osofsky, Gilbert. *Harlem: The Making of a Ghetto, Negro New York, 1890–1930*. New York: Harper and Row, 1966.

Ostendorf, Bundt. *Black Literature in White America*. Sussex, England: Harvester Press, 1982.

Ottley, Roi. *New World a Coming*. Boston: Mifflin Co., 1943.

Ottley, Roi, and William J. Weatherby, eds. *The Negro in New York: An Informal Social History*. New York: Oceana Publications, 1962.

Petesch, Donald A. *A Spy in the Enemy's Country: The Emergence of Modern Black Literature*. Iowa City: University of Iowa Press, 1989.

Pickens, William. *The New Negro: His Political, Civil, and Mental Status and Related Essays*. 1916. Reprint. New York: AMS Press, 1969.

Ramchard, Kenneth. *The West Indian Novel and Its Background*. New York: Barnes and Noble, 1970.

Rampersad, Arnold. *The Life of Langston Hughes*. Vol. 1, *I, Too, Sing America*. New York: Oxford University Press, 1986.

————. *The Life of Langston Hughes*. Vol. 2, *I Dream of a World*. New York: Oxford University Press, 1988.

Record, Wilson. *The Negro and the Communist Party*. New York: Atheneum, 1971.

Redding, J. Saunders. *To Make a Poet Black*. Chapel Hill: University of North Carolina Press, 1939.

————. *They Came in Chains*. New York: J. B. Lippincott, 1969.

Bibliography

Reid, Ira De A. *The Negro Immigrant: His Background, Characteristics, and Social Adjustments, 1899–1937*. New York: Columbia University Press, 1939.

Richmond, Al. *A Long View from the Left: Memoirs of an American Revolutionary*. Boston: Houghton and Mifflin Co., 1974.

Ross, Joyce B. *J. E. Spingarn and the Rise of the NAACP, 1911–1939*. New York: Atheneum, 1972.

Rudwick, Elliot M. *W. E. B. Du Bois: Propagandist of the Negro Protest*. 1960. Reprint. New York: Atheneum, 1969.

Singh, Amritjit, S. William Shiver, and Stanley Brodwin, eds. *The Harlem Renaissance: Revaluations*. New York: Garland Publishing, 1989.

Sitkoff, Harvard. *A New Deal for Blacks: The Emergence of Civil Rights as a National Issue: The Depression Decade*. New York: University Press, 1978.

Smith, Bernard, ed. *The Democratic Spirit: A Collection of American Writings from the Earliest Times to the Present Day*. New York: Knopf, 1941.

Solomon, Mark. *Red and Black: Communism and Afro-Americans, 1929–1933*. New York: Garland Publishing, 1988.

Spero, Sterling D., and Abram L. Harris. *The Black Worker*. 1931. Reprint. New York: Atheneum, 1969.

Tarry, Ellen. *The Third Door: The Autobiography of an American Negro Woman*. 1955. Reprint. Westport, Conn.: Negro Universities Press, 1971.

Treadgold, Donald W. *Twentieth-Century Russia*. Chicago: Rand McNally and Co., 1972.

Wagner, Jean. *Black Poets of the United States: From Paul Laurence Dunbar to Langston Hughes*. Urbana: University of Illinois Press, 1973.

Wald, Alan M. *The New York Intellectuals: The Rise and Decline of the Anti-Stalinist Left from the 1930s to the 1980s*. Chapel Hill: University of North Carolina Press, 1987.

Walvin, James. *Black and White: The Negro and English Society, 1555–1945*. London: Allen Lane/Penguin Press, 1955.

Weinstein, James. *The Decline of Socialism in America: 1912–1925*. New York: Monthly Review Press, 1967.

Whitney, Robert M. *Reds in America*. New York: Beckwith Press, 1924.

Wickersham, Harvey. *The Impuritans*. New York: Dial Press, 1929.

Wilkins, Roy. *The Autobiography of Roy Wilkins: Standing Fast*. New York: Viking Press, 1982.

UNPUBLISHED MATERIALS

Calverton, V. F. "The Negro." V. F. Calverton Papers. New York Public Library.

Conroy, Sister M. James. "Claude McKay: Negro Poet and Novelist." Ph.D. diss., Notre Dame University, 1968.

BIBLIOGRAPHY

Cooper, Wayne. "Claude McKay: The Evolution of a Negro Radical, 1889–1923." Master's Thesis, Tulane University, 1965.

———. "Stranger and Pilgrim: The Life of Claude McKay, 1890–1948." Ph.D. diss., Rutgers University, 1982.

Federal Bureau of Investigation, Claude McKay File. Number 61-3467. Washington, D.C.

"Interview with George Schuyler." Manuscript. Oral History Collection. Columbia University.

Johnson, James Weldon. "Brief Biography of Claude McKay." Manuscript. Harmon Papers, Library of Congress, Washington, D.C.

Johnson, R. J. "The Poetry of Dunbar and McKay: A Study." Master's Thesis, University of Pittsburgh, 1950.

Kornweibel, Theodore, Jr. "The Messenger Magazine: 1917–1928." Ph.D. diss., Yale University, 1962.

Lang, Phyllis Martin. "Claude McKay: The Later Years, 1934–1948." Ph.D. diss., University of Illinois at Urbana-Champaign, 1972.

Robinson, Harry. "The Negro Immigrant in New York." Works Progress Administration Research Paper, Schomburg Collection, New York Public Library, New York, New York.

Schomburg, Arthur. "Prospectus for the Establishment of a Negro Magazine." Schomburg Collection, New York Public Library, New York City, New York.

Tillery, Tyrone. "Claude McKay: Man and Symbol of the Harlem Renaissance." Ph.D. diss., Kent State University, 1981.

U.S. Department of Justice, Investigative Activities of the Department of Justice, Exhibit no. 10, "Radicalism and Sedition among Negroes as Reflected in Their Publications." 66th Congress, 1st Sess., Sen. Ex. Doc. 153, vol. 12 (1919, serial no. 7607), 161–187.

Zinoviev, Gregory E. "Zinoviev on National and Racial Problems." Typescript letter to Claude McKay, American Negro guest to the IV Congress of the III International, NAACP Administrative Files, Library of Congress, Washington, D.C.

Index

INDEX

Du Bois, W. E. B., 25, 36, 45, 47, 53, 73, 74, 87, 90, 92, 95, 100, 101, 108, 111, 112, 113, 117, 118, 122, 123, 151, 155, 174

Eastman, Crystal, 40
Eastman, Max, 12, 39, 51, 54, 59, 60, 66, 79, 112, 120, 126, 127, 128, 136, 137, 138, 140, 143, 144, 145, 146, 162, 168, 176, 179, 180, 182
Edwards, Eli (McKay nom de plume), 31, 32
Edwards, Eulalie Imelda, 27
Emancipator, 49
Embree, Edwin R., 146
Emperor Jones (E. O'Neill), 104
"Enigmatic Expatriate, The" (McKay), 145, 146
"Enslaved" (McKay), 70
Extension, 180

Fadiman, Clifton, 135
Fauset, Jessie, 92, 99, 103, 116, 117, 119, 153, 155
Federal Bureau of Investigation, 68, 69, 70, 71, 162
Federal Writers' Guild, 149
Ferris, William H., 41
Fire in the Flint (W. White), 96
Fisher, Rudolph, 81, 155
Fourth Congress of the Third International, 62, 69, 70, 71
Frank, Waldo, 104
Freeman, Joseph, 49, 56, 58, 158
Friendship House, 177, 178

Garland Fund, 146
Garrison, William Lloyd, 41
Garvey, Marcus, 17–19, 51, 52, 61, 87, 88, 108
Gingertown (McKay), 84
Glasgow, Ellen, 99
Gold, Michael, 58, 59, 60, 158
Gompers, Samuel, 47, 67
Greycourt, 144–46, 148
Gropper, William, 55
Gross, Bella, 141

Hall, Otto, 50
Hamid, Sufi Abdul, 165–68, 173
Harlem: Negro Metropolis (McKay), 149, 162, 163, 167, 168, 173, 176
"Harlem Dancer" (McKay), 30, 31, 113
Harlem Labor Union, Inc., 169–71, 172

Harlem Liberator, 141, 157
Harlem Renaissance: debate over, 95, 97, 98, 99, 100; nature of, 82–94
Harlem Shadows (McKay), 54, 76, 78, 83, 174
Harmon Gold Medal for Literature, 114
Harris, Abram, 73, 148
Harris, Frank, 12, 32–33, 39
Harrison, Hubert, 53, 54, 57
Hausen, Harry, 108
Haywood, Harry, 51–52, 161
Herbst, Josephine, 12, 84
Herndon, Angelo, 159, 176
He Who Gets Slapped (L. Andreyev), 55–57
Heyward, DuBose, 104
Hicks, Granville, 158
Hill, Robert, 52
Hitler, Adolph, 148, 156, 159
Hitler-Stalin Pact, 160
Holiday (W. Frank), 104
Holman, Carl M., 37
Home to Harlem (McKay), 18, 76, 83, 84–87, 88, 89, 96, 97, 100, 101, 104–22, 127–29, 141, 154, 166
Hope, John, 119
Hope, Rhonda (McKay nom de plume), 32
Huggins, Nathan, 85
Hughes, Langston, 79, 81, 88, 92, 101, 102, 103, 105, 113, 116, 148, 155, 157, 174
Huiswood, Otto, 50, 89
Hurston, Zora Neale, 105

"If We Must Die" (McKay), 33–37, 41, 51, 66, 68, 69, 70, 76, 115
Impuritans, The (H. Wickersham), 88
Industrial Workers of the World, 34, 69
"In Memoriam: Booker T. Washington" (McKay), 22
International Club, 42
International Literature, 157
"Invocation" (McKay), 30–31
Irish Republican Brotherhood, 50–51, 61
Izvestia, 157

Jackman, Harold, 182
Jekyll, Walter, 10–13, 19, 23–24, 40, 79, 131, 132
Jewish Frontier, 168
Jewish Writers' Guild, 150
Johnson, Charles S., 174

232

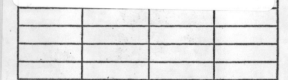